DIGITAL LIBRARY DEVELOPMENT

Sunil Kumar

RAJAT PUBLICATIONS
NEW DELHI - 110 002 (INDIA)

RAJAT PUBLICATIONS
4740/23, Ansari Road, Daryaganj
New Delhi- 110 002 (India)
Phones : 23267924, 9811484973
E-mail: rajat_publication@yahoo.com

Digital Library Development

Edition 2025

ISBN 978-81-7880-393-7

PRINTED IN INDIA

Published by Mrs. Seema Wasan for Rajat Publications, New Delhi and Printed at Asian Offset Press, Delhi.

Preface

Digital Libraries deal with the creation and management of information sources, the dissemination of information across global networks and the effective use and development of information. These libraries are extension and enhancement of information storage and retrieval systems.

Aim of this book is to provide to our readers innovative and important aspects of the digital library development. Every care has been taken to confirm to the course contents of library science.

In preparing this work we have incurred gratitude and indebtedness of the authorities on the subject. We record our acknowledgements.

Librarians and their staff-members have been kind and cooperative. We thank them.

My publisher and his staff-members at various level have rendered every possible assistance. They deserve my readers patronage.

—Editor

Contents

1

What is a Digital Library?

In 1993, the British Library initiated the "Electronic Beowulf Project" to capture, enhance, and preserve forever this cultural artifact in digital form. Not only has the manuscript been captured in its current form, but it is now available for study anywhere. This is only one example of how, throughout the world, libraries, museums and archives are digitizing the important documents and images of our culture, both to preserve them for future generations and to make them more accessible to our own.

As digital imaging technology has advanced, so have opportunities for preservation of irreplaceable artifacts. The Dead Sea Scrolls, written as early as the second century B.C. and discovered fifty years ago, were considerably degraded by their centuries of exposure to the elements. Conditions in the caves where they were discovered had caused the parchment scrolls to deteriorate, obscuring the text and causing parts of the writing to transfer to adjacent parts of the scroll. A specialized camera and filters developed by Eastman Kodak for the space programme were used to image fragments of the scrolls and reveal new characters previously invisible in normal light, allowing researchers to reconstruct new parts of the text.

The barriers of space and time in the search for knowledge are also being eliminated. Today, students, researchers, information professionals, and the general public can directly access many of the world's rarest artifacts—from high-quality images of each page of the Gutenberg Bible to a digital likeness of the Mona Lisa—right at the desktop or other Web-enabled device, at any time and from any location. Audio recordings of historic speeches or exotic birdcalls. video clippings from televised news programmes, geospacial data, and more are being delivered directly to the desks of students and researchers. Thanks to the creation of digital libraries, scholarly research is accelerating dramatically without the limitations of physical access.

Through the 1990s, digital library projects were largely experimental activities. As shown in Figure 1.1, many important advances in digital library techniques came about through research sponsored by the U.S. National Science Foundation (NSF) and the U.K. Join Information Systems Committee (JISC). In 1999 these projects began expanding internationally when NSF linked its digital library research programme with similar activities being undertaken by JISC, resulting in the JISC-NSF International Digital Library Initiative. The objectives of this three-year programme were to:

- Assemble collections of information that were not otherwise accessible or usable because of technical barriers, distance, size, system fragmentation, or other limits.
- Create new technology and the understanding to make it

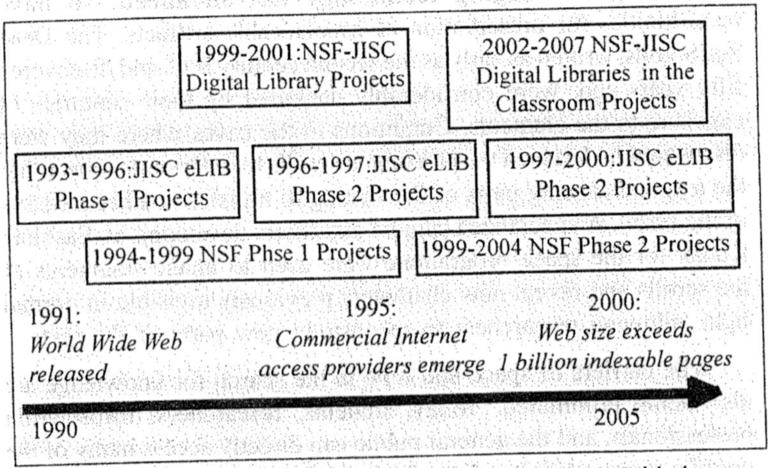

Figure 1.1: Key U.S./U.K. Digital Library Research Initiatives

possible for a distributed set of users to find, deliver, and exploit such information.

- Evaluate the impact of this new technology and its international benefits.

Since then, many other groups have become involved in the expansion of digital library technologies and techniques, including the European Union, Association for Computing Machinery (ACM), the Institute of Electrical and Electronics Engineers (IEEE), the International Federation of Library Associations (IFLA), the American Library Association (ALA), the Coalition for Networked Information (CNI), and the Digital Library Federation (DLF).

Library automation software vendors have also introduced the first commercial products developed from the experimental work. These products are aimed at educational institutions that seek easy-to-install and easy-to-maintain solutions based on industry standards and best practices to date.

Defining the Digital Library

Debate ranges among librarians and knowledge professionals as to what constitutes a digital library. There are many definitions, ranging from the electronic catalog that describes physical items in a "brick and mortar" library to advanced multimedia environments housing all-digital collections. H. Thomas Hickerson, Cornell University's Associate University Librarian for Information Technologies & Special Collections, believes it is time to erase the line between physical and digital libraries. "A major portion of library activities are technology-supported and have been for years. The Internet has had an incredible impact, but libraries have a history of managing large systems and using technology to deliver bibliographic information." Hickerson says.

Still, there has been tremendous progress in adapting new technologies to library use over the past decade. Bernie Hurley, the Director for Library Technologies at U.C. Berkeley, draws the distinction between traditional library automation and digital libraries. Hurley notes that "digital libraries are different in that they are designed to support the creation, maintenance, management, access to and preservation of digital content." He sees the work by U.C. Berkeley and other large research libraries as the first generation of digital library development. "Once the specifications settle out, the commercial vendors can more successfully enter the market with competitive products," Hurley says.

Sun Microsystems defines a digital library as *the electronic extension of functions users typically perform and the resources they access in a traditional library*. These information resources can be translated into digital form, stored in multimedia repositories, and made available through Web-based services. The emergence of the digital library mirrors the growth of e-learning (or distance learning) as the virtual alternative to traditional school attendance. As the student population increasingly turns to off-campus alternatives for lifelong learning, the library must evolve to fit this new educational paradigm or become obsolete as students search for other ways to conveniently locate information resources anywhere, any time.

Goals

Digital libraries began to appear on the campus in the early 1990s as research and development projects centered within computer science departments, sometimes funded by government grants. Campus librarians were often uninvolved in these early projects, which focused on digitization technology, metadata schemes, data management techniques, and digital preservation. Dan Greenstein, former director of the Digital Library Federation and now head of the California Digital Library, characterizes this experimental period as the "second-generation digital library," exploring new opportunities and developing new competencies. With this new knowledge in hand, Greenstein suggests that the third-generation digital library abandoned this experimentation and the "build it and they will come" philosophy that characterized early digital collections, focusing instead on fully integrating digital material into the library's collections through a modular systems architecture. "This modular approach is fundamentally librarian since it permits libraries to think creatively about how to build upon services supplied by others."

As these projects matured and led the way toward more practical digital library implementations, the library began to take a more central role. Digital library use shifted to a large and diverse campus audience, and information technology (IT) groups began to partner with the library to develop campus-wide standards for the deployment and operation of digital libraries as an integral part of the education enterprise. This development paralleled the development of heightened student requirements for access to library resources.

With the advent of the Internet, individuals' expectations for access to information have increased dramatically. It is no longer considered practical or acceptable to travel to a specific location during certain hours to locate needed information. Library patrons are not satisfied to locate an item of interest that is housed at yet another physical location, request the item, and then wait days or weeks for the item to arrive at the building where it was requested. Patrons increasingly expect instant access to all the information resources they require, from any location, at any time, and from any device. This is the objective that the digital library is fulfilling.

With digital libraries, an individual can:

- Gain access to the holdings of libraries worldwide through automated catalogs.
- Locate both physical and digitized versions of scholarly articles and books.
- Optimize searches, simultaneously search the Internet, commercial databases, and library collections.
- Save search results and conduct additional processing to narrow or qualify results.
- From search results, click through to access the digitized content or locate additional items of interest.

All of these capabilities are available from the desktop or other Web-enabled device such as a personal digital assistant or cellular telephone. Additionally, the user can customize his or her information request so that search results reflect individual needs and preferences. Sun considers personalisation the next killer application, creating a more valuable and richer user experience in the digital library environment.

Key Components

As shown in figure 1.2, a fully developed digital library environment involves the following elements:

1. Initial conversion of content from physical to digital form.
2. The extraction or creation of metadata or indexing information describing the content to facilitate searching and discovery, a s well as administrative and structural metadata to assist in object viewing, management, and preservation.
3. Storage of digital content and metadata in an appropriate multimedia repository. The repository will include rights management capabilities to enforce intellectual property rights, if required. E-commerce functionality may also be present if needed to handle accounting and billing.
4. Client services for the browser, including repository querying and workflow.
5. Content delivery via file transfer or streaming media.
6. Patron access through a browser or dedicated client.
7. A private or public network.

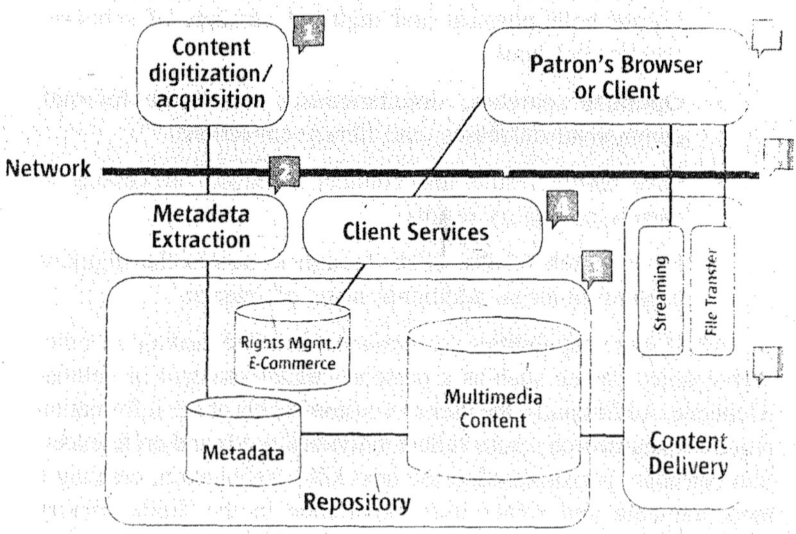

Figure 1.2: Functional Components of a Digital Library

These components might not all be part of a discrete digital library system, but could be provided by other related or multi-purpose systems or environments. Accordingly, integration is a consistent issue cited by digital library developers.

To interoperate with the existing library infrastructure, the digital library must be designed to work with existing library catalogs and incorporate industry standards, formats, and protocols. The term "digital library" is often used to describe any multimedia management system holding digitized information, but this does not mean it will deliver true library application functionality. Thus, these digital library components must also be tailored to capture, encode, and deliver information according to the standard practices adopted by the library industry. Because of the rapid pace of technological change, some standards are concrete and others are emerging.

Link to e-Learning and the Campus Enterprise

The development of digital libraries must be considered in the overall context of initiatives to unify the IT structures of the campus and to transform the learning process through innovative technology.

Economic, social, and cultural pressures are forcing schools and universities to reinvent themselves. As in the business process re-engineering activities of the last decade that transformed corporate enterprises, education organisations are now viewing themselves in a new light. New types of students and changing student expectations are driving the integration of core campus functions and deployment of student services on the Web. Fragmented, monolithic approaches are falling away as educators realize the need to link learning and administrative resources in a more effective way to become a "knowledge enterprise," the 21st century version of the traditional campus.

During the past decade steep declines in the cost of commodity components, combined with the availability of high bandwidth networks, have made sophisticated IT applications for education affordable. A mix of sophisticated digital and Internet-based services and rapidly expanding global digital content have made possible a "virtual learning environment" (VLE) that delivers the capability to enhance the classroom experience or conduct learning apart from a physical campus. The digital library is a core component of this VLE.

"These developments are extending the role of the library, and changing the relationships between the library and other parts of the academic enterprise," according to Clifford Lynch, Director of the Coalition for Networked Resources and a noted authority on digital libraries. "I think we will see a continued evolution from thinking about digital collections to thinking about networked information services, which will integrate authoring, analysis, and distribution tools that facilitate the reuse and repurposing of digital content. In almost all cases, the collections and services must be integrated into the institutional, national, and worldwide fabric of research and teaching."

The NSF in the United States has joined with the JISC in the United Kingdom to sponsor a major research programme called "Digital Libraries and the Classroom: Test beds for Transforming Teaching and Learning." This programme will promote the use of large-scale, distributed digital content and advanced networking technologies for learning. Running from 2002 to 2007, the sponsored projects are expected to demonstrate how integrating recent technical developments with digital content improves the learning experience of students and provides new models for classroom instruction. Evaluating the impact of these projects on student achievement, retention, recruitment, and on institutional structures and practices will be important elements of the initiative.

The Open Digital Library

Technology Platform Requirements

By its nature, digital collection development requires extensive use of technological resources. In the early days of digital library development, when collections were typically small and experimental, a wide variety of hardware and software was utilized. Today, the leading digital library developers are putting substantial collections online. Some of these collections include millions of digital objects; collections are being planned that will require storage measured in petabytes—the equivalent of more than 50,000 desktop computers with 20-gigabyte hard drives.

As digital libraries scale in size and functionality, it is critical for the underlying technology platform to deliver the performance and reliability required. Many digital libraries are considered "mission critical" to the overall institution. In addition, patrons expect high service levels, which means that downtime and poor response time are not tolerable. Moreover, because cost is a foremost concern, scalability and efficiency with a low total cost of ownership are also key requirements. This type of digital library implementation requires a scalable enterprise-level technology solution with built-in reliability, availability, and serviceability (RAS) features.

Storage capacity also must be scalable to adapt to rapid growth in demand, and must be adapted to the mix of media types that may be stored in a digital library, such as:

- Text, which is relatively compact.
- Graphics, which can be data-intensive.
- Audio, which is highly dynamic.
- Video, which is highly dynamic and data intensive.

Storage capacity should be expandable in economical increments and should not require redesign or re-engineering of the system design as requirements grow.

An open systems architecture provides both a robust platform and the best selection of digital media management solutions and development tools. The inherent reliability and scalability of open platforms have made them the most popular choice of IT professionals for Internet computing. This computing model features an architecture that is oriented totally around Internet protocols and stresses the role of Websites for a vast and diverse array of services that follow a utility model.

The Sun™ Platform

The use of new Internet and portal computing models, the explosion of off-campus, lifelong learners, and the growing need to better manage heterogeneous, round-the-clock IT environments has fueled the move to Sun technologies. Sun Microsystems™ continues to lead the way in RAS, resource management, real-world performance capabilities, and cost of ownership, setting a standard that other technology platform offerings cannot match. Among other achievements:

- Sun's 64-bit UltraSPARC® III processor received Micro Design Resources (MDR) Microprocessor Report 2001 Analysts Choice Award in the Best Server/Workstation processor category.
- The Solaris™ Operating Environment was declared the Best Server Operating Environment in 2001 by *Network Computing;* it was also ranked as the top UNIX® Operating System by industry analyst firm D.H. Brown Associates.
- In UNIX markets, Sun leads its competitors in both unit shipments and revenue in the entry, midrange, and high-end server segments.

The Solaris™ Operating Environment includes many features that deliver the scalability and RAS required for the digital library environment. Near-libear performance increases are achieved as processors are added to servers, and high-reliability clustering is supported for extremely high uptime environments. According to the results of the *2001 Unix Function Review* performed by D.H. Brown Associates, Solaris 8 Operating Environment is the highest rated operating system among five leading UNIX-based operating systems.

Sun midrange and high end servers also offer high availability features such as full hardware redundancy, fault-isolated dynamic system domains, concurrent maintenance, and clustering support. Exceptional performance is achieved through fast processors, outstanding system interconnect performance, fast I/O, and linear scalability.

Sun also offers one of the industry's most economical storage environments, providing modular storage capacity that can be added incrementally. Sun's flexible storage products enable the user to purchase precisely the increments needed. Spindle limits, capacity, and bandwidth can be increased with a simple upgrade. Sun's enterprise storage products are designed to have no single point of failure. For example, Sun StorEdge™ arrays incorporate hot-swappable, redundant components and dual controllers, providing built-in backup systems and easy serviceability.

Total investment protection is achieved through Sun's reliance on a common chip architecture, a common operating environment, and complete binary compatibility. The same application can scale from a single CPU to hundreds of CPUs, spanning generations of product releases without the need for modifications or recompilations.

The Education Portal

Increasingly, IT specialists are implementing campus portals. In a portal environment, the client connects to a portal server via a browser or other device. The portal server presents an authentication screen to the user (whether student, faculty, or staff). With the connection running https, all user name and password information is encrypted in transport. If the user name and password is accepted and verified within the directory services, the portal serer can then read all dynamic attributes for the customer from the directory services and start to build the primary screen. This screen will include all services and applications that the customer has permissions to access – including library services. Meanwhile, the portal server establishes connections to all the back-end application servers while waiting for the customer to choose where to go next. All of this functionality can create a management nightmare, which is why it is important to support a scalable management and policy base mechanism.

The Sun™ Open Net Environment (Sun ONE) product set (see Appendix) provides this functionality by administering access based on community. It ensures that student information stays with students (via a Student Portal), that faculty sees only applications for the faculty (via a Faculty Portal), and that administrative personnel view only relevant applications and content personnel view only relevant applications and content (via an Administrative Portal). Each portal is customised and tailored to the community. Once the portal server has been configured initially, whenever an application or service needs to be added it is simply a matter of adding the resources, having the services run in the backend, and then adding the access control entries to the portal. The next time the user connects, the service will be available. This provides the flexibility to dynamically modify the customer environment, supporting thousands to tens of thousands of devices or more.

In addition, an easily integrated Sun ONE product set provides modular directory and security services, e-commerce functionality, and campus-wide messaging and calendar services for a total campus infrastructure solution.

Evolution to Web Services

Software is evolving from local desktop and client-server software applications to Web applications. Today, it is very common for organisations to more their local applications to the Web, and in some cases to subscribe to additional application services over the Web from external service providers. The next phase of this evolution is the development of true Web services. A Web application offers a service that requires the intervention of a user, while a Web service facilitates direct programme-to-programme interaction without user intervention. Web services are functional components that can combine with other services dynamically to create a more useful or powerful application.

The digital library of the future will deliver "smart media services"; that is, Web services that can match "media content" to user "context" in a way that provides a customised, personalized experience. Media content is digital content that includes elements of interactivity. Context includes such information as the identity and location of the user.

Several key technologies must interact to allow Web services to work in this way. Extensible Markup Language (XML) and Standard General Markup Language (SGML) are important standards influencing our ability to create broadly interoperable Web-based applications. SGML is an international standard for text markup systems, and is very large and complex, describing thousands of different document types in many fields of human activity. XML is a standard for describing other languages, written in SGML. XML allows the design of customized markup languages for limitless types of documents, providing a very flexible and simple way to write Web-based applications. This differs from HTML which is a single, predefined markup language and can be considered one application of XML. The primary standards powering Web services today are XML-based. These include:

- Simple Object Access Protocol (SOAP).
- Universal Description, Discovery and Integration (UDDI).
- Web Services Description Language (WSDL).
- Electronic Business XML (ebXML).

These standards are emerging as the basis for the new Web services model. While not all are fully defined standards, they are maturing quickly with broad industry support.

Digital Library Development

An educational institution's digital library environment will likely encompass both local collections and externally provided resources from such sources as subscription services and other libraries. There is often a desire to structure this blend of internal and external resources as a unified collection from the user's point of view, with a single gateway and a comprehensive set of support services. Some resources are "born digital" while others originate in physical form and require transformation into digital form, a process that can be difficult and costly. Most of today's digital library environments are the result of custom development, but as packaged library solutions are now available, the next group of digital library adopters must reach a "make versus buy" decision. Much of the utility and long-term ease of maintenance of digital collections is dependent upon the types and quality of metadata that is stored with the digital objects, but agreed-upon standards for metadata are only beginning to emerge.

The first organisations to build large-scale digital libraries encountered many challenges in organising, funding, managing, and ensuring the long-term maintenance of the digital library environment. The objective of this section is to discuss some of these challenges and share experiences of the early adopters. Some of these experiences may help others avoid pitfalls and take advantage of evolving best practices.

Funding

The funding issue is probably the single largest barrier to digital library development; this is why most existing collections are essentially pilot projects or R&D activities. The challenge of mounting a large-scale digitization effort, encoding, appropriate metadata to ensure ease of discovery and use, and making a commitment to long-term preservation can be daunting to libraries already struggling to pay for existing activities.

Some institutions like Harvard University have been able to generate start-up funding with the philosophy of "build it and they will come." Most will have to shift funding from existing programmes or activities—never an easy task. "It's hard to change what you're doing when you have to achieve that change by moving existing funds from one spot to another," comments Cornell University's H. Thomas Hickerson. "Not all library leaders have been willing to do that." Cornell has sought initial seed money for digitization projects, but establishes cost recovery models that will eventually allow the digital programmes to become self-funding.

Custom Development vs. Packaged Solutions

Custom development has been the predominant means of constructing digital libraries simply because off-the-shelf solutions have only become available relatively recently. Leading digital library implementers who have gone this route consistently cite the lack of commercially available solutions that met their requirements as the reason for developing customer systems.

There are both benefits and drawbacks to doing custom development. On the plus side, there is a high degree of assurance that the completed system will closely fit the specific user requirements, since three are (theoretically, at least) no competing communities with different needs or opinions about the best way of accomplishing a certain task. The up-front cost of development can be spread over a long period of use, with no further license fees or charges to be paid as time goes on. Future development is completely controllable and predictable, and there is no doubt about continued availability of the system. On the other hand, the cost of developing and maintaining a complex multimedia management environment is very high. Says a veteran digital library implementer, commenting on one particularly well-funded project: "Even a million dollars doesn't go very far in developing this kind of a system." Another experienced digital library developer says, "If you're going to do it by yourself, bring your checkbook." There is also the threat that evolving standards would result in one-off systems that lack interoperability with other digital environments.

The school of thought advocating the development of commercial digital library solutions revolves around the value of a large number of buyers supporting the research and development required to bring a robust "turn-key" solution to market. The nature of the marketplace will dictate that the system for sale will meet a majority of the buyers' needs at a more reasonable price than developing unique systems. The continuing force of the market will exert pressure for improvement and evolution of the product to continue to meet users' requirements, protecting the buyers' long-term interests. Many libraries simply do not have access to the types of technologists required to develop and maintain these systems, nor do they have any interest in staffing to maintain a complex digital library system. These arguments in favour of commercial systems have motivated many would-be digital librarians to wait...but the wait may be over.

At least four library automation companies now offer digital library solutions, and other general multimedia management technology companies are starting to target the educational institution/ library market. Stanford University Librarian Michael Keller's advice is: "Don't reinvent the wheel. Don't write code or try to be leading edge unless you have strong support from your computer science department. Buy off the shelf from reliable suppliers."

The following section introduces several commercial entries from Sun software partners in this emerging digital library software market.

Package Solutions

These products are available from established library automation vendors:

Endeavour Information Systems, the vendor of the integrated library system "Voyager," has introduced its digital library offering "ENCompass." Endeavour involved a small group of customers as product co-developers. Cornell University, supported by a hardware grant from Sun Microsystems, Inc., became the first co-developer,. Other co-developers now include the Getty Research Institute, Kansas State University, and the University of Pennsylvania. The first commercial release of ENCompass was in March 2001. Endeavour is currently working on the third release of this product.

Endeavour describes ENCompass functionality as including:

- Search and discovery.
- Object management.
- Collection management.
- License and rights management.
- Linking.

Information about ENCompass products can be found at Endeavour's Website, *www.endinfosys.com*

EX LIBRIS. Provider of the integrated library system "ALEPH," has entered the digital library market with "DigiTool." Ex Libris has also taken the approach of involving users. In October, 2001 the University of Maryland Libraries was announced as a Premier Partner to further development of the DigiTool digital asset management software. This Ex Libris programme actively fosters participation in the ongoing design, development, and testing of new features within DigiTool.

Ex Libris describes DigiTool as a means of ensuring that digital data can be acquired, manipulated, shared, searched, and distributed in conformance with industry standards:

- Data structures such as Dublin Core (DC), MARC21, MAB, Text Encoding Initiative (TEI), and Electronic Archive Description (EAD). Future support is planned for Visual Resources Association (VRA), Computerized Interchange of Museum Information (CIMI), and Records Export for Art and Cultural Heritage (REACH).
- Data content of pages in TIFF, GIF, JPEG, or PDF formats;

text in SGML, HTML, or XML formats.

- Data interchange viz. Z39.50, SQI, HTTP, Dienst, and Open Archive Initiative.
- Information industry syntaxes (SGML, HTML, XML. And Resource Description Framework [RDF]).

DigiTool product information can be found at Ex Libris' web site, www.exlibris.co.il or www.exlibris-usa.com

Sirsi, vendor of the "Unicorn" integrated library system has a digital library offering called "Hyperion" Digital Media Archive." The Hyperion Digital Media Archive is a tool for building, storing and maintaining collections of digitally captured material—most often scanned documents, photographs, maps, drawings, artwork, sound, and movie clips. Hyperion can also serve as a repository for computer generated material such as technical documents, multimedia presentations, and engineering drawings. More information on Sirsi's Hyperion Digital Media Archive can be found at *www.sirsi.com.*

VTLS, developer of the "Virtua" integrated library system, has a slightly different approach, offering "visual MIS" (Multimedia and Imaging Solutions), professional services for digitizing and making available a variety of materials such as documents, maps, glass plates, slides, photographs, catalog cards, manuscripts, and microfilm. VTLS believes that outsourcing the digitisation process ensures high-quality, professional scanning results without the necessity for a long-term investment in equipment, staff and time. The Visual MIS services address all aspects of the digitization process from collection analysis to database creation and interface design. For more information, see the VTLS Web site at www.vtls.com.

The following offerings are examples of products from mainstream multimedia vendors who are targeting the education market:

Artesia Technologies is a generalised multimedia management system vendor targeting the library market. Artesia's "TEAMS™" product is being used by Stanford University as the basis for its digital library initiative. Artesia describes TEAMS as a digital asset warehouse that serves as the hub for media files as well as for the vital information related to them. TEAMS integrates with other asset-intensive applications like Web content management, digital rights management, customer relationship management, syndication, and e-learning. TEAMS product information can be viewed at www.artesia.com.

Luna Imaging's "Insight®" high-resolution digital imaging software is used to digitize image collections, license digital images from existing image collections, or share content with other institutions. The Andrew W. Mellon Foundation is adopting Luna's Insight software as the platform to distribute ArtSTOR, a new independent, not-for-profit organization that will make a large body of digital resources for the study of art, architecture, and other fields in the humanities available for subscription. More information is available at www.luna-imaging.com.

MuseGlobal, Inc. specializes in information connectivity solutions. Its flagship product, MuseSearch™, is a broadcast search technology that allows unlimited numbers and types of information sources to be searched simultaneously with a single user query. It also incorporates linking features to take users from record results to category indices, content, and references. More information is available at www.museglobal.com.

Metadata

The key to locating, using, and preserving digital content is metadata, or structured data about digital objects and collections. Many digitization efforts have been unsuccessful due to inadequate metadata. There are three different types of metadata, all essential to ensure the usability and preservation of the collection over time.

1. *Descriptive Metadata*

This metadata provides information that (a) allows discovery of collections or objects through the use of search tools, and (b) provides sufficient context for understanding what has been found. When collections become large or when searching multiple collections (such as over the Internet) the discovery of objects of interest becomes a "needle in a haystack" exercise. Without agreed-upon metadata standards and the discipline of capturing and storing appropriate descriptive metadata, all but the smallest digital collections would be useless.

Metadata for individual objects varies by the type of object, but would include such things as its title, what it is, who created it, contributors, language, when it was created, where it is located, the subject, etc. At the collection level, users should be able to determine the scope, ownership, any access restrictions, and other important characteristics that would assist in understanding the collection. Probably the best-known descriptive metadata standard for libraries is MARC (Machine-readable Catalog) used for cataloging books and other publications. MARC has served the traditional library well, but was not designed for describing images, sound files, and other new media types.

An important emerging descriptive metadata standard for images and other multimedia objects is Dublin Core, a group of 15 items of information designed to be simple to understand and use. Dublin Core was designed to provide a very widely accepted mechanism to allow discovery, but with the option for different communities of users to adapt and customize it by adding more fields of particular importance to the community. In this way, the same base standard can be used for a wide variety of purposes and business modles. Figure 1.3 describes the elements of the Dublin Core metadata standard.

2. *Structural Metadata*

The second type of metadata is structural metadata. This describes the associations within or among related individual information objects. A book, which consists of pages and chapters, is one of the most straightforward examples of structural metadata. The structural metadata would explain how individual page images make up individual chapters, and how chapters make up the book. There could also be individually imaged figures, and structural metadata could also relate these to chapters or to a list of all figures in the book. Structural metadata aids the user in navigating among individual objects that comprise a compound object.

3. *Administrative Metadata*

Administrative metadata facilitates access, management, and

Name	*Identifier*	*Definition*	*Comment*
Title	Title	A name given to the resource.	Typically a Title will be a name by which the resource is formally known.
Creator	Creator	An entity primarily responsible for making the content of the resource.	Examples of a Creator include a person, an organisation, or a service. Typically, the name of a Creator should be used to indicate the entity.
Subject and Keywords	Subject	The topic of the content of the resource.	Typically, a Subject will be expressed as keywords, key phrases, or classification codes that describe a topic of the resource. Recommended best practice is to select a value from a controlled vocabulary or formal classification scheme.
Description	Description	An account of the content of the resource.	Description may include, but is not limited to: an abstract, table of contents, reference to a graphical representation of content or a free-text account of the content.
Publisher	Publisher	An entity responsible for making the resource available	Examples of a Publisher include a person, an organisation, or a service. Typically, the name of a Publisher should be used to indicate the entity.
Contributor	Contributor	An entity responsible for making contributions to the content of the resource.	Examples of a Contributor include a person, an organisation, or service. Typically, the name of a Contributor should be used to indicate the entity.
Date	Date	A date associated with an event in the life cycle of the resource.	Typically, Date will be associated with the creation or availability of the resource. Recommended best practice

Name	*Identifier*	*Definition*	*Comment*
			for encoding the date value is defined in a profile of ISO 8601 [W3CDTF] and follows the YYYY-MM-DD format.
Resource Type	Type	The nature or genre of the content of the resource.	Type includes terms describing general categories, functions, genres, or aggregation levels for content. Recommended best practice is to select a value from a controlled vocabulary (for example, the working draft list of Dublin Core Types [DCT1]). To describe the physical or digital manifestation of the resource, use the format element.
Format	Format	The physical or digital manifestation of the resource.	Typically, Format may include the media type or dimensions of the resource. Format may be used to determine the software, hardware or other equipment needed to display or operate the resource. Examples of dimensions include size and duration. Recommended best practice is to select a value from a controlled vocabulary (for example, the list of Internet Media Types [MIME] defining computer media formats).
Resource Identifier	Identifier	An unambiguous reference to the resource within a given context.	Recommended best practice is to identify the resource by means of a string or number conforming to a formal identification system. Example formal identification systems include the Uniform Resource Identifier (URI) (including the Uniform Resource Locator (URL)), the Digital Object Identifier (DOI) and the

Name	Identifier	Definition	Comment
			International Standard Book Number (ISBN).
Source	Source	A reference to a resource from which the present resource is derived.	The present resource may be derived from the Source resource in whole or in part. Recommended best practice is to reference the resource by means of a string or number conforming to a formal identification system.
Language	Language	A language of the intellectual content of the resource.	Recommended best practice for the values of the Language element is defined by RFC 1766 [RFC1766] which includes a two-letter Language Code (taken from the ISO 639 standard [ISO639]), followed optionally, by a two-letter Country Code (taken from the ISO 3166 standard [ISO3166]). For example, 'en' for English, 'fr' for French or 'en-uk' for English used in the United Kingdom.
Relation	Relation	A reference to a related resource.	Recommended best practice is to reference the resource by means of a string or number conforming to a formal identification system.
Coverage	Coverage	The extent or scope of the content of the resource.	Coverage will typically include spatial location (a place name or geographic coordinates), temporal period (a period label, date, or date range) or jurisdiction (such as a named administrative entity). Recommended best practice is to select a value from a controlled vocabulary (for example, the Thesaurus of Geographic Names [TGN]),

Name	*Identifier*	*Definition*	*Comment*
			and that, where appropriate, named places or time periods be used in preference to numeric identifiers such as sets of coordinates or date ranges.
Rights Management	Rights	Information about rights held in and over the resource.	Typically, a Rights element will contain a rights management statement for the resource, or reference a service providing such information. Rights information often encompasses intellectual Property Rights (IPR), Copyright, and various Property Rights. If the Rights element is absent, no assumptions can be made about the status of these and other rights with respect to the resource.

Figure 1.3: Dublin core Metadata Element Set[1]

preservation of the digital resource. It can describe the viewer or player necessary to access the object, automatically opening that viewer or player when a user selects that resource. It can describe attributes such as image resolution, file size, or audio sampling rate. It can provide a record of how and when an object was created as well as archival and rights management information.

An important emerging standard for interoperability of digital collections is the Metadata Encoding and Transmission Standard (METS), which provides a uniform framework for managing and transmitting digital objects. The Making of America II project (MOA2) developed an encoding format for descriptive, administrative, and structural metadata for textual and image-based works. Supported by the Digital Library Federation and the Library of Congress, METS builds upon the work of MOA2. It provides a format for encoding metadata necessary for both management of digital library objects within a repository and exchange of such objects between repositories (or between repositories and their users). Leading academic and research libraries are citing METS as an important standard for digital library interoperability, and seem to be rallying behind this standard.

Identity and Rights Management

As libraries increasingly focus on building gateways that direct patrons both to the library's own content and to networked digital resources owned or controlled by other entities, rights management becomes a major concern. "In constructing a digital library service environment, the library becomes responsible for configuring access to a world of information of which it owns or manages only a part." says the California Digital Library's Dan Greenstein. "Accordingly, the digital library is known less for the extent and nature of the collections it owns than for the networked information space it defines through a range of online services." In this type of cooperative resource-sharing environment, mechanisms for identifying information users and their access privileges are essential.

With increased use of the Internet to buy, sell, or license the use of documents, images, video, and other copyrighted content in digital form, comes the need to protect that content from unauthorized use once it is outside the control of the publisher or distributor. Digital content is very easy to copy and disseminate with little or no loss of quality. Accordingly, the ability to positively identify library patrons and their associated access privileges is required to assure that materials are being accessed and used by the appropriate parties. From a more practical perspective, it is also useful to integrate these identification and authorisation mechanisms with other campus requirements, providing an environment where individuals can use a common facility for a "single sign on" identification process shared with other campus computing applications.

Ideally, a common authentication/authorization process would be capable of positively identifying any computer user, linking that user to groups of other users with similar access requirements, and passing the user's identity and access profile to all campus computing applications that require such intelligence. A student enrolled in a particular class should be able to seamlessly access reserve materials in digital form (held in the digital library system) as well as online course materials available through the curriculum management system, the student's enrollment in the course being verifiable through the course registration system. The Sun ONE framework discussed in Appendix A provides these common identify and policy facilities—deployed to an open directory, available to all campus computing applications, and delivering this seamless ability to give students access to all resources to which they are entitled.

Preservation

Libraries place high value on preserving the irreplaceable contents of their collections making the historical and cultural artifacts of our civilization available for future generations. Stanford University's Michael Keller comments, "Libraries are communications devices from preceding generations to succeeding generations. Debates about preservation of scholarly publications are tremendously important."

Fire prevention systems, environmental controls, and microfilming initiatives guard against catastrophic loss of irreplaceable items. Even the move from acid to alkaline paper in publishing has worked for long-term retention of printed items. In 1991, the American Library Association published a preservation policy outlining the responsibilities of the library profession for preserving access to information of all forms. In 2001, that policy was updated to reflect changes brought about by the Internet. The preamble of the revised policy states:

"Librarians must be committed to preserving their collections through appropriate and non-damaging storage, remedial treatment of damaged and fragile items, preservation of materials in their original format when possible, replacement or reformatting of deteriorated materials, appropriate security measures, and life-cycle management of digital publications to assure their usefulness for future generations."[2]

With digitized resources, it would seem that preservation would be much easier to achieve, especially since an unlimited number of copies can be created of the individual object. There are, however, a number of issues that complicate the maintenance of digital objects over long periods of time:

- *Deterioration of media.* Stone tablets have a considerable advantage over today's digital media for long-term storage. The problem of deterioration limits the useful life of today's digital media to between 5 and 50 years, while librarians debate how to retain the artifacts of our civilization for thousands of years to come.
- *Evolution in type and format of media.* In addition to the concerns of physical deterioration of media, we must be aware of the challenges posed by changes in media type and format. In the relatively recent history of personal computer use, we have seen an evolution from 5¼" floppy disks to higher density 3½" diskettes to high-density zip disks, all requiring different physical disk drives and reader software. Optical storage technology is next, and there will undoubtedly be continual change in storage technologies.
- *Changes in applications and operating systems.* New software constantly appears on the horizon, rendering older versions obsolete. The hardware required by applications and operating systems, software also changes over time. Any information stored in a given software/hardware environment will eventually be rendered obsolete through technological obsolescence, most likely before deterioration of the actual storage media occurs. Today, locating a system capable of reading 20 year-old Visicalc spreadsheet files or Multimate word processing files is a difficult proposition: in 50 years' time it will likely be impossible.
- *Preservation of processing results.* Some digital resources exist only fleetingly as a programme runs and cannot be preserved as static objects. Preservation of such resources requires maintenance of the programme and the surrounding operating environment in operable form.

Of course, not all digital resources have the same preservation requirements. "We are more concerned about persistence and authenticity of the collection of images than the long-term preservation of the surrogate," explains David Bearman, director of the Art Museum Image Consortium (AMICO). "Museums are in the business of preserving the real thing." The skill set of the archivist, establishing criteria for selection of content to be preserved, will become even more essential as the amount of digital content expands.

Today, most digital libraries follow a schedule of copying archived digital resources to address the issue of media deterioration. As organisational standards for formats and applications evolve, many libraries also convert the objects over time to maintain readability. Specific preservation policies and best practices, however, are not well developed. The Research Libraries Group (RLG) is an international member alliance, including universities and colleges, national libraries, archives, historical societies, museums and independent research collections, and public libraries dedicated to "improving access to information that supports research and learning." In early 1998. RLG funded a study by Dr. Margaret Hedstrom and Sheon Montgomery to determine the state of digital archiving among 54 of its member institutions. Only 13 institutions reported they had established methods in place for digital preservation.

The National Library of Australia sponsors an initiative called "Preserving Access to Digital Information" (PADI) with the goal of providing mechanisms that help ensure that digital information is managed with appropriate consideration for preservation and future access. PADI recommends these strategies for long-term preservation of digital collections:

1. The migration of digital information from one hardware/ software configuration to another or from one generation of computer technology to a later one offers one method of dealing with technological obsolescence.
2. Adherence to standards will assist in preserving access to digital information.
3. Technology emulation potentially offers substantial benefits in preserving the functionality and integrity of digital objects.
4. Encapsulation, a technique of grouping together a digital object and anything else necessary to provide access to that object, has been proposed by a number of researchers as a useful strategy in conjunction with other digital preservation methods.

5. It is universally agreed that documentation is an important tool to assist in preserving digital material. In addition to the metadata necessary for resource discovery, other sorts of metadata, including preservation metadata describing the software, hardware and management requirements of the digital material, will provide essential information for preservation.[3]

Sun Microsystems has teamed with Stanford University, the National Science Foundation, and the Andrew W. Mellon Foundation to develop an approach to preserving web-published materials (with a focus on electronic journals). The resulting technology LOCKSS™) "Lots of Copies Keeps Stuff Safe"), depends upon cooperation among multiple organisations with a common goal of maintaining access to the same content. A LOCKSS system run by each organisation manages multiple web caches of the content and continuously compares the copies. If any cache appears to have been lost or has suffered disruption, the content is automatically replaced from the publisher or other caches.

A beta test is being conducted by more than 50 libraries worldwide, with a revised version of this software expected to be available through open source late in 2002. More information is available at http://lockss.stanford.edu/.

Portals

Deployment of portal technology has occurred side-by-side with digital collection development and access. As seen in Figure 1.4, portals are unified views into a set of disparate information sources and research tools, with the goal of providing users a simple way to locate and access all the information content they need and have authority to access. As libraries create, license, or negotiate access to more and more digital content, the need for an easy-to-use interface becomes increasingly important.

Library portals typically include an online catalog of materials as well as gateways to collections of digital resources accessible to the user. Broadcast search tools allow library users to search all of these sources simultaneously with a single query. Portals may include electronic reference services ("ask a librarian"), personalization features ("my bookshelf," custom intelligent searches), and other

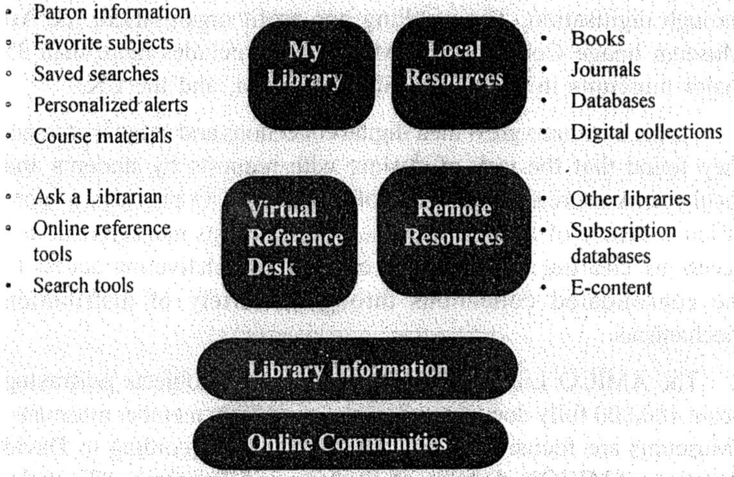

Figure 1.4: Library Portal Components

research tools, Enriched content, such as author biographies and book reviews, tables of contents, and jacket images can be provided to supplement the online catalog. Some libraries have built interactive features into their portals, allowing development of virtual communities.

Portals also provide an excellent opportunity to capture use statistics. "We still know very little about how many of the new systems are being used, who is using them, and who is not using them," says CNI's Clifford Lynch. "Good instrumentation will help you to refine the systems that you develop over time to be more responsive to your user community, and will also allow you to contribute to the collective knowledge base about how to best design and engineer such systems in the future." It must be recognized, however that concern about access to personal information continues to grow and any plan to capture data about individuals' activities must assure them adequate privacy.

Digital Library Programme Profiles

Art Museum Image Consortium

www.amico.org

In 1997 a group of museum directors agreed to collaborate on making more museum collections available to educational institutions through digitisation. The resulting non-profit organisation, the Art Museum Image Consortium (AMICO) now includes more than 35 major museums in the United States, Canada, and the UK.

As the museums grew their digital collections and usage increased, they found that the task of dealing with requests by students and faculty took increasing amounts of time. AMICO provides a more efficient means of dealing with the work of rights management and access by clearing a licensed set of rights and delivering access to the consolidated collections through a variety of distribution mechanisms.

The AMICO Library™ includes multimedia objects portraying about 100,000 fully documented works of art from member museums. "Museums are focused on use, not discovery," according to David Bearman, AMICO's director of Strategy and Research. "To make scholarly use of digitized works of art, you need to maintain a lot more data than what is needed for mere discovery," he says. More than three million AMICO Library subscribers access not only the images, but also find detailed provenance information, curatorial text, multiple views, and other related multimedia for many of the works.

AMICO maintains the half-terabyte master repository in a custom-developed relational database that is growing by 20,000 works per year. Current challenges include expanding the multilingual capabilities of the user interface to encourage more internationalisation of membership and use, as well as encouraging the inclusion of more multimedia items in the collection. Clearing digital rights for works sought for inclusion in the AMICO Library also remains a continuing challenge.

University of California at Berkeley

http://elib.cs.berkeley.edu
http://sunsite.berkeley.edu

The University of California at Berkeley has been in the forefront of digital library innovation for many years. Projects begun at Berkeley included the creation of specifications for encoding electronic finding aids that are used to access special collections and archives. These specifications later evolved into the XML—based Encoded Archival Description (EAD).

The Making of America II project, which proposed a standard encoding for digital objects, was also lead by Berkeley. This project has since evolved into the Metadata Encoding and Transmission Standard (METS).

U.C. Berkeley has also become a significant resource for digital library researchers and developers worldwide. In 1996, with the support of Sun Microsystems, U.C. Berkeley created a SunSITE (Sun Software. Information, and Technology Exchange). Since that time the U.C. Berkeley SunSITE has provided:

- Catalogs and indices to electronic content.
- Links to significant digital collections.
- Digital library information resources.
- Links to significant digital library research and development.
- Information on tools used to build digital libraries.

Current work involves development of a modular object management environment, called GenDL (for "Generic Digital Library"). GenDL includes three components that can be thought of as three separate systems:

- The Web-based content management system, where creation and maintenance of the digital content is controlled. Descriptive, administrative, and structural metadata is created and linked to digitized or born-digital content. The resulting digital library objects are then encoded to the METS standard.
- The preservation repository (a joint project with the California Digital Library), where the digital content is managed to ensure its integrity and longevity.
- The access system, which is used to discover, display, and navigate objects that may have complex internal organisations (i.e., structural metadata).

Figure 1.5 shows the general architecture of GenDL.

The research and development thrust at U.C. Berkeley does not discount the efforts by software vendors to develop commercial tools that tackle these problems. "A large part of what we do in our initial

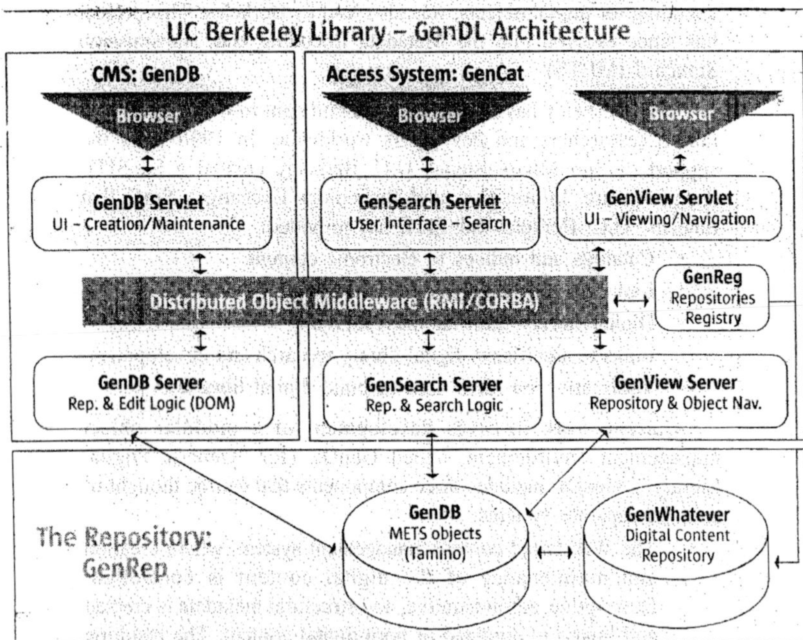

Figure 1.5: GenDL Architecture

development is to define the requirements and procedures that need to be supported in a Digital Library System," comments U.C. Berkeley Library's Director of Library Technologies, Bernie Hurley, pointing out that this allows commercial vendors to focus on introducing successful products.

Cornell University

http://campusgw.library.cornell.edu

"An article in the *Chronicle of Education* has claimed that the libraries are empty. That isn't true at Cornell. We're working very hard to keep that from happening. Although we are aggressively building digital collections and services, at the same time we are supporting greater ranges of use of library space", according to H. Thomas Hickerson, Associate University Librarian and head of Cornell University's digital library programmes. Through the Library, Cornell provides advanced information technology tool sets to the students and supports faculty innovations in using technology to aid in teaching.

Having undertaken one of the world's most aggressive digitisation programmes. Cornell has been a developer of best practices and a leader in the field of digital libraries. As a Sun Center of Excellence for Digital Libraries, Cornell has served as a co-developer with Endeavour Information Systems for the Product "ENCompass", a specially tailored multimedia management system intended for library implementations. Although Cornell has gained international recognition for its computer science advances in digital library technology, this university also recognises the value of off – the shelf-products. "We would rather have this product supported by someone else. We don't want to maintain our own system any more than we have to," says Hickerson.

Cornell has attained recognition for the substantial digital collections it has developed. One of the best known is the "Making of America" collection, a multi-institutional digitization initiative making available primary sources of 19th century American culture and history, including popular magazines like *Harper's Atlantic Monthly*, and *Scientific American*. To date, more than 900,000 pages, which are full-text searchable and freely accessible over the Internet, are in the collection. More than 40 other digital collections have been established, ranging from audio recordings of rare birdcalls to digital facsimiles of essential works in the literature of witchcraft and demonology, drawn from Cornell University's Rare Book Collection.

There are several strategic digital library priorities. One is to establish a central repository for all information resources deemed worthy of long-term maintenance. The repository's aim is to support the total lifecycle of those materials.

A Sun case study on Cornell's digital library programme is available at http://www.sun.com/products-n-solutions/edu/success/cornell.

Harvard University

http://lib.harvard.edu

Harvard University has a very large and decentralized library system including more than 100 libraries and 35 major research collections. There is no hierarchy typing these libraries into a single organisational group. Harvard University's Librarian reports to the University President with a mission to provide services, including information technology, to the libraries. Accordingly, Harvard's digital library activities are designed to provide a common technology infrastructure, consulting assistance, and guidance on policy issues to all of the Harvard libraries.

Unlike many universities. Harvard has established major funding to support the development of a comprehensive infrastructure for digital libraries. The $12 million. 5-year programme is called the "Library Digital Initiative," deliberately emphasizing the library orientation of the programme. The goal of centrally funding this initiative to serve the decentralised network of libraries is to create incentive for participation in a common, standardized solution featuring a robust production IT environment and common practices for digitizing, reformatting metadata creation, digital licensing preservation, and migration of objects, etc. "We are tackling new and hard issues, and by developing this locus of expertise, setting up digital collections becomes easier for all the libraries," says Dale Flecker, Harvard University Library Associate Director for Planning and Systems.

There central Oracle repository supports all types of multimedia objects and a set of catalogs. A portal sits over the catalogs, allowing cross-catalog searching. Although born digital information is at the heart of the programme, a programme of internal grants has also been established to foster additions to the collection. Figure 1.6 gives a graphic representation of Harvard's digital library architecture.

The are active discussions under way with learning management groups about how to make digital library resources more directly relevant to learning and teaching. It is expected that there will be a lot of activity devoted to the interface with learning systems in the future. There will also be increased emphasis on scholarly

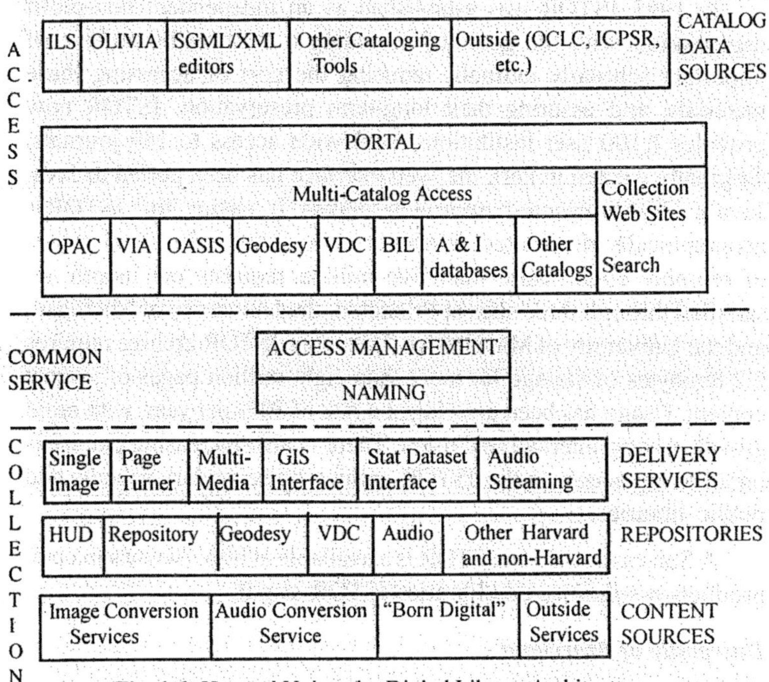

Fig. 1.6: Harvard University Digital Library Architecture

communication and the libraries' role in capturing the university's intellectual output.

JSTOR

http://www.jstor.org

The problems associated with storing back issues of printed journals and locating articles of interest in those back issues led to the creation of JSTOR, an eletronic archive of scholarly journals. JSTOR began as a pilot project sponsored by the Andrew W. Mellon Foundation in 1990. Ten journals in economics and history were selected initially, and all back issues were digitized. High-resolution images of each page were captured and linked to a text file generated with optical character recognition software. Table of contents indices were developed as well, to provide search and retrieval of journal content of interest. When five test libraries showed enthusiasm about the space savings and ease of access, JSTOR was born.

In 1995 JSTOR was established as an independent non-profit organisation with the goals of providing a trustworthy archive of important scholarly journals, reducing the cost of accessing these materials, and assuring their long-term preservation. JSTOR now provides 1,100 user institutions worldwide access to 169 journals. Originally written in Perl, the Web interface has been ported to Java. Java's object-oriented approach makes it easier for JSTOR's geographically distributed developers to quickly write small pieces of reusable code. More than five million requests per month are satisfied through three sites at Princeton, the University of Michigan, and the University of Manchester. The entire JSTOR archive requires 2.2 terabytes of storage for more than eight million pages of journal content. Usage has been growing at a rate of 50% per year, with rapid growth among international users. There is also increasing emphasis on allowing access to the JSTOR archive by secondary schools and public libraries.

A Sun case study on JSTOR is a available at http://www.sun.com/products-n-solutions/edu/libraries/JSTOR-ss.pdf.

University of Maryland

http://www.lib.umd.edu

The University of Maryland has opportunistically grown its unique digital collections, beginning with the Performing Arts Library and the Broadcasting Archives. Both were highly motivated to make their holdings more accessible and usable. Target collections range from original piano roll recordings of early 20th century concert pianists, to a complete wire-recorded collection of the Arthur Godfrey Hour radio broadcasts, to early rock 'n' roll recordings.

A 1996 implementation of a commercial multimedia management platform had mixed results, due to the difficulty of integrating the product into the existing environment and the lack of specific library functionality. The University of Maryland has since taken a different approach, becoming an Ex Libris "Premier Partner" for the Ex Libris "DigiTool" product. This involves full implementation of the Ex Libris digital asset management product, as well as ongoing participation in product design, development, and testing, The implementation will emphasize streaming audio and video, as well as images. The university's goal is an environment that handles all types of digital objects.

Advanced object management technologies are envisioned to assist users in accessing the Performing Arts Library audio collections. An example of an enhanced digital service is the capability of displaying sheet music images simultaneous with the music being played.

"It's good to have a vendor who works with library problems as a mainline business. Other commercial products don't necessarily map to the library business," says University Dean of Libraries Dr. Charles Lowry. Lowry also cites the ability to integrate the digital library software into the Web-based user interface as a benefit, so users can access the physical collection catalog in the same way as the digital collections. It is also important to the University of Maryland that the digital library software supports National Information Standards Organisation (NISO) and National Institute of Standards and Technology (NIST) standards and protocols.

Stanford University

http://www-sul.stanford.edu

http://highwire.stanford.edu

Stanford University is well known for its pioneering work in digital library development and electronic publishing. Stanford has participated in both phases of the NSF Digital Library Initiative, provided online publishing services to nearly 100 scholarly societies, developed extensive digital collections, and is currently implementing an advanced digital repository.

Stanford has entrusted the responsibilities of University Librarian. Publisher of the University Press, Publisher of the HighWire Press, and Director of Academic Computing to a single individual at Stanford. This assignment has fostered functional synergy that has integrated many information management activities across these disciplines and facilitated coordination between related activities such as digital repository and learning management system development. "We don't need to invent a separate digital library programme at Stanford because the digital aspects are an accepted and pervasive part of library support for research and teaching," says University Librarian Michael Keller.

After putting up many digital collections on custom-developed systems, the Stanford Libraries have selected the "TEAMS" multimedia management software from Artesia Technologies as the base for its new digital repository. It is also utilizing Luna Imaging's "Insight" software for managing high-resolution images, and it will utilize the METS sandard for managing multimedia objects. "METS is tremendous, an XML implemented generalised metadata

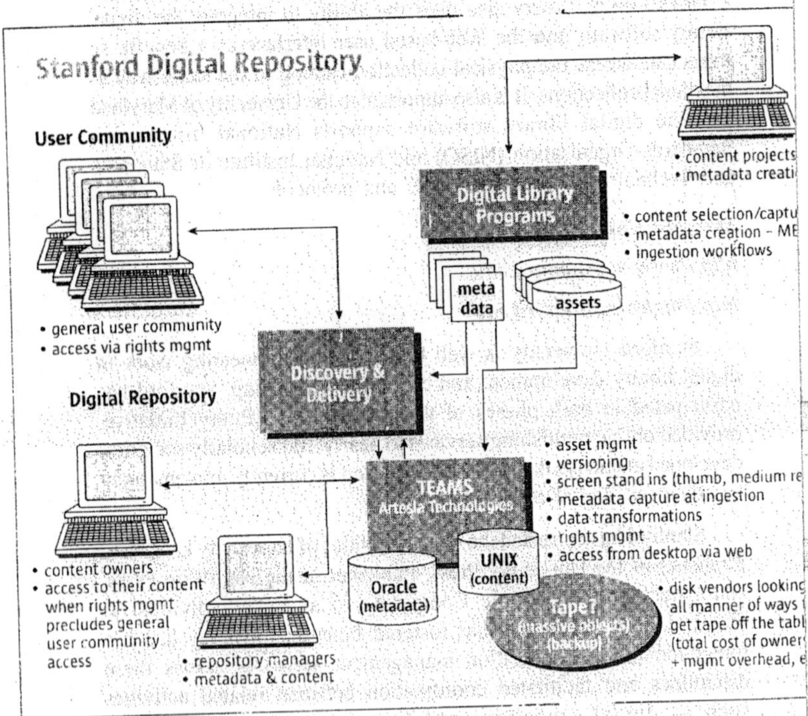

Figure 1.7: Stanford Digital Respository Architecture

environment that lets you describe and interrelate any digital entity. We'll be able to store objects one time in one repository, encode them using different descriptive metadata, and make them available to all different types of applications on campus," explains Stanford Libraries' Chief Information Architect Jerry Persons. The repository will handle authentication using Kerberos certificates and will include rights management and charging mechanisms. Figure 1.7 illustrates the architecture of Stanford's Digital Repository.

Another well-known Stanford venture is HighWire Press, a very successful electronic co-publisher of more that 300 scholarly journals. HighWire Press was started in early 1995; its goal was to assist scientific societies in the transition to new technologies for scholarly communication by providing a common infrastructure. Small not-for-profit publishers are able to take advantage of economies of scale in making the transition to online delivery, thus giving them parity with for-profit publishers.

HighWire is known for its advanced functionality, creating value beyond what would be available in a physical publication, through:

- Links among authors, articles and citations, particularly featuring Toll-Free Linking, which allows readers of an article also to read the full text of other articles cited by the first without charge, whether or not that reader has subscription rights to the journals in which the cited articles appear.
- Advanced searching capabilities, high-resolution images and multimedia.
- Interactive functionality.
- More content (including more articles) than can be physically published in hard-copy.

Originally written in Perl and C++, HighWire migrated to Java in 1998. With the challenge of rapidly scaling the number of publishers supported, Java allowed HighWire programmers to develop application code much faster and more effectively. Performance and availability is critical; HighWire's web site serves 180,000 users and averages nine million hits weekly.

A Sun case study on HighWire Press is available at http://www.sun.com/products-n-solutions/edu/success/paperless.

Future concerns at Stanford include:

- How to improve the digital environment for teaching online, supplementing the teaching, and managing the teaching process.
- How to do data mining across all the different formats of digital information they have to improve the research process.
- How to make it possible for students and faculty to customize their views and take them wherever they go.

Future Directions

The pace of change in digital library technology and its applications has accelerated in recent years as the focus has begun to shift from R&D to full-scale deployment.

Several key trends are emerging and will continue to gain momentum:

- The shift from text and image-based systems to audio and video will continue. As network bandwidth becomes more economical and streaming technologies improve, increasing numbers of institutions will have access to the practicality of full multimedia solutions.
- Broadly accepted best practices will emerge for digitization, rights management, preservation, metadata encoding, and other key digital library processes. The library discipline is highly collaborative and has a history of sharing successful approaches. Debate about these issues will recede as proven techniques mature and spread.
- Standards will move from the discussion and trial stage to widespread adoption. As library industry thought leaders work through existing standards organisations to agree on common approaches, software vendors focusing on the library market will incorporate these agreed-upon standards into their product lines.
- As the center of digital library activity shifts from computer science experiments back to mainstream library implementations, the next generation of digital library development and deployment will focus on standardization,

usability, and productisation—providing greater usability for library patrons, increased inter-operability among digital collections, and more cost-effective choices for institutions just beginning digitisation programmes.

- New technology services will enhance the scholarly communication process just as they have assisted consumers in making purchases from online merchants and auction houses. Referring to the user-provided book reviews and evaluations of sources, CNI's Clifford Lynch comments, "Recommender systems and reputation management systems allow us to augment traditional information review approaches with new methods that mimic social practices and offer additional tools for helping users to deal with the ever growing flood of information." He cites an initiative where a thousand highly rated life scientists were asked to post their recommendations on new articles, which instantly created an expert panel that became an authoritative source for those interested in keeping current with the most important developments in life science.
- Growing dependence on digital information resources will create market pressure for the creation of cooperative solutions for long-term preservation. The charter of library consortia will enlarge to accommodate development of mass storage facilities serving a range of institutions. This will be more cost-effective and more reliable than individual solutions.
- Even now, course management systems providers and textbook publishers are starting to work together. As more texts are published electronically, this linkage will become stronger. In time, digital libraries and learning management systems will be routinely integrated, repurposing the same digital content as both course content and reference material. E-learning will continue to blur the lines between course content, textbooks and reserve materials provided by libraries as these all become digital content managed in common repositories or through common gateways. Digital libraries will be routinely linked to campus e-learning and administrative systems to provide a one-stop virtual campus.

It is clear that digital library technology is becoming an essential enabler of library services. In fact, one recent posting to a digital library e-mail list commented that the term "digital library" is starting to sound as anachronistic as "horseless carriage." Just as the term "electronic banking" lost favour and was subsumed by the more generic "banking," so we will see "digital libraries" discussed less and less often as employment of these technologies becomes universal. It is certain that all libraries of the future will be characterized by technology-based information services that extend and enhance the traditional mission of libraries in our society.

APPENDIX

Sun™ Open Net Environment (Sun ONE)

Based on these industry standards, Sun has defined an open software architecture to support interoperable services on demand across diverse devices. The Sun™ Open Net Environment (Sun ONE) provides an

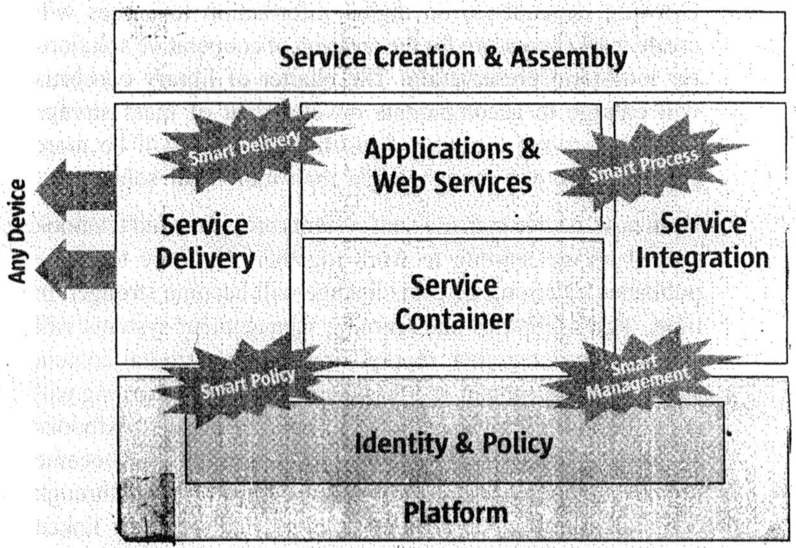

Fig. 1.8: Components of the Sun ONE Smart Web Services Architecture

ideal model for deploying the rich media services that comprise the digital library functionality. Sun ONE provides an open framework for deriving information about a device user's identity, role, and location as well as security, privacy, and permissions requirements that allow the delivery of smart media services within the overall context of the organisation's IT environment. Figure 1.8 summarises the components of the Sun ONE smart Web services architecture.

The Web services architecture includes these elements:

- Service creation and assembly facilities create discrete micro services and assemble them into composite services, or macro services.
- Service delivery facilities provide basic connection, location, discovery, and communication functionality.
- Service integration facilities enable the service to access other Web services and resources such as databases, files, directories, and legacy applications.
- Applications and Web services are the Web services that can be deployed on any type of platform or intelligent device.
- Service container is the runtime environment for the service and provides persistence and state management services, as well as process management facilities that manage service workflow and event processing.
- Identity and policy facilities are deployed to an open directory that manages identity, security, and policy.

The capability of a Web service to understand "context" or the situation it is in allows it to share this information with other services in order to perform as requested. Smart Web services operate within the Sun ONE architecture in four facilities:

- Smart delivery facilities will be able to aggregate, customize, and personalize service results based on context in the digital library of the future.
- Smart process facilities use context to affect business service workflow.

- Smart policy facilities coordinate activities according to policies associated with identity, context, and roles.
- Smart management facilities manage, monitor, and maintain a Web service for inter-service registration, pay-per-use and subscription agreements, service provisioning, and management and runtime policies.

The open, modular, standards-based approach of Sun ONE is allowing the educational community to achieve continuous access to its information resources, an integrated infrastructure, and connectivity to disparate campus information systems through a single user sign-on. The Web-based Sun ONE platform extends the life of existing IT investments while making it easy to add new application services through the re-use of components and services.

See the Sun ONE web-site for more information at www.sun.com/sunone.

NOTES AND REFERENCES

1. This is the reference description, version 1.1 of the Dublin Core Metadata Element Set. See the Dublin Core Home Page *(http://dublincore.org)* for further information concerning the Dublin Core Metadata Element set.
2. American Library Association Preservation Policy, Revised 2001.
3. See the PADI website at www.nla.gov.au/padi for additional information.

2

Relationship Knowledge

The Term and the Concept

When using the term *relationship* we assume that there is an implicit and common understanding of what this term actually means. Although most people have a certain understanding of this term, we nevertheless find that it is difficult to be specific when explaining its meaning. The actual understanding is often vague and sometimes even diverse. When exploring relationships – what they are and how they can be represented – there is however a need to be precise by using definitions or explanations that express or describe the essential nature of the concept.

When examining the actual meaning of a term, it is often useful to refer to Ogden and Richards' triangle of meaning depicted in Figure 2.1 [156]. The triangle of meaning is a model that distinguishes between *symbol, thought or reference*, and *referent*. The model states that the connection between a symbol and what the symbol refers to, is an indirect one that depends on the meaning that each person associates with the symbol.

A symbol has both intension and extension [17]. The extension of a symbol means the referent – the object or the set of objects in the real world to which the symbol indirectly refers. The intension of a symbol is its sense: that which a person normally understands by the expression. A major problem when discussing relationships in information technology is that neither the intension nor the extension is clearly defined. The term *relationship* is merely a symbol that denotes the idea of relationships – an idea that can be highly personal and domain dependent. The extension of this term is all the possible relationships that may exist – a rather large set since almost anything can be related to everything else in the real world. For this reason, an extensional analysis of relationships is a difficult task. An analysis of relationships rather has to be based upon the intension of the term – what is generally understood by this term and how this influences the expressing and processing of relationships in information systems.

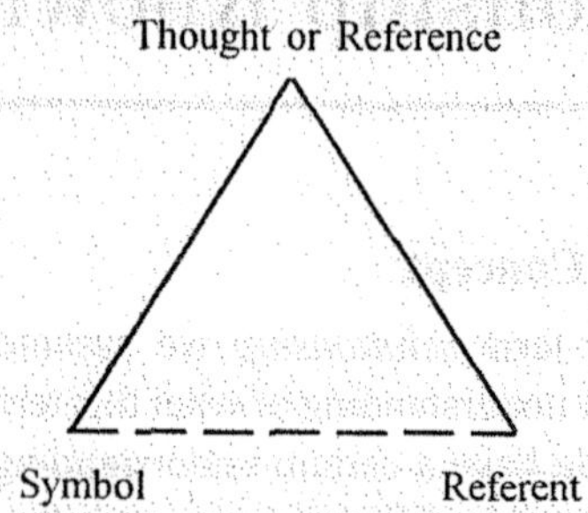

Figure 2.1: The triangle of meaning

A main problem in human discourse is that we use different terms with the same intension (synonyms), or that we use the same term but with different intension (homonyms). This problem is highly relevant when examining literature and theories concerned with relationships. Terms like *association, relation*, and *relationship* denotes, in many cases, the same concept, while in other cases they represent different views or different concepts. When referring to ideas and solutions from different domains, this work will conveniently use the original authors' terminology, despite the problem that two domains may use different terms for the same concept. When referring to theories and solutions developed in this work, the term *relationship* is the preferred one. Correspondingly, the term *related* is used to describe the idea of relationship participation. If there is a relationship between two objects, these objects are related to each other. The term *link* often occurs in computer science, and this work interprets *link* as the implementation of a relationship instance.

Relationship as Knowledge

Understanding human knowledge and reasoning has occupied scientists for centuries, but despite the efforts to understand knowledge and cognition there is no consensus understanding in this field. Rather, there is a set of theories emphasizing the various capabilities of human cognition and discourse where each theory is coloured by the context it is developed in and the purpose it serves. The concept of relationships is, however, present in many of these theories.

In the field of science philosophy as it is a presented by M. Bunge in [27, 28], knowledge and meaning are defined by the notion of *concepts*. Concepts can be defined as a unit of thought, and accordingly the theory of concepts should be the philosophical equivalent to the atomic theory. Like for the atoms of atomic theory, we are not able to see concepts, but concept theory exists because it is a convenient model of the world of human knowledge according to available evidence. Bunge makes a further distinction between different concept types and includes relation concepts as one of the four categories:

- Individual concepts
- Class concepts
- Relation concepts
- Quantitative concepts

Individual concepts apply to individuals, whether definite (specific) or indefinite (generic), like the concept of the definite person "Einstein" or the concept of the mathematical indefinite symbol "X"

Relation concepts apply to relations among objects and can further be divided into *comparative* and *non-comparative* relations. A relation pairs the elements of two (or more) sets and comparative relations, like $<$, are relations that reflect a specific ordering of elements; 2 *is less than* 3, John is *higher than* Paul, based on some measurable quality of the individuals.

A comparable model of knowledge can be found in the field of artificial intelligence exemplified by Han Reichgelt's two main categories of knowledge in [170]:

- Domain knowledge
- Strategic knowledge

Domain knowledge is the information about a domain that a computer needs to manipulate to reason about this particular domain. Strategic knowledge, on the other hand, is knowledge about how to use the domain knowledge to solve particular problems in the domain. One can further distinguish between two kinds of domain knowledge:

- Structural knowledge
- Relational knowledge

Domain knowledge often has a very specific structure that consists of entity types possibly arranged in a classification hierarchy – structural knowledge. Relational knowledge is concerned with the relations between the entities that are distinguished in the structural knowledge.

Statements comparable to Bunge's analogy to the atomic theory can be found in the artificial intelligence discipline as well. According to Davis *et al.* in [52], all knowledge representations are surrogates of the real world. Reasoning, whether it is in programme or in the human mind, is an internal activity, while most things that are reasoned about exist only externally. Representations are imperfect approximations to reality, and each approximation attends to some things and ignores others. In selecting representation, we are necessarily making a set of decisions about how and what to see in the world.

The above examples from science philosophy and artificial intelligence both indicate that relationships are a fundamental category of knowledge that is different from the knowledge we have about atomic entities. Ronald W. Langacker argues in [122] that this distinction is reflected in language itself by the distinction between:

- Nominal predications which designate things and correspond to nouns.
- Relational predications which designate states and processes and correspond to adjectives, adverbs, prepositions, and verbs.

Relationships may be considered a fundamental aspect of knowledge in the sense that it enables higher-level, coherent and complex knowledge to be constructed from the knowledge we have about singular entities. The existence of relationships as a specific category of knowledge, however, is not based on physical laws or neutral observations, but is determined by our inclination to categorize and distinguish between different types – in this case different types of knowledge. The distinction between relationships and the entitles they relate is fundamental in many fields of computer science. This is reflected in information and knowledge representation models like:

- The nodes and arcs of semantic nets
- The terms and propositions of the first order predicate calculus
- The entities and relationships in data modeling.
- The objects and relationships in object-oriented modeling

This is equally important for the field of digital libraries where we may distinguish between the basic entities that we deal with and the numerous relationships that may hold between them. Relationships are the main enablers for building larger knowledge or information structures form the more atomic entities of documents and other content objects.

Where Do Relationships Come From?

Despite this presence of relationships in knowledge models, there is no well-accepted account for the origin of relationships. What are relationships made of? How are they made? This is emphasised by Gaser et al. in [67] by the presentation of five common facts about how relationship knowledge is adapted and interpreted by humans:

- *Fact 1: Language matters.* The relational knowledge we develop is influenced by language. The fact that different languages contain different spatial relation concepts is one proof of this. The German language distinguishes between *an* and *auf* where the English uses the single term *on*. The Korean language, on the other hand, uses the concept of tight fit and loose fit. These and similar discrepancies between the relational terms of different languages show that the various relational concepts are learned, and it seems clear that the individual languages determine the possible relations that can be expressed.

- *Fact 2: Object categories are easier and earlier than relational categories.* In the process of language acquisition children tend to learn object terms earlier and more easily than relation terms. This is not evident in all languages, but all in all there is a bias towards learning nouns over relational terms in early word learning. Studies on other aspects of language acquisition show that common categories are for the most part trivial for children to acquire whereas relational terms exhibit a protracted and erroneous course of development.
- *Fact 3: Understanding relations is dependent on the specific objects entering into those relations.* Children's attention to relations is at first highly dependent on the objects involved but becomes less so with development. The understanding of relational terms is an understanding that develops from a specific similarity-based knowledge at an early stage and then towards a more abstract understanding across diverse kinds of objects and settings.
- *Fact 4: Object properties are relevant to understanding relations.* Studies have shown that object properties matter when people make relational judgements. The real-world use and recognition of relations requires an understanding of the objects that participate in the relationship.
- *Fact 5: Relational concepts have a category structure.* Research indicates that relational concepts seem to be like object concepts in having a graded similarity structure. Studies of how both children and adults perceive relations like higher and lower show that some instances of a relation are better instances, even with respect to relations that do not appear to be graded.

Together, these facts reflect some general observations of how relationships are learned and interpreted by humans. One general conclusion is that there is no predefined set of relationships that are globally understood. Relationships are highly influenced by learning which for instance should imply that relationship mechanisms need to be support ways in which users can learn the meaning of unfamiliar relationships. Another observation is that the understanding of a relationship is depending on the participants of the relationship, which should imply that first-class relationships need to include relevant information about the participants if this information is unavailable by other means.

The Mathematical Relation

One contribution that strongly has influenced the notion of relationships in computer science is the mathematical relation which can be viewed as a formal abstraction of order among things. In contrast to other approaches, we find that in mathematics the relation primitive is defined in terms of other more fundamental elements in the mathematical set theory [206].

A relation is a set of ordered sets. In this context, ordered means that the elements of the set are positioned. The first coordinate stands in a particular order to the second etc. Ordered sets are usually referred to as tuples, and the size of the tuple is referred to as the degree. A binary relation is a set of ordered pairs, a ternary relation is made up of ordered triples, etc. For sets $A,B \subseteq U$, any subset of the Cartesian product $A \times B$ is called a relation from A to B. Any subset of $A \times A$ is called a binary relation on A. Whereas the Cartesian product represents all possible unique combinations with one element from each set, the relation is a subset that reflects the actual truth conforming combinations. A relation corresponds to the extension of a predicate. Given a domain of discourse containing all humans, called H, the Cartesian product $H \times H$ is formed. The predicate $F(x.y)$, interpreted as x is the father of y. is true for certain ordered pairs in $H \times H$ and false for others. The set of ordered pairs for which $F(x.y)$ are true is called the extension of the predicate $F(x.y)$ or the relation of fatherhood in H. A function is a specific kind of relation. A relation F in $A \times B$ can be called a function when every member of A occurs exactly once as the first coordinate in the set of ordered pairs of the relation from A to B.

A mathematical relation does not necessarily correspond to a relationship as a conceptual knowledge primitive. The coordinates of a tuple may be attribute values from different domains used to describe an entity, in which case each tuple represents an entity, alternatively the coordinates may be keys – entity identifiers – in which case the relation reflects a relationship. This is quite evident in the implementation of data using database relations. The database relation is a lower level structure that can be used to represent many kinds of information in an organised way.

In mathematics a relation is said to specify the set of tuples for which the relation holds. Each tuple can be interpreted as instances of the relation. In mathematics, however, the set is the relation. When discussing relationships in the context of information systems a comparable distinction can be made between the relationship as a class-level definition or set and the instances of the set – relationship instance. The Unified Modeling Language defines the individual connection among two or more objects as a link – a tuple of object references [176]. This corresponds to how a link generally is understood in other disciplines such as hypermedia. Links, however,

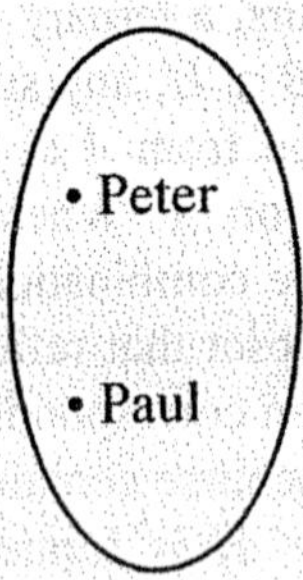

Humans

The Cartersian product:

Peter	Peter
Peter	Paul
Paul	Paul
Paul	Peter

$C = H \times H$

The relation of fatherhood:

Peter	Paul

$Fatherhood \subseteq H \times H$

Figure 2.2: Relation and Cartesian Products

are not always explicitly belonging to a particular class or set other than the universal set of all links.

The Relationship as a Modeling Primitive

The introduction of the relationship as a distinct modeling primitive in computer and information science can be traced back to the emerging of the semantic data modeling languages of the 1970-80's. Unlike the earlier data models, such as the hierarchical data model and the network model, which mostly were used to specify the structure of data for storage in record based file formats, the essence of semantic modeling is that the model should reflect the way humans conceptualise a domain. To achieve this many modeling languages have introduces a relationship modeling primitive, and the ability to describe relationships is by several described as one of the main characteristics of semantic data models [164, 166]. A major contribution was given by P. Chen with the introduction of the Entity-relationship model [37], which distinguishes between entities and the relationships they participate in.

In semantic modeling languages and the later object-oriented modeling languages, relationships are supported by specific primitives. One example is the Unified Modeling Language which defines different relationship primitives including aggregation and generalization. The expression of user defined relationships is supported by the generic association primitive. Relationship modeling follows a comparable pattern in many languages. Aspects of a relationship commonly expressed in models may include:

- *Related entities*: Entities or classes are in most cases prior and the relationships are specified between specific entities or classes.

- The relationship *degree* is the number of participating entities or objects of a relationship. A relationship between 2 entities – by far the most frequently occurring incident – gives a relationship with the degree of two; a binary relationship. Relationships, as well as mathematical relations, can however include more than two entities, *e.g.*, a ternary relationship that relates three entities. Any degree higher than two is often referred to as relationships of n-ary degree.

- *Cardinality,* also called multiplicity, is another characteristic used when modeling relationships. The cardinality constraint indicates the number of relationships instances that a given object is allowed to participate in. If an object only can participate in one relationship of a specific kind, the cardinality constraint is 1. Other numbers may be used to specify other cardinality constraints. If the number is undefined, the cardinality constraint is often said to be N.
- *Participation* is a constraint that is used to express whether the entity is required to participate in a relationship or may exist within the system without participating in a relationship. It can either be expressed using specific notational symbols for this purpose, or it can be combined with the cardinality constraint by the specification of a cardinality ratio. The cardinality ratio of 1..N expresses that an object has to participate in at least one relationship. The participation constraint 0..N defines that relationship participation is optional.
- *Names* are often used to express the meaning of a relationship. A single name for the relationship can be used and role names can additionally be used to enrich the relationship with additional semantics that describes the participant of the relationship.
- Relationship may additionally be defined with *class-like capabilities*. The difference between a relationship and an entity is not a very distinct one, and intermediary solutions may include the modeling of relationships that include attributes and methods of their own.

A more comprehensive support for relationship modeling can be found in other languages like the Referent language for conceptual modeling [186]. This language supports the formal definition of a rich set of conceptual structures and includes the ability to model relational compositions and derived relationships.

In the context of modeling languages, the relationship primitive is merely one out of several primitives. Together these primitives make up the vocabulary that is used when capturing and describing the domain of discourse in the software engineering process. The actual usage of these primitives can, however, be diverse. A marriage may be defined as a relationship between the two involved persons, but a marriage may also be defined as a class. Choosing between the relationship and the class primitive to represent a specific kind of information is, in this case, a design issue.

A more extreme approach can also be used in modeling by rephrasing other commonly used constructs as relationships. Compound objects and collection objects like lists, bags or sets can be interpreted as specific relationship constructs, with each object as a participating member in a relationship. The objects participating in an aggregation are typically of different types, whereas for a collection object the participating objects are topically of the same type.

The Meaning of Relationships

The emphasis so far has been on the general concept of relationships. However, in real-world applications the focus is on specific relationships with specific semantics. The mere notion of things being related to each other is quite useless without knowing the meaning of the relationship, as pointed out by Rebecca Green in [73]:

> *To specify a relationship, we must be able, first, to designate all the parties bound by the relationship and, second, to specify the nature of the relationship.*

In mathematics, the relational operators like equals (=), less than (<) or greater than (>) express specific and precise meaning that is well understood by those who are familiar with numbers and mathematics. The ideal solution for any deployment of relationship knowledge is to be able to interpret relationships at the same level of preciseness. This is, however, far from the situation when it comes to common knowledge and information. As argued by Gasser *et al.*, [67], there is no universal set of innate relations hard-wired into biology. The relationship vocabulary is determined by the language and the interpretation of a relationship is depending on the objects involved. Relationship types that are considered fundamental in modeling languages include categories like:

- Classification and instantiations which are used to specify the relationship between an entity and the class that this entity belongs to. Generalization/specification which is used to express the relationship between classes where one class is a more general super-type and the other is a more specific subtype.
- Aggregation and composition that are used to express the relationship between the higher level whole and its subparts.
- General associations that are used to model application specific relationships.

The development of relationship vocabularies in other domains may conclude with other fundamental relationship categories, or the interpretation of what constitutes the fundamental categories can be a variation over the same theme. In thesauruses, relationships are used to express the various dependencies and connections between the terms of the thesaurus. Three general classes of fundamental relationships have been established [39]:

- The equivalence relationship that denotes the relationship between a preferred term and the non-preferred term.
- The hierarchical relationship that represents pairs of terms in their superordinate or subordinate status. The superordinate term represents the whole and the subordinate represents the part. This includes both whole/part relationships and categories of generalization hierarchies.
- The associative relationship denotes the relationships between terms that are neither hierarchical nor equivalence.

In domains related to digital libraries there have been quite many attempts to define typologies of application-specific relationships. The ACM/SIGIR[1] workshop "Beyond Word Relations" examined a number of relationship types significant for information retrieval systems and concluded with the following list of relationship types [94]:

- Word-based relationships that denote documents that share the same vocabulary or word.

- Attribute-based relationships that denote relationships based on shared characteristics as same author or same place of origin etc.
- Document-document hierarchical relationships that denotes situations where one document is a sub-set or super-type of the ohter.
- Document-document hierarchical relationship and include relationships that denote conceptual equivalence, sequences, etc.
- Document-to-document influence relationships that denote relationships where one document has affected the writing of another.
- Topic-based relationships that exist between documents that are related through less obvious topical resemblances.
- Usage-based relationships that exist between documents that are related through the use of the documents.

The field of relationships between bibliographic entries has been examined by Tillet in [196, 197] and by Leazer in [125]. Tillett identifies the following categories:

- Equivalence relationships which hold between exact copies of the same object.
- Derivate relationships which hold between the original and the modified version.
- Descriptive relationships which hold between a bibliographic entity a description, criticism evaluation, or review.
- Whole-part relationships which hold between a bibliographic entity and a component part of that entity.
- Accompanying relationships which hold between a work and the accompanying material.
- Sequential relationship which holds between bibliographic entities that continue or precede one another.
- Shared characteristic relationships that hold between entities that happen to have the same subject, author, etc.

A rich set of bibliographic relationships partially based on this is in the bibliographic information model proposed by the IFLA Study Group on the Functional Requirements for Bibliographic Records [100].

A different discipline that has a comparable concern in relationship typologies is hypermedia. Several taxonomies for hypermedia link types have been proposed and overviews are given by Kopak in [119] and by Verbyla in [203]. A hypermedia link is essentially only a connection between hypermedia nodes. A link type is needed to express the semantics of the link and in the way enable the link to become a meaningful relationship. One early attempt to define a link typology for hypermedia can be found in the TEXNET system [199] which included a list with over seventy different link types. This extensive list was motivated by the desire to provide for a sufficiently rich set of link types that users could select among, and to prevent the need for users to create new user-defined types. A more general categorisation of link types is identified by Lisa Baron in [131]. She identifies two general types of links:

- Organisational links that are used to describe the "surface" structure of documents, for example the links used to organize the presentation of documents; links to and from the table of contents, and previous and next links to browse sequential structures.
- Content-based links that deals with the relationships between nodes of the text.
- Content-based links can further be categorised as:
- Semantic links that describe the semantic association between words or concepts.
- Rhetorical links that are used by the author to lead the reader through a sequence of information elements.
- Pragmatic links that are concerned with practical results like warnings and errors.

A different concern in the field of relationship semantics is *how* to express the meaning of a relationship. When modelling a relationship it is often labelled with a single term that denotes the intended semantics of the relationship. The mere purpose of this label is to capture and signal the semantics of the relationship to the principals and to the implementers.

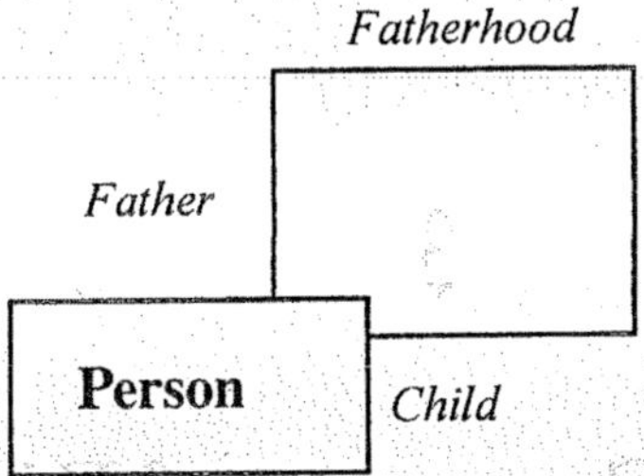

Figure 2.3: Relationship naming

Certain modeling languages introduce a richer semantic typing of relationships by allowing for roles to be associated with the participants of a relationship, if two persons are related to each other by the *Fatherhood* relationship, it is difficult to determine who is the father and who is the child without any further knowledge of the persons. The role type denotes the role the participant plays in the relationship, *e.g.,* that one participant is the *father* and that the other is the *child* as illustrated in Figure 2.3. The use of more complex typing of links has been explored in the field of hypermedia as well [143]. A different convention found in both modeling languages and hypermedia is the use of direction to indicate the origin and the target of a relationship.

As pointed out by Gasser *et al.,* the understanding of relations is dependent on the specific objects entering into those relations. This implies that a relationship type can be insufficient for expressing the full semantics of a relationship. In addition to rolenames there can be a need for even more information about the participants if information about the objects of the relationship is unavailable or insufficient for the proper interpretation of a relationship.

NOTE

1. Association of Computing Machinery/Special Interest Group in Information Retrieval.

3

General Concepts of Digital Libraries and Information Retrieval

Introduction

This report is focused mainly on further development of document classification algorithms and their potential applications in various areas of digital library world. Special attention is also paid to clustering and summarisation technologies.

Previous chapter constitutes a description of a real world digital library implemented at a regional power utility company. A brief introduction to existing document classification methods, presenting advantages and disadvantages of existing categorisation technologies, thus reasoning development of yet another method. *Itemsets categorisation*, a new document classification method, is the prime topic of my further research. Automatic document sumarisation is the topic of this is prerequisite for *itemsets categorisation.* Other potential applications of *itemsets* method are briefly introduced in this book.

Development of *itemsets* classifier, a method suitable for short documents, was motivated by presence of freely accessible abstracts on the web. Digital collections of abstracts can be developed cheaply, avoiding the risk of copyright infringement.

Our further research work will concentrate namely on the following: Domain-independent optimisation of itemsets categorisation method and its application in full-length text files, and testing *itemsets* method on additional document collections (both in Czech and English). Categorisation of full-length documents by *itemsets* classifier will require my involvement in research on suitable document summarisation methods. I will also look for specific applications of *itemsets* method (and their implementation), namely modification of Naïve Bayes classifier, itemsets-based document clustering, unsolicited e-mail filtering and information querying.

Needed to note that some of the new ideas and concept contained in this report have already been implemented. Other ideas, suggestions and paradigms will be subject to my further research and, hopefully, also implemented. The prime topic of this report is permanently tested on a real intranet application, which is undergoing quite dynamic day-to-day development.

Numerous information sources on digital libraries and document management systems can be found on the web, such as www.dlib.org (including renowned *D-Lib Magazine*). See Section 8 – Web Information Sources for further references. The issue of digital libraries is also the topic of the well-known *European Conference on Research and Advanced Technology for Digital Libraries* (ECDL).

Basic Terminology

Let's define several key terms to be used in the following sections of this report. *Corpus* is an extensive, structured and comprehensive collection of documents in a given language. Corpuses can include either plain or tagged documents. *Morpheme* represents an elementary language element, such as root, prefix, or suffix. *Morphological analyzer* is an automation providing a set of basic forms (lemmas and grammar rules) for each form of a word. *Morphological normalisation (stemming)* denotes a process of converting word forms into corresponding basic forms. *Morphological variations* are inflected word forms (*word declensions*) occurring at some languages, such as Czech. *Vocabulary problem* denotes potential use of different synonyms by document authors and users entering their queries. *Phrase* is a short sequence of significant words bearing some meaning.

Phrase search can be implemented by full-text search of phrases in a document collection. *Stop list* is a list of non-significant words, *i.e.*, words bearing no semantics (prepositions, conjunctions, etc.). *Classification* (or *categorisation*) is the process of arranging specific items (such as words, documents, messages) into classes, or categories, using (combination of) features depending on specific classification method. A priori definition of classes (categories) by a librarian is required. *Clustering*, on the other hand, is used to arrange specific items into groups that are defined along the way, without prior definition of categories. A *Itemset* denotes a set of items (such as words, goods in a supermarket, etc.) of some kind.

Various authors often confuse the meaning of *keyword*, term and descriptor. To be exact, *keywords* represent the simplest expressions (*e.g.*, "liberalisation", "price", etc.). whereas *terms* and *descriptors* denote multiword language a phrases, such as "bipolar transistor" or "structured query language".

Quantitative and Qualitative Assessment of the Search Process

In order to assess the quality of a search engine, we need to define some basic parameters and criteria. Elementary measurements include *precision* and *recall* coefficients.

$$\text{Precision : } P = \frac{N_{Rrel}}{N_R} \qquad \text{Recall : } R = \frac{N_{Rrel}}{N_{DBrel}}$$

Where:

N_{Rrel} = Number of retrieved documents relevant to the user,

N_R = Total number of documents retrieved.

N_{DBrel} = Total number of documents in the document collection relevant to the user.

In order to quantify the above coefficients, users must declare how many documents are relevant to them. It order to determine *recall*, we need to know the number of relevant documents in the whole collection, which is often impossible (such as in case of www).

Taxonomy of Search Methods

Statistical Analysis of Absolute Term Frequency

Quantification of *absolute term frequency* is the elementary method used by search engines. It entails monitoring the number of matches between the word entered and its frequency in the text database. Such a definition of relevance is quite unreliable, however it is considered sufficient for giving a basic hint. Document *ranking* by search engines is often expressed in percent or by a number. Documents are then sorted according to their ranking, starting with those considered most relevant to the user.

In many languages, such as Czech and other Slavic languages, we are coping with derived word forms (declensions). This is a problem not only for querying, but also for document indexing, namely when we deal with *irregular* word declensions. We must also take into account non-significant words, *i.e.*, words with grammatical function only, lacking any semantics.

Syntactical Methods

Syntactical methods are based on comparing syntactical text structures with structure templates stored in a special database. Basic document structuring is based on document heads, sections, parts, chapters, paragraphs, etc.

Semantic Methods

Document retrieval by means of semantic methods is based on analysis of the semantic structure of document content. Semantic analysis of the text database must be performed. Information retrieval system can be represented, for example, by a semantic tree structure including various topics of interest.

Some search engines display query terms in retrieved documents using different typeface or by means of highlighting (such as *Uniseek* search engine described in section 2.5). Metadata are often displayed in addition to text information in order top provide further semantics.

Full-text search in very large document collections is not very efficient unless it is accompanied by support techniques, such as document structuring, hypertent, thesauri, domain dictionaries, etc.

The language of lawyers, for example, is constantly changing by not only introducing new words, but also by altering the semantics of existing terms [22]. Some words, seemingly unambiguous, can have as much as a dozen of different meanings, often contradictory ones. Ambiguity of legal speak is widely known, being less of a problem in strictly technical libraries, such as the one of a power utility company.

Taxonomy of Search Models

Boolean Model

Boolean model facilitates queries consisting of several words associated by logical operators, as well phrases. By implementing logical operators, we end up with a system based on Boolean logic, *i.e.*, system supporting Boolean search model.

User's query must be passed to lexical and syntax analysers that must separate terms from logical operators depending on systax rules, recognize phrases and parenthesized expressions.

Indexing is implemented by means of a sparse Boolean matrix of k x n (k documents, n terms). Logical operations on terms correspond to Boolean vector operations (using bit arithmetic), with highly efficient processing time. Bitmap indexing can be expressed as follows:

d_1 (t_{11}, t_{12}, ..., t_{1n})

d_2 (t_{21}, t_{22}, ..., t_{2n})

...

d_k (t_{kl} t_{k2} ..., t_{kn})

Where t_{ij} = 1 if term j is contained in document i, otherwise t_j = 0. For domains of a large cardinality (*i.e.*, high number of terms) we can apply compressed bitmap indexing, using a suitable compression method, e.g., *RLL* encoding.

User's query $\boldsymbol{Q}$ = (q_1, q_2, ..., q_n) is represented by a Boolean vector of the length n, which is matched against Boolean vectors of individual documents d_i = (t_1, t_2, ..., t_n). For queries containing *AND* operators only (*i.e.*, conjunctive queries, *AND*-queries), d_i is included in the result iff $\boldsymbol{Q}$ && $d_i == \boldsymbol{Q}$. Should a query include OR operators only (*i.e.*, disjunctive query, OR-query), document is retrieved iff $\boldsymbol{Q}$ && $d_i <> 0$. Relevance coefficient can be simply defined by the scalar product of a Boolean query vector $\boldsymbol{Q}$ and the Boolean vector representing document d_i. Documents retrieved upon applying an *OR*-query can be ranked in descending order according to the above scalar product.

In general, Boolean queries can be defined in conjunctive normal form (CNF,) conjunction of disjunctions of terms or their negations), or disjunctive normal form (*DNF*, disjunction of conjunctions of terms or their negations). The length of a query is then defined as the number of disjunctions (*CNF*), or conjunctions (*DNF*).

A query vector can be subject to query expansion (application of thesaurus and inference rules), converting the original query vector to a modified Boolean vector.

The above Boolen matrix can be refined by specifying exact location of each term in the document. In place of logical values $t_{ij} = 0/1$, each matrix cell can represent a record {*0/1*; *offset*}, where *offset* is the displacement from the origin of the document, according to applicable granularity level (chars, sentences, paragraphs, sections, etc.).

The table below presents customary logical and positional operators and symbols used in definitions of general regular expressions:

Table 3.1: Logical and positional (proxy) operators

Operator	*Meaning*
X AND Y *X & Y*	Documents containing both term X and term Y (conjunctive query)
X OR Y X/Y	Documents containing term X or term Y (disjunctive query)
NOT X *!X* *–X*	Documents not containing term X
X NEAR Y	Documents containing term X in the vicinity of term Y (at the distance

X ~ Y	less then a predefined number of words)
X (n) words Y	Documents containing term *X* and also term *Y* at most *n* words after term *X*
X adj Y	Documents containing term *X* followed by term *Y* (the same as *X (0) words Y*)
X sentence Y	Documents containing terms *X* and *Y* in the same sentence
X paragraph Y	Documents containing terms *X* and *Y* in the same paragraph
(expression)	Expressions in parentheses
"phrase"	Documents containing a specific phrase (several terms delimited by quotes)
+*X*	Documents that must contain term *X*
X category	Documents containing term *X* at a specific category, e.g.
Delphi/Software -	Full-stop represents any character
*x**	Star indicates an arbitrary (also zero) number of occurrences of character *x*
x+	Plus sign indicates arbitrary (1 or more) number of occurrences of character *x*
[s]	Arbitrary character (exactly one) of string s
[^s]	Arbitrary character, except chars contained in string s
[x-y]	Arbitrary character in the range from *x* to *y*. Several ranges can be defined simultaneously, *e.g.*, [a-z0-9] indicates an arbitrary lower case character or number,
Other search specifiers or functions	
Language	User can specify the language of document being searched
Family filter	User can leave out documents not suitable for children
Results per page	Users can specify the number of documents per page
Customised settings	*e.g.*, character set, document size, etc.

The disadvantage of the Boolean model is unsatisfactory relevance ranking of documents when displaying query results. Definition of user queries is not intuitive and expressive power of the Boolean model is relatively limited.

Vector Model

Vector model is in fact an extension of the Boolean model, trading logical weights for weight coefficients expressed by real numbers. In vector model we can use more intuitive queries, or even queries in natural language. We are making use of the concept of relevance, which is not covered in the Boolean model. The original system must be enhanced by index tables of significant terms (sparse matrices in a compressed form), weight definitions and efficient index file management. Methods of computing document relevance against query are the issue of proprietary algorithms implemented by search engines.

The following general approach applies:

Let's consider *k* documents and *n* index terms. We will assign weights

W_{ij} = $TF_{ij} \times IDF_j$ (the weight of term t_j in document d_i), where:

TF_{ij} = *Term Frequency*, frequency of term t_j in document d_i

DF_j = *Document Frequency*, the number of documents containing term t_j

$$IDF_j = \log\left(\frac{m}{DF_j}\right) + 1$$

IDF_j = *Inverse Document Frequency*, the function inversely proportional to the number of documents containing term t_j, where *m* is the total number of documents in the collection.

Prior to processing a query, we need to compute query term weights q_j in the range [0;1], by applying the following formula (Salton and Buckley, 1988):

$$q_j = \frac{0{,}5 + (0{,}5 \times TF_j)}{TF_{max}} \times IDF_j$$

where TF_j is the frequency of query term t_j, TF_{max} is the maximum frequency of an arbitrary query term, and IDF_j represents *IDF* of term *tj* in the document collection.

Index Structure and Similarity

Index is represented by the following data structures: weight matrix W (containing weights w_{ij}), term frequency matrix TF (TF_{ij}), document frequency vectors DF (DF_j), and inverse document frequency vectors (DF (IDF_j). Context (such as headings, text body, keywords) of terms should be taken into account while associating weights with document terms. Indexing granularity can be refined by replacing "pointers" to documents by pointers to specific paragraphs or sentences.

Similarity $Sim\ (Q.\ d_i)$ can be quantified by various coefficients with subsequent impact on precision (P) and recall (R) of information retrieval.

The simplest (not normalized) method of computing *similarity coefficient* is a plain scalar product of query and document weight vectors:

$$Sim\ (Q,d_i) = \sum_{j=1....n} (q_j \times w_{ij})$$

Another popular method is *cosine similarity function*, which can be illustrated by geometrical distance between query and document vectors in vector pace of dimension n:

$$Sim\ (Q,d_l)\ \frac{\sum_{j=1....n}(q_j \times w_{lj})}{\sum_{j=i....n}(q_j)^2 \times \sum_{j=i....n}(w_{lj})^2}$$

Documents representing result of a query are sorted per relevance, placing first documents with the highest $Sim\ (Q,\ d_i)$ values.

Conjunctive and disjunctive queries are not distinguished in vector model. *NOT* operator can be implemented by extending the range of query term weights from [0; 1] to [-1; 1].

The main advantage of vector retrieval model as opposed to Boolean model is document ranking per relevance with respect to user's query. Retrieval usability is thus significantly better compared to the Boolean model.

Searching for Similar Documents

The above formula for computing q_j, can be used to implement "*find similar documents*" feature. Should it be the case, query is represented by the document (or an abstract) itself – we are trying to quantify similarity between the original document (*i.e.*, the query) and documents in the collection.

Index terms result from the linguistic analysis of all documents in the collection. The number of terms should reflect our effort in reaching compromise between the search speed and full semantic coverage.

Fuzzy Model

Users can specify weights associated with query terms – resulting in a special case of vector search model (fuzzy search). Specification of these weights by users is both difficult and subjective.

The advantage of fuzzy concept is the ability to simulate words in natural language, which is extremely important for query languages. Majority of query languages is based on two-value logic [0;1], with no opportunity to convert adequately vague (*fuzzy*) requirements to the query. The expressive power of the Boolean model is rather limited; therefore we can anticipate increased recall of the search engine by using fuzzy (multiple-valued) logic in the query. Response will include also those items that did not fit into strict two-value criteria. The expressive power of a non-procedural query language containing fuzzy logic elements will therefore increase.

Linguistic Aspects in the Context of a Digital Library

Morphological Analysis of Queries

A search engine can make automatic query term expansion by synonyms, or possibly other morphological variations of query terms (reverse stemming). Unsophisticated query expansion can, however, result in significant drop in precision (while increasing recall). Further ramification requires user's feedback, often taking place in several query-response phases.

Stemming

Stemming (*lemmatization, morphological normalisation*) denotes the process of forming basic word forms. Stemming can be used not only for creating normalised index terms, but also for converting query terms into their corresponding base forms. It is common wisdom in IR that stemming improves *recall* with at most a small reduction in *precision.*

The simplest stemming method consists in trivial *cutoff* of word endings (using a database of predefined word endings), so that the resulting word fraction included at least three or four characters. As follows from our practical testing on document collection of Czech technical documents, trivial stemming is quite satisfactory, considering the ease of its implementation. *Dictionary* approach, on the other hand, is based on a brute-force searching in an extensive database of all derived word forms, substituting base forms for corresponding original terms. As stemming is performed off-line, time is not a problem in this case. Quality of stemming clearly depends on the quality of language corpus used. We have implemented dictionary-based stemming using i-spell corpus distributed under general public license (GPL). For more information on stemming by means of *i-spell* see section further improvement in this chapter.

According to Dumais *et al.*, [32] speaking in the context of document classification by inductive learning algorithms, the simplest document representation (using individual words delimited by white spaces with no stemming) was, surprisingly, at least as good as representations involving more complicated syntactic and morphological analysis. However, these results apply to Reuters collection of short English newswire stories. Application to Czech documents leads to largely different results.

Practical stemming algorithms can be found, for example, at http://snowball.sourceforge.net/index.php (stemmers for English, French, Spanish, German, Russian and other languages).

Stop-List

Stop-list (dictionary of non-significant words) is applied to text corpus in order to eliminate words bearing no semantics, *i.e.,* words playing grammatical role only. Application of a stop-list is a must in every digital library. Stop-list used for our digital library (see Section 2) currently contains non-significant English terms listed in the figure below. These terms are used both during the indexing phase and user query processing.[1] A suitable stop-list for the Czech language can be found in [17].

an	the	for	be	is	am	are
you	he	she	it	we	they	them
do	to	in	at	on	if	as
by	of	and	or	then	than	so
which	their	was	were	will	how	when
here	there	not				

Figure 3.1: Example stop-list for the English language.

Stop words are removed from text corpus by the lexical analyzer. Collection of non-significant words can be created ad hoc on the basis of a frequency vocabulary, as this task is largely *domain-dependent*. Final content of the stop-list must be fine-tuned manually.

Right-hand Word Expansion

This concept is related to using wildcards in the user query (such as *,%,?,_). We can modify lexical analyzer to expand query terms with wildcards to corresponding full terms (stored in a database – upon stemming). Search engine is then provided with expanded query without any wildcards. As a result we achieve higher recall (with likely smaller precision).

Thesaurus

Terms contained in a *thesaurus* (a hierarchical dictionary of synonyms) are classified into synonym classes. Thesauri are often used not only for text corpus indexing, but also for information querying. Should a system respond by too few documents, we can apply thesaurus to expand the query by additional terms.[2] By analogy, should the response be too extensive, we can use thesaurus to make query more specific. Systems, integrating a thesaurus are sometimes denoted as third-generation full-text search engines. Design of a thesaurus can be simplified by concentrating on a specific domain only.

When expanding user's query, we should take into account the length of the original query: the longer the query, the more synonyms we can add and vice versa.

Well-defined thesaurus can improve system's response significantly. The system can demonstrate some intelligence, depending on the content and quality of thesaurus database.

Thesaurus can solve, at least partially, the *vocabulary problem i.e.,* use of different terms for the same concept by document authors and digital library users.

Thesaurus can also solve the issue of ever-changing grammar rules, such as concurrent use of Czech terms like "liberalisace" and "liberalisace", "impulz" and 'impuls", etc.

Digital Library of ZapadoCeska Energetika

The purpose of this technical digital library is to enhance knowledge and skills of company employees, who should regularly monitor the latest trends and advancements in their area of specialty. Majority of employees does to have the time to monitor information resources. This issue is comprehensively tackled by the intranet digital library, storing information and providing it conveniently to all users. Materials can be stored directly by a person having the information, a designated group of people, or an external data provider.

We will consider a real-life information system called *InfoServis* used by Zapadoceska energetika, *a.s.,* a regional power utility. The system was installed in the commercial environment in early 1999. Author of this report is on the team responsible for the design and development of the library described herein.

Main Features

Solution is based on a three-tier architecture with thin clients (web browsers) accessing relational database. The system has gradually developed into a full-fledged object-oriented multi-platform client server application. Text data are stored in a semi-structured object form.

All data in InforServis are classified into topic trees, which can be defined by a librarian arbitrarily. Tree nodes hold the actual data (called materials). Materials can take various forms, usually consisting of several text fields (*e.g.*, title, short description or an abstract, keywords) and one or more attached files in any format (PDF, MS Word, MS Excel, MS PowerPoint, HTML. XML, etc.).

Main features of InforServis:

- Document classification using customer-defined taxonomy;
- Immediate access to new materials, quick list of abstracts, full-text available upon request;
- Integration with a search engine (*uniseek*);
- Individual user settings (profiles – automated notification of new or updated materials;
- Automated replication of data between two InfoServis installations via e-mail;
- All data are treated as objects linked by semantic networks – guaranteeing maximum flexibility and extensibility;
- Automated archiving of outdated documents and corresponding database records. Integrating InfoServis with Uniseek (search engine) allows users searching for information in text fields of materials as well as in documents attached. Search can be restricted to sub-trees only. Uniseek is described in detail in section *Search Engine—Uniseek*

Technical Features

Implementation is based on a relational database using a tree-like taxonomy. Technical solution includes a non-distributed text database, software tools for graphical database administration using standard web browser, customer-specific taxonomy (based on keyword analysis, customer requirements and domain expert, and software tools for generating dynamic web pages using C++/Java code.

From users' viewpoint, there are typically no write operations (except administrative data); therefore transaction integrity problems are not an issue. Transaction control would be a problem, as web server is a stateless entity (there is no context maintained for individual clients). The SQL server used (*MySQL*) currently does not support transaction processing, which is well balanced by its significant speed in day-to-day usage.

InfoServis can be linked to file server's directory tree to maintain additional information on individual documents. The system can detect new document and ask their authors to enter the required data.

Software Requirements include *Linux* operating system, *MySQL* database server, Apache web server, *PHP 4*, and Sendmail. By using MySQl Database server we can generate text form of the complete database by single mysqldump command, and thus transfer the database to another server easily. By analogy, we can restore the complete database in a batch from a single plain-text file.

Hardware Requirements: Web applications running under Linux are known for modest hardware requirements. InfoServis can run on a modest Pentium II server fitted with 128 MB RAM and IDE hard drive.

Object-Oriented Design

Each element in InfoServis is treated as an object. Attributes (features) are defined for each object. Object handling depends on the object type (*e.g.*, "article", "company", "product", "process", etc.). Object steps are summarized in the object catalog (see below).

Objects are inter-connected by semantic links (such as *translation* link between two objects of *document* type, *topic* link between object of document type and object of *topic* type, parent link between two objects of *topic* type, defining tree-like topic hierarchy).

Object Catalog

The following major object types are used:

Topics define the area of interest. Topics form a hierarchy, facilitating multi-criterion information classification. Documents: Instances of Document lass represent materials as such (including attributes such as title, language, etc.). *Source*: Source objects are necessary for expanding the information base. We can create links between topics build taxonomy of sources, create source "rings", classify sources into topic trees, etc.

Links Catalog

Types of links are defined by means of *links catalogue*. It is a list of available links and detailed description of these. Defferent links are used for different object types; however, some links are used for all objects. We have defined links between topics, between documents, between documents/sources and topics, and between documents and sources.

Object-oriented solution incorporating semantic networks provides opportunity for future development, such as defining inheritance hierarchy of object types (e.g. company – customer – wholesale customer), facilitating various analyses over the data.

Auto-Links

InfoServis also includes a special form of references called *autolinks*. These facilitate document classification into tree hierarchy. If we have, for example, an autolink from "Wind power plants" to "Renewable energy", documents classified to the first class will be also automatically classified into the latter. One. It is an example of *unidirectional autolink. Bidirectional outlinks* are also utilized widely. Semantically speaking, unidirectional autholinks mostly represent *is-part-of* relationship (such as "e-commerce" topic *is-part-of* "e-anything" topic), whereas bi-directional autolinks represent is-identical-to or is-similar-to relations, namely when making references from one knowledge tree to another, saving librarian from making multiple classifications.

System's Architecture

Implementation of the digital library is based on a three-tier architecture depicted in figure 3.2. Thin client (interface layer) is represented by a standard web browser. Apache web server plays the role of an application server (second layer), communicating via PHP scripts with MySQL database server (third layer). Administrator can also communicate directly with database server by using either command line or MyAdmin management tool. Three-tier model is suitable for applications accessing data from various heterogeneous sources, which is the case.

Cliet's role (MSIE, Netscape, Opera) consists in presentation functions only (displaying HTML code distributed by the web server, and sending data entered by users). Platform-independent web application server, Apache, takes care of the business logic (SQL, input data processing and forwarding these data to DB server, management of user profiles, etc.). MySQL database server takes

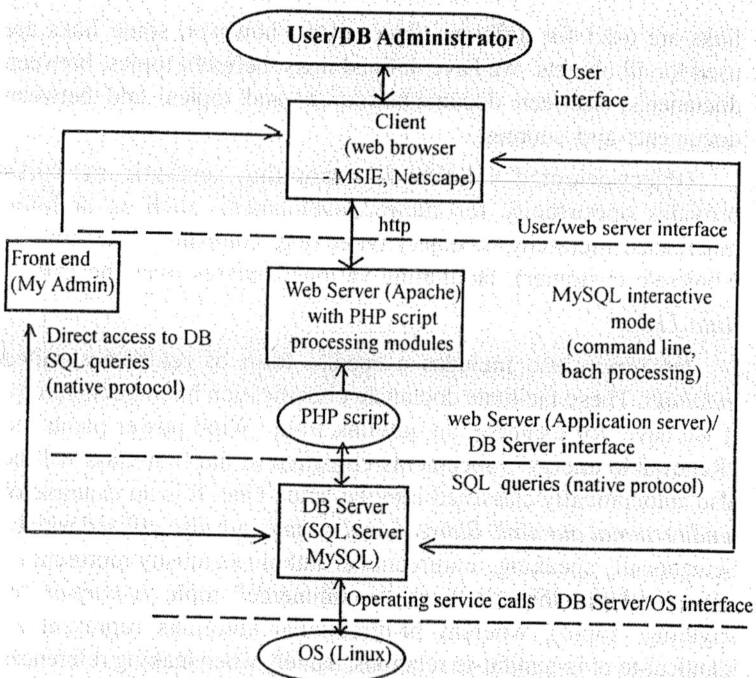

Fig. 3.2: Three-tier architecture of InfoServis

Flow of documents, parameters and queries is depicted in fig. 2.3.-2. Users working on the Internet cannot add their own documents into the shared library directories.

On-site installation – company intranet

client ———— application server ———— DB server
(web browser) documents ←→ queries →
parameters, queries → data ←→

Off-site installation —Internet (server housing)

client ———— application server ———— DB server
(web browser) documents ← queries →
parameters, queries → data ←

Fig. 3.3: Information flow in the digital library

care of the data logic (*i.e.*, applicable data model), data services (input and output of raw data) and file services (operating system calls).

By segmenting the application into presentation logic, business logic and data logic we can achieve much higher flexibility level. Integration of an application server makes connectivity and interoperability among heterogeneous network components much simpler. The middle layer provides for uniform API for all connected clients and the database server.

HTTP transactions between the server and a client take place by opening a connection by the client and sending an applicable URL address. Server get the request, extracts file requested by the user from the URL address, sends reply information back to the user and closes the connection.

Querying and User Interface

Users can enter their queries without any a priori knowledge of data structures or location of data being looked up. Users can browse through the topic tree (navigation), optionally displaying all abstracts at the current level and all sub-levels. Navigation results can be ranked per various criteria, such as the date (from the oldest to the most recent), title, users' ranking, or the number of times an abstract was read. Users can also invoke (advanced) full-text search. Search can be invoked globally (in the root of a tree), or at the required topic tree level.

Information search is based on *uniseek* search engine developed especially for multi-lingual digital libraries. It is particularly efficient for east-European languages, such as Czech and Slovak. Readers can use the following search criteria:

- Limiting search to a particular digital library, location or language;
- Limiting search to any topic or combination of topics;
- Exact phrase search;
- Boolean operators (AND, OR, NOT);
- Positional operator NEAR
- Wildcards -*,?

Entry dialog of the search portal is depicted in the figure below.

Zde vypinte vyhledavaci dotaz

Hledany text:

[ ] Vyhledat

Hledat;

ⓞvinfoServisu O Dokumenty • Zdroje [ ]
ⓞ bez omezenl nazeyoblesti obsahuje [ ]
O aktuaii oblast ajeji podstrom

naintemetu	ceske katalogy	fultext deske stranky
(sluzba archon)	svetove katalogy	fulltext cely internet
	vobchodnim rejstriku	

Technika

- — Technika siti pro prenos elektricke energie (17)
- —Vyroba, zdroje, skladovani a spotreba energie (44)
- — Zivontni prostredi a jeho ochrana (72)
- — Informacni technologie (54)
- — Trh a obchod (26)
- — Legislative (30)
- — Telekomunikace (51)
- — Terminologie, nove trendy a vyzkum (51)
- — Geografie (30
- — Organizace (7)

Fig. 3.4: Dialogue box of the search portal

Novinly obarech

Oblasti	Technika		
Casovy rozsah:	posledni novinky	razeni	Datum (nove-> stars)

1. M Kornto garancliho fondu energetiky je prazdne
Vlozeno 7.12.2001 cislo10585 konentaru 0 ctenosi 1 Originalni cl ..... stromy Byznys+technika
Na Uctu Energetic keho regulacniho uradu (ERU), ktery, ma hradit prokazatele ztraty dodavatelu energie, nejsou v teto chvill zadne penize. Zdrojem prijmu du tohoto fondu by mely byt prispevky od.

2. M Konkurenchni zpravodajstvi — legalni spionaz
Vlozeno 6.12.2001 scislo 1059 komentaru 0 ctenosi 0 originalni stromy byzsys + tecnika + manazer
konkurencni zpravoda zstvi by se dalo s trochou nadsa zky prirovnat ke spionazi s tim rozdilem ze je pine legalni. Jedna se o shromazdovani o konkerencnich firmach (napr.z financnich.

3. M Volani z voleje - virtualni call cenntrum vyuziji i male a stredni firmy
vlozeno 6.12.2001 cislo 10545 komentaru o ctenost 1 originalni cl - stromy Byznys+technika
Mezi nast roje pro zlepseni pece o zakazniky se radi vseobecne znama call centra. Jsou nezbytna zejmena u vetsith spolecnosti, ktere obsluhuji mnoztvi zakazniku call centra jim umoznuji urd zet kontakt

4. M Energeticke spolecnostl v USA se pripravujina nedostatek techniku
Vlozeno 05. 12. 2001 Cisio: 10531 1 Komentari0 0 1 Ctenost 1 Originaini cl Stromy: Byznys + Technika
anglricky
Konkurence v americke elektc energetice zacala rok pote, na University of Louisiana ziskal diplom posledni inzenyr elektrotechniky. Tento adalsi duvody zpusobily. ze nedostatek techniku v voboru elektroenergetk zacinaji pocitrovat.

5. M Supravodice jsou prislibem nove infrastruktury
Viozeno 04.12.2001 Cisio: 10561 L Kometraru 01 Ongnaini cl -- angricky Stromy. Technika

Fig. 3.5: Survey of the latest abstracts in InfoServis.

Search portal can be further improved by introducing *context-specific search, i.e.,* users can specify entities to search in headlines, bodies, or keywords, for example, depending on the structure of documents in the library.

Abstracts are displayed in form of HTML pages generated dynamically from MySQL database. By default, the latest abstracts are displayed first (see the figure 3.5).

The interface has been designed to facilitate full utilisation of enterprise document taxonomy, featuring functionality such as intra- and inter-document links, tree browsing, automatic (semantic) inter-topic links, etc.

Data Update

Data in the library are updated continuously, as librarians and new items into the collection. Overnight update is performed as well, storing all new documents supplied by information provider. E-mails informing of new items are broadcasted on daily basis. This model is based on 1:1 information delivery, *i.e.,* one source of information distributes data to one owner of the profile. We can make an enhancement to 1:N model, sending news to all employees of a department, using generic departmental profile.

Search Engine – Uniseek

The indexing and search server is designed to allow searching defined information sources (with the company or outside). The system features the following characteristics:

* Reading data from various sources (file server, database engines, intranet/Internet, etc.);
* Transferring the data on the indexing server;
* Converting files into a text representation;
* Controlled indexing with saves into a database;
* Searching using a web interface – no need to install any dedicated client software;
* Support for Boolean operators, multiple-word expressions, lexical forms;
* Sorting by relevance, date.

Searching

Search function are interfaced via a web browser. Users enter their search queries, select individual data locations, and send information to the server. For each object found, a title and a short description are displayed. Selected terms found in the document collection are *highlighted* using various colors, so that user can judge relevance of the reply.

Search time depends on complexity of the search query. Even complicated queries do not take more than several seconds. For a vague query the server can locate thousands of documents – users can gradually refine their queries to find the required information.

System's design

The search engine usually runs on a dedicated machine, reading data across local networks or the Internet. Searching is usually invoked

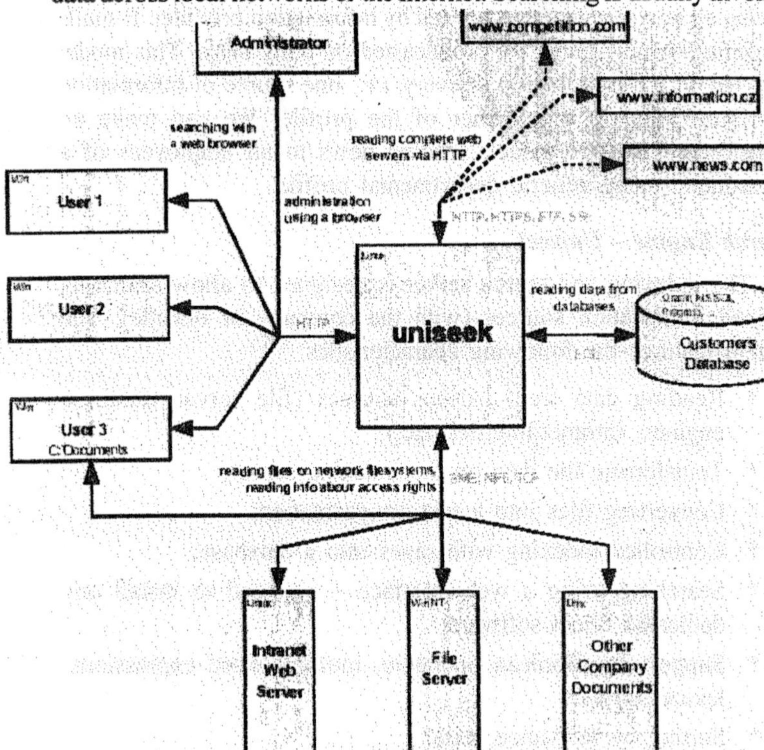

Fig. 3.6: System's design

via a web interface. A network client communicating with the search server is available, allowing customers' existing or new applications easily interface into the system – results are generated in form of an XML, document.

Indexing

Uniseek can handle multi-language documents. Each language is supported by an extensive dictionary defining lexical relations among individual words (declination, various word forms, singular/ plural). The following languages are currently supported:

- Czech (the dictionary contains almost 3,000,000 words);
- English (over 150,000 words);
- German (over 500,000 words).

Since these dictionaries are based on freely available international spell-checker *i-spell*, it is possible to extend support to other languages easily.

During indexing phase, all words are converted into their base form (equivalent of a nominative). Words not covered by the dictionary have their language identified by heuristic algorithms and are converted into their base form using a database of suffices and endings from a given language.

Linguistic Aspects

The library includes various documents in Czech, English, German and Slovak. Vast majority of documents is either is Czech or English, mostly coming from the web. In order to index and process these documents correctly, we need suitable, linguistic tools for both Czech and English. Working with English documents has another advantage: we can compare, for example, classification results with those achieved on Reuters[3]-21578 collection.

It is often the case that a document cannot be classified into a single topic only (in our case this holds true for 8% of documents only. Most documents are assigned to 3 topics, the average is 2, 7, although this number ranges from 1 to 10 (in case of Reuters collection, this parameter ranges from 1 to 16).

Stemming and Stop-List Application

Upon application of a stemmer, the number of distinct significant terms dropped by 42%, with consequent impact on size of database index files. We have used *i-spell* text corpus for Czech stemming, currently containing approx. three million words. All terms are subject to morphological normalisation, including terms with irregular declension. As we expected, stemming applied to the English corpus resulted in much less significant drop (20%).

We have applied both controlled-indexing-based stemmer (*i-spell*) as well as trivial word-endings' cutoff stemmer. Controlled indexing is more complicated, requiring continuous update of the dictionary databases.

By leaving out non-significant words from the index of Czech collection, library volume was reduced by 18% (in number of terms). Observing this parameter in a long term, there was very little variation, regardless of the total collection volume (always ranging around 20%). By leaving out five most frequent non-significant terms, the number of terms dropped by more than 10%. In case of Reuters collection, we have observed drop by 32%. Impacts of using stop-list have been much more significant for the English language, in spite of using stop-list half the size of the Czech one.

Language	*Stop-list size*	*Number of suffixes used in trivial stemming process*	*I-spell volume (number of terms)*
Czech	484	108	Almost 3 million
English	64	29	500 thousand
German	108	127	150 thousand

According to tests described in [22], a sample of 5,000 full-text documents contained approx. 2,00,000 various terms (all morphological variations), represented by 80,000 distinct words in their base form (upon stemming).

It is clear that ever-growing volume of the digital library results in adding new technical terms (with constantly slowing speed, as word stock gets saturated), such as chemical substances, foreign words and some special medical terms.

The most frequent significant words in law documents include "low", "republic", "court", "contract", "state", and "legal" [22], as opposed to „system“, „electrical“, „energy“, „market“, „device“, „control“ and „power“ occurring in our digital library of a power utility company.

Further Improvements

Digital library will be enhanced by some innovative and non-traditional functions results from research topics constituting focus of this report:

1. *Itemsets* classifier will be optimized to allow automatic categorisation of full-length Czech, English, German, and Slovak documents to *InfoServis* topics. The classifier will be also used for pre-classification of specific e-mail messages into knowledge-base topics (final classification will be confirmed by a librarian periodically).

2. *Itemsets clustering* will be tested on document collection, possibly using it for automatic grouping of discussion group submissions and e-mail messages.

3. *Itemsets-based information push* technology will be tested within the context of InfoServis.

4. Search for similar documents will be further enhanced, possibly using itemsets for this purpose.

5. Results of automatic document summarisation research will be utilized in order to create document abstracts automatically, as this work currently occupies one full-time employee.

6. I am planning to look for new features that can be used for information classification, such as identification of the sender, personal profile of message authors, previous submissions of document originators, keywords, titles, behavioral patterns of *infoServis* users, pre-defined auto-links, etc.

Document Classification

The Task of Document Classification

Classification is used to split data into groups, taking into account specific criteria, attributes, or features. Should these criteria be a priori known for at least a sample of data, we can apply predictive modeling methods and develop a model with classification variable at its output. In the case of text classification, the attributes are words contained in text documents. Feature (attribute) selection is widely used prior to machine learning to reduce the feature space, as the number of features in consideration might become prohibitive.

We are often working with *uncontrolled* classifier, *i.e.,* criteria are not a priori known, making the classifier find these criteria. *Cluster analysis* techniques are applied in these cases.

Learning a classifier (*supervised machine learning*) means inducing a model from the training data set that we believe will be effective at predicting class in new data for which we do not know the class.

In general, we distinguish between *rule-based classifiers* (rules are constructed manually, and the resulting set of rules is difficult to modify) and *inductive-learning classifiers*. Classifiers based on inductive learning are constructed using labeled training data; these are easy to construct and update, not requiring rule-writing skills. In this report I will focus on inductive-learning approach in classifier construction only.

Besides document categorisation, we can come across the issue of web page and *link classification*, as introduced by Hasas and Grams [37], with useful applications in searching and authoring.

Existing Document Classification Methods

An interesting survey of five (supervised learning) document classification algorithms is presented by Dumais *et al.* [32], focusing namely on promising *Support Vector Machines* (SVM) method. *Find Similar, Naïve Bayes, Bayesian Networks*, and *Decision Trees methods* are also discussed. Another detailed test of text categorisation method is presented by Yang and Liu [33], discussing various algorithms such as SVM, kNN, LLSF (linear lest-squares fit), NNet and *Naïve Bayes*.

Selected existing document classification methods are briefly examined in the table below:

Method	K nearest neighbour (KNN), "Find Similar"
Principle	To classify a new object, find the object in the training set that is most similar, Methods utilising such principle are sometimes called "memory based learning" methods. *tf*idf* term weights are used, computing similarity between test examples and category centroids. The weight assigned to a term is a combination of its weight in an original query, and judged relevant and irrelevant documents. It is a variant of Rocchio's method for relevance feedback. Cosine value of two vectors (or any other similarity measure) can be used to measure similarity between two documents.
Advantages	Easy to interpret. One of the top performing methods on the benchmark *Reuters* corpus (*Reuters-21450, Apte set*).
Dis-advantages	No feature space reduction. Lazy learner – defers data processing until classification time (no off-line preprocessing).
Method	Decision trees
Principle	Model based on decision trees consists of a series of simple decision rules, often presented in form of a graph. These graphs can be quickly modified even by those lacking deep knowledge of statistics. It is a probabilistic classifier – *confidence* (class) represents a probability distribution.
Advantages	Easy to interpret.
Disadvantages	Number of model parameters is hard to find. Error estimates are difficult.
Method	Naïve Bayes (Idiot Bayes)
Principle	Constructed from the training data to estimate the probability of each class given the document feature

	values (words) of a new instance. Bayes theorem is used to estimate these probabilities. It is a probabilistic classifier – confidence (class) represents a probability distribution.
Advantages	Works well even when the feature independence assumed by Naive Bayes does not hold. Surprisingly effective.
Disadvantages	Simplifying assumptions (conditional independence of words).
Method	Unrestricted Bayesian classifier
Principle	Assumption of word independence is not applied. Its alternative – semi-naïve Bayesian classifier – iteratively joins pairs of attributes to relax the strongest independence assumptions.
Advantages	Simple implementation, easy interpretation.
Disadvantages	Exponential complexity due to assuming conditional dependence of words.
Method	Neural networks (perceptrons)
Principle	Separate neural network per category is constructed, learning a non-linear mapping from input words (or more complex features, such as itemsets) to a category.
Advantages	Design is easy to modify. Various models can be constructed quickly and flexibly. Subject to intensive study in artificial intelligence.
Disadvantages	Model based on neural networks does not provide any clear interpretation. High training cost (more time consuming than the other classifiers).
Method	Linear SVM
Principle	An SVM is a hyperplane that separates a set of positive examples from a set of negative examples with maximum margin. The margin is defined by the distance of he hyperplane to the nearest of the

	positive and negative examples. SVM (optimisation) problem is to find the decision surface that maximises the margin between the data points in a training set.
Advantages	Good generalisation performance on a wide variety of classification problems. Good classification accuracy, fast to learn, fast for classifying new instances.
Disadvantages	Not all problems are linearly separable.
Method	Itemsets Modification of Naïve Bayes – see Section *Naive Bayes Classifier and its Modification based on Itemsets Method*

Development of yet another classification method was motivated by the need of *processing short-documents* (abstracts). It is likely that size of digital libraries will increase rapidly in the near future and proper classification of abstracts will become even more important. Efficiency of universal document categorisation methods will gradually decrease, necessitating ad-hoc classification methods, such as *itemsets*, offering easy adjustment to a particular document collection.

Test Document Collections

Classification algorithms are tested on large sample document collections in order to assess their viability and compare one to another. *Reuters-21578* collection[4] is gaining popularity among researchers in text classification,[5] becoming a widely used benchmark corpus. Collection includes short newswire stories in English, classified into 118 categories (*e.g., earnings, interest, money*, etc.). Each story is assigned to 1.3 categories on the average (maximum is 16); however there are many unassigned stories as well. Original classification is highly skewed, as a very large portion of stories is assigned to *earnings* category only. Top 10 categories include 75% of all instances, and 82% of the categories have less than 100 instances.

We have also made various tests on our proprietary collection of technical documents from the digital library of a power utility (more than 4,000 text documents in Czech, English, German and Slovak). There are other widely used collections, such as MEDLINE[6] (medical texts in English), UCI ML Repository,[7] or Czech national corpus.[8]

The size of test collection is an important issue. When testing a classification algorithm, we need to examine how many positive training examples are necessary to provide good generalization performance. According to Dumais *et al.* [32], twenty or more training instances provide stable generalisation performance.[9] According to Yang and Liu [33], *SVM* and *kNN* classifiers significantly outperform *NNet (neural nets)* and *Naïve Bayes* when the number of positive training examples per category are small (less than ten). The required number of training examples is therefore specific for each classification algorithm.

As opposed to testing classification algorithms on collections of short abstracts, various tests on full text document collections have been performed, such as the one by Beney and Koster [38], testing *Winnow* classifier[10] on patent application supplied by the European Patent Office (documents about 5,000 words each).

Assessment of Classification Algorithms

Classification algorithms are evaluated in terms of speed and accuracy. Speed of a classifier must be assessed separately for two different tasks: *learning* (training a classifier) and *classification* of new instances.

Many evaluation criteria for classification are proposed. *Precision* and *recall* criteria are mentioned most often. *Break-even* point is proposed by Dumais et al. [32] as an average of precision and recall. Decision thresholds in classification algorithms can be modified in order to produce higher precision (at the cost of lower recall), or vice versa – as appropriate for different applications. Averaged F_1 measure[11] is commonly used for classifier evaluation. Single valued performance measures (p, r, F_1) can be dominated by the classifier's performance on common categories or rare categories, depending on how the average performance is computed [33] (*micro-averaging vs. macro-averaging*).

In the case of mono-classification, some researchers (*e.g.*, [38] report error rate measure, which is percentage of documents misclassified.

Yang and Liu [33] report an interesting controlled study with statistical significance tests on five text categorisation methods. As categories typically have an extremely non-uniform distribution (such as the case of *Reuters-21578*), it is meaningful to assets a classifier with respect to category frequencies. With respect to *Reuters-2157* benchmark corpus, ApteMod version is often used, which is obtained by eliminating unlabeled stories (*i.e.*, unclassified instances) and selecting the categories which have at least one document in the training set and the test set.

It is important to note that classifier's performance largely depends on splitting the corpus on training and testing data. Testing the classifier on training data used for learning the classifier often leads to significantly better results.

The problem with evaluating classifiers is their domain dependence. Each classifier has a particular sub-domain for which it is most reliable [35]. In order to overcome this issue, multiple learned classifiers are combined to obtain more accurate classification. Separating the training data into subsets where classifiers either succeed or fail to make predictions was used in Schapire's Boosting algorithm [36]. A decision tree induction algorithm (such as C4.5) can be trained and applied to distinguish between cases where the classifier is correct and those where it is incorrect.

Itemsets Classifier

Association Rules

The topic of association rules is of key importance for many document classification algorithms. Association rules, and the related concept of itemsets, constituted my motivation for developing a new document classifier.

It is imperative to find a method for automatic generation of association rules over the word domain. We can start with keywords, checking which word pairs are present in more than τ documents (τ is a threshold value), or possible documents classified to a specific topic. We can also look for associations among terms with specific semantics (semantic tags can be supplemented by means of a special lexical analyzer). We can define weights of association rules by frequency of occurrence, or possibly by distances between terms in an association. Association among terms cannot be regarded as causality relationship, as we do not know the direction.

Itemsets Classifier

Original classification method, called *itemsets classification*, has been developed to facilitate automatic classification of short-documents in the digital library of Zapadoceska energetika. Majority of traditional document classification methods is based on repeated word occurrence, which is impractical to use in case of very short documents (less than 100 significant words in this case).

Our aim was to produce a taxonomy reflecting information-seeking behaviour of a specific user population, *i.e.*, employees of a regional power utility. Functionality of the digital library simplifies creation of enterprise information portal (EIP). Automatic classification (auto-categorisation) engine facilitates continual monitoring of the information generated by the company (or external sources) and organizing it into directories.

Itemsets method resulted from our basic assumption, that objects belonging to the same concept (class) demonstrate similar features. Learning paradigm based on such an assumption is called *similarity-based learning*. Objects representing instances of the same concept constitute "clusters" in the concept space. The task of modeling is to assume finite number of instances and find general representation[12] of these clusters, which we call *classes, topics*, or *categories*, Classification algorithm looks for knowledge that can be used for classifying new instances.

We are using inductive inference based on *inductive learning hypothesis*: Any hypothesis found to approximate the target (classification) function well over a sufficiently large set of training examples (abstracts in the training set, in this case) will also approximate the target function well over other unobserved examples (abstracts to be classified).

Itemsets method is robust to errors (alike decision tree learning methods) – both errors in the classification of training documents (made by a librarian manually) and errors in the attribute values (significant terms) that describe these documents.

Abstracts of technical articles are mostly freely accessible on the web. It is therefore possible to create an extensive library of these abstracts. Users of the library can then make a request to buy a full copy of a document or its translation. The task of document searching in the digital library is similar to the one of categorisation, being solved by means of similar principles.

Apriori Algorithm for Itemsets Generation

The *apriori algorithm* (Agrawal *et al.*) is and efficient algorithm for knowledge mining in form of association rules [25]. We have recognized its convenience for document categorisation. The original apriori algorithm is applied to a transactional database of market baskets. In the context of a digital library, significant terms occurring in text documents take place of items contained in market baskets (*itemsets* searching is equivalent to term clustering process) and the transactional database is in fact a set of documents (represented by sets of significant terms). Consistently with the usual terminology lets's denote terms as items and sets of items as *itemsets*.

Let π, is an item, $\Pi = \{\pi_1, \pi_2, \ldots, \pi_m\}$is an *itemset* and Δ is our *document collection (representing transactions)*. The itemset containing *k* items is called *k-itemset*. Each itemset Π is associated with a set of transactions $T_\Pi = \{T \varepsilon \Delta / \Pi \subseteq T\}$ which is a set of transactions containing itemset Π. Frequency of an itemset is defined as a simultaneous occurrence of items in data in consideration. Within our investigation we often utilise the threshold value employed for the minimum frequency (*minsupport*) of an itemset. *Frequent itemsets* are defined as those whose support is greater than or equal to *minsupport*. The (transaction) *support* in our case corresponds to the frequency of an itemset occurrence in the (transaction) database $\Delta(\Delta = \{T_1, T_2, \ldots, T_n\}$, *T* representing transactions). The support supp(Π) of an itemset Π equals $|T_\Pi| / |\Delta|$. Support is defined over the binary domain $\{0, 1\}$, with a value of 1 indicating the presence of an item in a document, and the value of 0 indicating absence of an item (frequency of an item is deemed irrelevant, as opposed to traditional TF×IDF methods)[13]. Support fails as a measure of relative importance whenever the number of items plays a significant role. We have found that this is not a problem for short-document classification task.

Declaring itemsets *frequent* should they occur in more than *minsupport* number of documents in a particular class is correct[14], with no need of normalisation like in case of IDF concept (we do not eliminate those in the upper frequency range, as itemsets are to characterise a class based on their frequent appearance). At this phase we have already eliminated stop (non-content) words; moreover, we are deciding on, being frequent" within the scope of a class, not the whole document collection. Co-occurrence of terms representing an itemest is domain-restricted, domain being as class (category).

Our goal is to discover frequent itemsets in order to characterise individual topics in the digital library.

Frequent itemsets' searching is an interactive process. At the beginning, all frequent 1-itemsets are found, these are used to generate frequent 2-itemsets, then frequent 3-itemsets are fund using frequent 2-itemsets, etc.

Let's suppose we have *TDs* distinct significant terms in our document collection *Δ*. Firstly we generate candidates of frequent 1-itemsets (shortly „candidate 1-itemsets"). These are stored directly index files in *DF* (Document Frequency) table. Consequently, we computer frequent 1-itemsets. In the next step, we generate 2-itemsets from frequent 1-itemsets. Generation of subsequent candidate and frequent *n*-itemsets continues until the process of frequent itemsets' searching terminates with regard to apriori property ("all non-empty subsets of a frequent itemset must be frequent"). While implementing this method, we utilise a technique similar to *transaction reduction* method: a document that does not contain a k-itemset can be left out of our further consideration, since it cannot contain any of (k+1)-itemsets.

Let C_k denote a set of candidate k-itemsets and F_k a set of frequent k-itemsets. Generation of F_k from F_{k-1} is based on the following algorithm (our modification of the original Apriori algorithm by Srikant and Agrawal):

```
// For 1 – itemsets:
Ç1 : = all significant terms in Δ;
F1 := ∅;
for ∀Πi ε Ç1 do
for ∀ tj ε T do
   if (supp (Πi) in class tj is greater than or equal to minsupport)
         then begin
            add Πi to F1
             break;
            end;
// For k-itemsets, where k > 1:
Fk := ∅;
for ∀ Πi ε Fk-1 do
for ∀ Πi ε Fk-1 do
if (the first k-2 items in Πi and Πj equal, but the last items differ)
   then begin
  c : = Πi join Πj;
if (∃ subset s, s ⊃ c having k–1 elements, where s ∉ Fk-1)
    then break;
else for ∀ t ε T do
    if (supp (c) in class t is greater than or equal to minsupport)
      then begin
              add c to Fk
              break;
           end;
         end;
```

Document Classification Using Itemsets

The following notation will be used in this section:

Π	Frequent itemset	D Πi	Set of documents containing itemset Π_i
| Π |	Cardinality of frequent itemset Π_i	| DΠi |	The number of documents containing the itemset Π_i
T	Topic (representing a categorisation class)	DTi	Set of documents associated with topic T_i
D	Document	| DTi |	The number of documents associated with topic T_i
$\tilde{D}$	A set of significant terms contained in document D	| $T\Pi_i$ |	Number of topics in which itemset Π_i is frequent
L	The number of topics	C_i	Set of itemsets characterising topic T_i
N_i	The number of frequent itemsets of cardinality i	| C_i |	The number of itemsets characterising topic T_i

The Classification Problem

The classification problem can be divided into two parts: *training phase and classification*[15] *phase.*

The training phase consists of the following:

* Define a set of topics (categories) by a domain expert[16], L categories are thus defined.
* Insert (manually) a certain number of documents into topics, i.e. classification attributes are defined for each class (training data set). A domain expert performs categorisation of all available training documents. Each topic should be assigned a statistically significant number of documents.
* Automatic generation of representative itemsets of different cardinality for each topic.

While performing classification, we utilize representative (characteristic) itemsets to classify documents into corresponding topics.

The classification algorithm can be evaluated in terms of accuracy (*precision* and *recall* parameters) and speed. Accuracy can be measured by means of a test-set, the members of which have a priori know classification. Precision: $P = p/q$: Recall; $Q = p/r$, where p is the number of classes determined correctly by the classifier (automatically); q is total number of classes determined automatically; r is the number of classes determined by a domain expert (manually, *i.e.*, correctly).

Note the analogy with corresponding parameters defined for search engines as well as association rules in databases of business transactions:

Classifier	*Search engine*	*Association rules*
Precision	Precision	Confidence
	$\frac{\textit{found relevant}}{\textit{found total}}$	$Conf\,(X \Rightarrow Y) = P\,(X/Y)$ $= \frac{\textit{number of transactions } X \cup Y}{\textit{number of transactions } X}$
$P = p/q$		
Recall	Recall	Support
$Q = p / r\Pi_i$	$\frac{\textit{Found relevant}}{\textit{relevant in database}}$	$Sup\ (X \Rightarrow Y) = P\ (X \cup Y)$ $= \frac{\textit{number of transactions } X \cup Y}{\textit{number of all transactions}}$

Where number of transactions $X \cup Y$ denotes the number of transactions containing both X and Y.

We are computing overall precision and recall parameters using *micro-averaging* method, *i.e.*, we are giving equal weight to each object (rather than each category, as in *macro-averaging*). P and R are computed for each new test document separately, then figuring out the average of all precision and recall values over the whole test set.

Quality of classification is often expressed by means of *F-measure* (or *F-score*):

$$F = \frac{1}{\alpha\frac{1}{P} + (1-\alpha)\frac{1}{R}}$$

α representing relative importance attributed to precision P.

The following F-measure is one used in the context of text retrieval and classification (by substituting $\alpha = ½$), denoting it as F_1 –measure (see also Assessment of classification Algorithms):

$$F = \frac{2 \times P \times R}{P + R}$$

Complexity of itemset classification algorithm

Complexity of classifying one document can be expressed approximately as $C_{AVG} \times L \times K$ (= $C_{TOT} \times K$), were C_{AVG} is the average number of itemsets in C, L is the number of classes, K is a constant representing average complexity of comparing itemsets in C with document being classified[17] and C_{TOT} is the total number of itemsets in all C files. Time requirements of classification as such are relatively low compared to complexity of the training phase.

Phases of Itemsets Method

Training Phase

The *training phase* can be also described as *feature selection phase* (reduction of the feature space). For each itemset Π_j we can find a corresponding set of documents containing Π_j. Let's designate this set of documents as $D\Pi_j$. It is obvious that cardinality of $D\Pi_j$ will be higher than a certain threshold value, since Π_j was selected as a frequent itemset.

By analogy, for each topic Ti there is a characteristic set of documents associated with this topic. Let's designate this set as DT_i. Altogether we will have L sets.

Our goal is to specify a certain number of itemsets for each topic, where each itemset is associated with a subset of the set of topics. Namely, itemset Π_j is associated with topic T_i corresponding to the values of w^{Ti}_{Π} exceeding some threshold value. The weight of w^{Ti}_{Π} can be computed as follows.[18]

$$w^{T_i}_{\Pi j} = \frac{|D\Pi_j \cap DT_i|}{|DTi| \times [1 + |D\Pi_j| - |D\Pi_j \cap DTi|]} \quad i = 1, 2 \ldots, L$$

Demoninator is used to normalise with respect to the number of documents associated with topic T_i. It takes into account whether an itemset occurs in other topics as well. Significance of terms occurring frequently in documents other than DT_i, is thus suppressed.

Upon associating itemsets with individual topics based on the formula above, we will acquire sets of itemsets *Ci* characterising a particular topic[19] *Ti*. On the whole, there will be *L* sets of itemsets.

Aside: As we look for itemsets of higher cardinality, we are, in a way, performing *latent semantic indexing* (although applied to classifier training phase rather than document indexing). Co-occurring terms are projected onto the same dimension, while non-co-occurring terms onto different dimensions (latent semantic indexing results in dimensionality reduction). LSI is sometimes useful for solving vocabulary problem, at least partially. It is important, as objects in the collection of abstracts are often created by many different authors using various synonyms. *End of aside*.

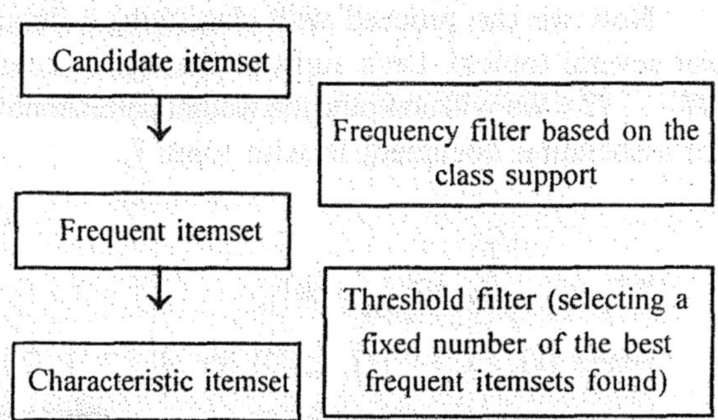

Classifier construction is summarised in the figure below:

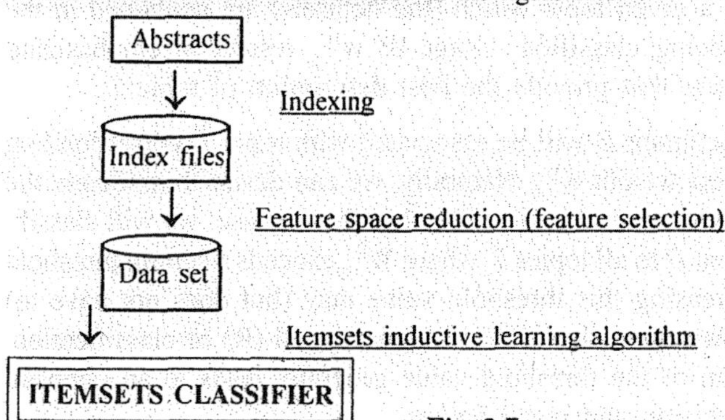

Fig. 3.7

Let's summarise notation used herein: *itemset* is a set of items (*i.e.*, terms). Candidate itemset is a potentially frequent itemset. Frequent itemsets are those appearing in more than *minsupport* number of documents of a given class. *Characteristic itemsets* are frequent itemsets declared characteristic for a given class (taking some fixed number of the best frequent itemsets associated with that class). See the figure 3.7.

Classification Phase

Over the course of document classification process, we must take into account cardinality of itemsets in order to distinguish between correspondence in pairs and correspondence in quadruplets, for instance. That is why we define a weight factor corresponding to the cardinality of an itemset. For pairs we will use wf_2, for triplets wf_3, for quadruplets wf_4, etc.

Now we can proceed with classifying a document into a topic (or several topics). Let's suppose that set C_j contains elements Π_1, Π_2, ..., $\Pi_{|k|}$. We will compute the weight corresponding to the accuracy of associating document D with topic T_j:

$$W^{D}_{T_i} = \sum_{j=i}^{|C_j|} wf_{|\pi j|} \times w^{T_i}_{\Pi j}$$

where $(\Pi_j \; \varepsilon \; C_j) \wedge (\Pi_i \subseteq \overline{D})$ for all $i = 1, 2, \ldots L)$

In other words, the classification weight is determined by the sum of products of weights $w^{T_i}_{\Pi j}$ with weight factors $wf_{|\Pi j|}$ for all itemsets of a given topic which (the itemsets) are contained in the document being classified. Usage of $w^{T_i}_{\Pi j}$ results in emphasizing those itemsets that provide the best description of topic T_j.

The document *D* will be associated with topic T_j corresponding to the highest weight w^{D}_{Π}. Naturally, we can desire to associate the document with several topics. Should it be the case, we will classify the document *D* to all topics T_j where W^{D}_{Π} exceeds a certain threshold value. Decreasing this threshold value may (but does not have to) result in lower precision (P) and higher recall (R) of classification. Modification of the threshold value generally leads to an opposite shift of precision and recall values.

Preliminary Results

Initial results achieved on a large collection of abstracts in English are quire promising. Results indicated in [32] were used for cross-method comparison, utilizing Reuters-21578 collection for this purpose. Classifiers in the test were used to categorize 12,902 documents into 118 classes, showing results for 10 largest categories, which include almost 75% of all documents. That is why I have run the tests only for classes containing more than180 documents (ranging from 212 to 2,779), to imitate approach of other authors. Documents were split to training and testing using 3:1 ratio.

Classifier	*Itemsets*	*Naïve Bayes*	*Bayes Nets*	*Linear SVM*
AVG(P,R)	91.36[20]	81.50	85.00	92.00

Preliminary results are motivating for further optimisation of itemsets classifier, namely on other document collections, potentially in other languages, with the ultimate goal of developing a domain/ language independent short-document classifier.

Automatic Document Summarisation

Introduction

Research in automatic document summarization is motivated by the need of applying *itemsets* classifier to full-length documents. As itemsets method is designed for short documents and abstracts, it is imperative to reduce the length of documents in the document collection by means of an intelligent summarizer. Documents "abbreviated" by automatic summariser can be then passed to classifier to proceed with categorisation.

Automatic document summarisation also constitutes a *classification problem*: each sentence (or paragraph) in a document to be summarised is either a summary sentence (paragraph) or a non-summary sentence (paragraph). Class collection is restricted to two categories in this case.

It is imperative to define basic summary types:

(a) *Indicative*: Indicative summaries give brief information on the central topic of a document (useful in IR applications, such as giving an indicative summary of documents retrieved by a search engine). Indicative summary is typically 5-10% of the original text.

(b) *Informative (substantive):* Informative summaries provide a substitute for full document ("surrogate", "digest"), retaining important details, while reducing information volume. Informative summary is typically 20-30% of the original text.

(c) *Evaluative*: Evaluative summary captures the point of view of the author on a given subject.

In the context of automatic document classification by itemsets method, we are interested primarily in *indicative* summarisation (indicative summariser has the ability to preserve the critical portion of the content); however, for automating the task of document summarising in a digital library, *informative* summarises are needed, in order to maintain coverage of a topic.

Approaches to Document Summarisation

Summary is either *fixed-length* (limited by some portion of document length, say 10%) or *best-length* (no length limit is applied). Fixed-length summary will be preferred for the purpose of subsequent document categorisation by itemsets method. *Optimum length* of documents being fed to itemsets-classifier is still a question of further research.

The following methodologies are most commonly used by document summarisers:

- Sentence length cutoff[21];
- Cue phrases[22];
- Sentence position in a document / paragraph;
- Occurrence of frequent words;
- Relative position of frequent terms within a sentence;
- Words in capital letters (uppercase words[23];
- Occurrence of title words[24];
- Author-supplied abstract[25];
- Intra-document links between passages of a document.

The importance of term frequency for document summarisation has been recognised by Luhn [26] as early as in 1958. Luhn observes that *relative position* of frequent terms within a sentence also furnishes useful measurement for determining significance of sentences. Significance of sentences can therefore be expressed as a *combination* of word *frequency* and *position* of these words. Intelligent summariser should take into account linguistic implications, such as grammar, syntax, and possibly logical and semantic relationships. Speaking strictly of word frequency and word position, wherever the greatest number of frequently occurring different words are found in the greatest physical proximity to each other, the probability is very high that the information being conveyed is most representative of the document [26]. It is important to set a limit for the *distance* at which any two significant words will be considered *significantly related.* We have coped with a similar problem while implementing sliding-window modification (see Hynek, Jezek [3]) of the itemsets classifier. *Summary by extraction* is mentioned by Kupiec. Pedersen and Chen [27]. The goal is to find a subset of the document that is *indicative* of its contents (sentences are scored and those with the best score are presented in a summary). It is important to note that extracted sentences rarely maintain narrative coherence of the original text. Sentence extraction is treated as a *statistical classification problem* in [27]. Classification function is developed in order to estimate the probability a given sentence is included in an extract. A training set of data (*i.e.,* corpus of documents with labeled extracts) must be prepared manually prior to inductive learning process. A set of potential features, the classification method and a training corpus of document/extract pairs must be established for this purpose. Simple Bayesian classification function has been developed by Kupiec *et al.,* [27] in order to assign for each sentence a score, which can be used to select sentences for inclusion in a generated summary. Resulting summaries are mainly indicative (give brief information on the central topic), with the average length of three sentences.

Strzalkowski *et al.,* [28] observed that much of the written text display certain regularities of organisation and style, which they call *Discourse Macro Structure* (DMS). Summaries are crated to reflect the components of a given DMS. Resulting summaries are coherent and readable. DMS-based summariser can generate both short indicative abstracts and well as longer informative digests that can serve as surrogates for the original text. In order to make a summary intelligible, it is necessary to extract text sections longer than simple sentences. Some studies [29] show that simply selecting the first paragraph from a document tends to produce better summaries than a sentence-based algorithm. Strzalkowski *et al.*, [28] work on paragraph-level instead of sentences. Summaries are made up of paragraphs extracted from the original text. Indicative summaries are scored for relevance to pre-selected topics and compared to the classification of respective full documents. A summary is considered successful if it preserves the original document's relevance or non-relevance to a topic. By analogy, we can use the same evaluation method upon classifying original documents and their summarized counterparts by the itemsets classifier.

An interesting approach to document summarization is presented by Salton *et al.*, [30], generating *intra-document links* between passages of a document, using these linkages to characterise the structure of the text. The knowledge of text structure is applied to perform automatic text summarisation by passage extraction. Intra-document links are generated by means of techniques used by most automatic hypertext link generation algorithms as well (see *Section Itemsets-based Document Clustering*). A text relationship map obtained by intra-document text linking may be used to isolate text passages that are functionally homogeneous [30]. These text passages represent contiguous piece of text that is well linked internally, but largely disconnected from the adjacent text.

Evaluation of Summarisation Systems

Quality of an automatic summariser can be measured by comparing *classification* of the original (full-length) document with that of the summarized document. Classification can be compared, for example, in terms of *precision, recall* or *F-measure*.

Besides evaluation based on classification, we may compare automatically generated extracts with those produced by humans. We must assume that a human would be able to identify effectively the most important sentences or paragraphs in a document. If the set of sentences/paragraphs selected by an automatic extraction method has a high overlap with the extract generated by human, the automatic summariser should be regarded as effective. However, there is fairly uniform acceptance of the belief that any number of acceptable abstracts could effectively represent the content of a single document [31]. The essence of an idea can be captured by more than one sentence or phrase.

Evaluation of text summarisation systems is discussed in detail by Firm in and Chrzanowski in [31]. Besides a number of other evaluation approaches, they mention degree of *domain independence*. Although most authors claim some degree of domain independence, they have performed tests only on a specific type of data, such as newspaper articles [29].

Quality of a summariser was calculated, for example, as percentage of sentence matches and partial matches between their automatic summary and manually generated abstract [27]. The problem with this approach is reliance on the notion of a single "correct" ("best") abstract.

Quality of an abstract can be also measured by time required to read it. Firm in and Chrzanowski [31] compare average time required for reading full-text documents, best summaries, and 10% summaries.

There are many improvements that can be made to the quality of the summaries, such as higher cohesion in sentence selection or sentence generation, and topic coverage across the set of topics mentioned within a document.

Other Applications of Itemsets Method

The following sections describe potential usage areas of the itemsets method. Further research will be performed to explore additional applications and new possibilities. Final results of practical implementation will be published.

Itemsets-Based Document Clustering

General Concepts of Document Clustering

The issue of clustering is closely related to classification. It will focus on document clustering based on textual contents of these entities. The goal of clustering is to maximise intra-class similarity while minimising inter-class similarity. Clustering thus facilitates taxonomy building, *i.e.,* information structuring into classes or a hierarchy of classes represented by similar entities. Clustering technologies are described in detail by Lukasova and Sarmanova [39] – clustering methods are divided into hierarchical (with further subdivision to agglomerative and divisive) and non-hierarchical (either optimising or mode analysis methods).

Inter-document similarity can be expressed by a coefficient, so that we can associate each document with at least one cluster. Should similarity exceed some threshold value, documents rank into the same class of equivalence (cluster). Each new document can be compared, for example, with (a) the first document of a cluster (b) an arbitrary document of a cluster (c) a representative document of a cluster (d) several documents from a cluster, etc.

Clustering can be implemented either as hierarchical (creating a tree[26] of document clusters) or non-hierarchical. We will consider non-hierarchical clustering only, If we desire to join clusters into a hierarchical structure, we can apply various binding methods, such as "simple binding" (*i.e.,* linking two most similar documents, each coming from a different cluster). By analogy, we can apply "full binding", comparing two clusters using two least similar documents.

Clustering technology is used, for example, by Altavista search engine for clustering of results. Query results are substituted by a single document representing the whole web site. Such a document can be expanded to all relevant documents by clicking on "More pages from this site" button

Document Clustering Using Itemsets

In order to enhance the original use of *itemsets* classification method, we can also consider its application to document clustering. The following paragraphs contain preliminary ideas, while practical application is the issue of my further research.

We can start document clustering process with an arbitrary document clustering method, such as *k-means* or its modification, and create a variable number of clusters using pre-defined number of documents (at least one thousand). The number of clusters thus created depends largely on threshold value applicable to clustering method chosen for this purpose (genetic algorithm can be applied at this phase).

Let's denote clusters containing at least, say, fifty documents, as *regular* clusters. Smaller clusters will be denoted as *non-regular*. We will use regular clusters for training the itemsets classifier, *i.e.,* for creating characteristic itemsets for each of these clusters. The same number of characteristic itemsets will be defined for every regular cluster. This number can range from 10 to 40, for example, so that we could guarantee existence of enough characteristic itemsets for each regular cluster.

We will retrain itemsets classifier on regular clusters every time the number of documents in a particular cluster grows by a pre-defined figure (by applying a trigger). Itemsets classifier is retrained for a particular cluster only, as remaining clusters are still either non-regular, or trained enough.

New documents are assigned to non-regular clusters using a traditional document clustering method (such as k-means), until these clusters become regular. Itemsets classifier must be trained on each new regular cluster. Time requirements should not be prohibitive, as we look for frequent (and thus characteristic) itemsets only within the pertinent topic, not the whole document collection.

"Cannot classify" criterion: This criterion is a must to decide whether we can classify a particular document at all. Let's define it as: "computed weight of document assignment to the worst class compared to weight applicable to the best class is greater than X %". Relatively narrow "weight band" means small difference between document assignments to various topics. An assignment in such a case is too fuzzy. Classifier decides: cannot classify. It is to be decided what "narrow weight band" means. We may alter the width of this band depending on the number of topics resulting from document clustering process. We may apply some form of genetic algorithm for this purpose.

The first implementation draft of a clustering algorithm is depicted in the figure on next page.

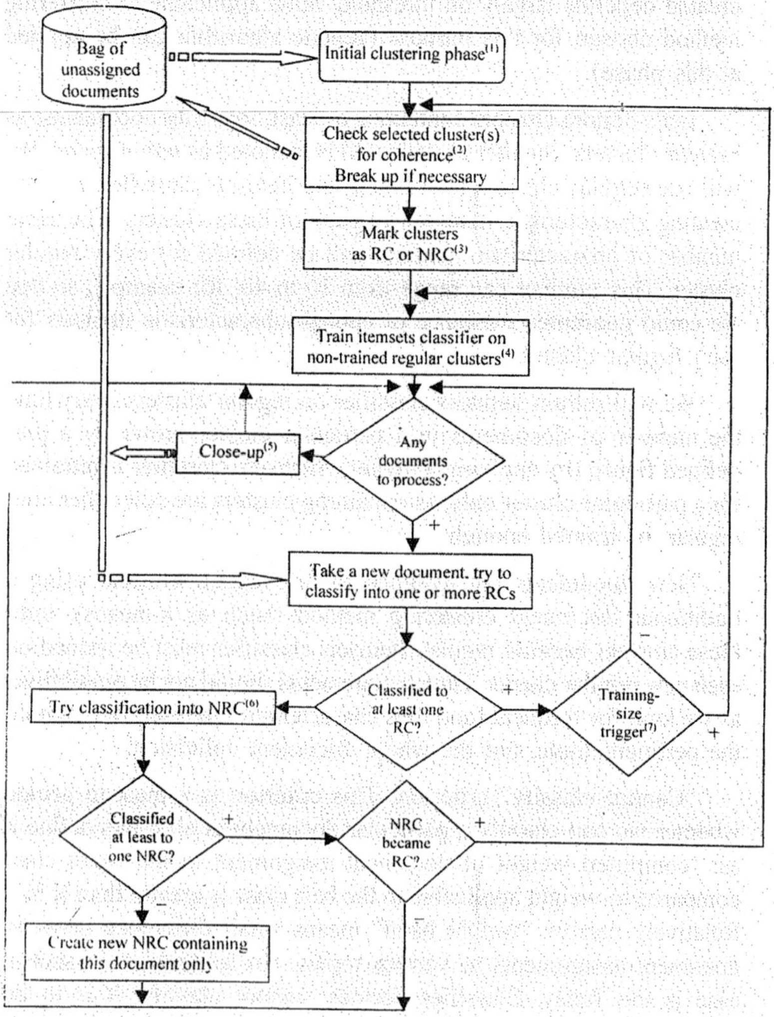
Bag of unassigned documents
Initial clustering phase(1)
Check selected cluster(s) for coherence(2) Break up if necessary
Mark clusters as RC or NRC(3)
Train itemsets classifier on non-trained regular clusters(4)
Any documents to process?
Close-up(5)
Take a new document, try to classify into one or more RCs
Classified to at least one RC?
Training-size trigger(7)
Try classification into NRC(6)
Classified at least to one NRC?
NRC became RC?
Create new NRC containing this document only

Notes:

(1) Initial clustering phase is performed by means of a modified "traditional" clustering mechanism, such as *k-means* using itemsets in lieu of single terms. We will first evaluate the whole corpus by some form of *if*idf* method, leaving out terms with extremely low or high frequency of occurrence, as well as applying stop-list and stemmer. We can then represent each document by several itemsets (achieving significant feature-space reduction).

(2) We need to ensure that one cluster does not contain semantically different documents. We can compare each pair of documents in the cluster. In case of inconsistencies, we must break up the cluster and put documents back into the bag.

(3) Regular clusters (RC) and non-regular clusters (NRC), depending on the number of documents assigned to the cluster.

(4) Clusters that were marked by training-size triggers are also considered non-trained regular clusters.

(5) Close-up operations: Browse cluster by cluster and look for similarity coefficients between each pair of documents (alike in step (2)). In the case of unsatisfactory semantic cohesion (*i.e.*, the range of similarity coefficient is relatively too wide), break-up the cluster, and put documents back into the bag of unassigned documents.

Identify extremely small clusters, say of 1 or 2 documents. Put these back into the bag and change threshold values applicable to assignment.

Run clustering for remaining documents in the bag.

Optional: Take each document from every existing (both regular and non-regular) cluster and try to reclassify it (using *itemsets* classifier) into other regular clusters. We will thus ensure document classification into those clusters that may have been created after document's initial classification. This is the final phase of our clustering algorithm.

(6) Using the same clustering method as in the initial phase (*e.g.*, modified *k-means*).

(7) The trigger is set ON if the cluster must be re-trained, *i.e.*, more than a specified number o documents have been added since the last training.

The above approach ensures creating new clusters on as-needed basis, as well a break up of clusters demonstrating low semantic cohesion.

Threshold values: By properly setting up clustering threshold values, we can tune up optimal number of clusters upon the initial phase, or the total number of clusters in general. Trial and error approach (a form of genetic algorithm) is viable in this case.

As an alternative, we may try to assign a new document into one class only, which results in a simpler clustering method.

In the sense of taxonomy presented by Lukasova and Sarmanova [39], the clustering algorithm proposed above ranks to the class of *agglomerative* algorithms, although we are not building a hierarchy of documents (even if we could redesign the algorithm to a hierarchical one).

Naïve Bayes Classifier and its Modification Based on Itemsets Method

General Principles

Naïve Bayes classifier can be applied in such tasks where each instance x is described by a product of attribute values (probabilities), and target function *f(x)* represents mapping to a finite set of values *V* (classes). If we describe the new instance *A* by n-tuple ($a_1, a_2 \ldots, a_n$), we can describe the target value of v_{MAP} as:

$$v_{MAP} = \arg\max_{v_j \varepsilon V} P(v_j \mid a_1, a_2 \ldots a_n)$$

Then, by applying Bayes theorem:

$$V_{MAP} = \arg\max_{v_j \varepsilon V} \frac{P(a_1, a_2 \ldots\ldots a_n \mid v_j) \cdot P(v_j)}{P(a_1, a_2 \ldots\ldots a_n)}$$

$$= \arg\max_{v_j \varepsilon V} P(a_1, a_2 \ldots\ldots a_n \mid v_j) \cdot P(v_j)$$

We can make an estimate of the parameters occurring in the above formulae:

- $P(v_j)$ – based on frequency of v_j values in training data;
- $P(a_1, a_2 \ldots a_n \mid v_j)$ – these values can be estimated for sufficiently large sets of training data.

The Naive Bayes classifier is based on a simplifying assumption of conditional dependence of attribute values of the target value. In other words, conjunction is represented by a product of probabilities of individual attribute values, *i.e.*: $P(a_1, a_2, \ldots a_n \mid v_j) = \prod P(a_j \mid v_j)$

By substituting to the above formula, we get **Naïve Bayes Classifier**:

$$v_{NB} = \arg\max_{v \varepsilon l'} P(v_j) \prod P(a_i \mid v_j)$$

Itemsets Modification

Instead of working with word attributes (a_1), we may use (characteristic) items C of different cardinality or for computing v_{NB}. Over the course of classification, we will utilize characteristic itemsets that have been determined for each class. This leads to significant feature space reduction. Only characteristic itemsets of a given class contained in the instance A being classified are utilized. The formula is therefore changed to

$v_{NBI} = \operatorname{argmax}_{v_j e V} P(v_j) \prod_j P(C_j^{vj} \mid v_j)$, where C_i^{vj} represents i-th characteristic itemset of the class v_j, that also occurs in the instance A being classified. An itemset C was declared frequent in the class v iff its $P(C \mid v)$ exceeded some minsupport value. For filtering *characteristic* itemsets out of *frequent* ones, we are utilizing the same concept as in the itemsets classifier.

We may as well combine both methods, *i.e.*, sum up the weights determined by NB and those determined by itemsets' modification of NB, designating this method *NBCI* (Naïve Bayes Combined with Itemsets).

Document Classification Using Naive Bayes classifier

In order to illustrate practical use of Naïve Bayes classifier, we will apply it to document classification. Let's have a document collection *X*, a set of training documents determining yet unknown target function *f(x)* and a finite set *V* of possible resulting values of the target function. Attributes $a_1, a_2 ... a_n$ represent individual words occurring in documents.

For the sake of simplicity, let's assume a set of 1,000 documents, 700 representing „interesting" documents, considering the remaining 300 documents uninteresting. The set *V* therefore represents two values only, $v_j \varepsilon$ {*interesting, uninteresting*}. We can take a new document containing *111* words, to be classified into one of these classes, containing the word „your" in the 1st position, the word „letter" in the 2nd position, etc., and the word „date" in the last position. Now we apply Naïve Bayes classifier:

$$v_{NB} = \underset{vj\ \varepsilon\{\text{interesting uninteresting}\}}{\arg\max} P(v_j): \prod_{I}^{III} P(a_i \mid v_j)$$

$$= \underset{vj\ \varepsilon\{\text{interesting uninteresting}\}}{\arg\max} P(v_j).\ P\ (a_1 = \text{"}your\text{"} \mid v_j).\ P(a_2 = \text{"}letter\text{"} \mid v_j)$$

$$\ldots P(a_{111} = \text{"}date\text{"} \mid v_j)$$

In the end, we will get the following results:

V_{NB} ... classification via NB classifier

V^{jk}_{NBI} classification using characteristic *k-itemsets* (k being 1,2,3)

(not necessarily one class, can represent a set of classes)

The basic assumption we are making is mutual independence among words occurring at various positions in the document. Now we must determine probabilities of $P(v_j)$ and $P\ (a_j = w_k \mid v_j)$. We assume that $P(a_1 = w_k|v_j)$, $P\ (a_2 = w_k|v_j)$, etc. are equal to probability $P\ (w_k|v_j)$, where w_k is k-th word in vocabulary compiled from training documents.

$$P(\text{interesting}) = \frac{\text{interesting}}{\text{all}} = 0.7$$

$$P(\text{uninteresting}) = \frac{\text{uninteresting}}{\text{all}} = 0.3$$

In order to determine the probability of $P(w_k|v_j)$ we will use formula (see [21]) for estimating probability of terms in document collection, *i.e.*

$$P(w_k \mid v_j) = \frac{n_k + 1}{n_j + |vocabulary|}$$

Where $|vocabulary|$ is the total number of distinct significant terms in the collection of training data.

By analogy for itemsets modification: the total number of distinct frequent *itemsets* in the collection

n_j – The total number of word positions in all training instances with the target value of v_j

n_k – The number of w_k occurrences over these word positions.

By analogy, the value of $P(C_j^{vj}/v_j)$ can be determined by algorithm *classify* (F,A) described in [24], potentially also applying the weight factor of w^{Ti}_{Π} specified in section Training Phase above.

Implementation of Naïve Bayes Document Classification Algorithm

Practical implementation is divided into training and classification phases.

Training phase

Input: Collection of training documents: Set of target values (categories, topics) V, where $v_j \varepsilon V$ Output: Files containing probabilities of $P(v_j)$ and $P(w_k|v_j)$

Procedure

1. Identify all significant terms (other than stop words) contained in collection of training documents (*examples*)
   - *Vocabulary* ← set of all distinct words from the collection of training documents
2. Compute required probabilities of $P(v_j)$ and $P(w_k|v_j)$

- $docs_j \leftarrow$ subset of documents from training collection with target value of v_j
- $P(v_j) \leftarrow \dfrac{|docs_j|}{|examples|}$
- $Text_j \leftarrow$ one document formed by chaining all members of $docs_j$
- $n^j \leftarrow$ total number of different word positions in $Text_j$
- For each word w_k from *Vocabulary*
    - $n^j_k \leftarrow$ number of w_k occurrences in $Text_j$
    - $P(w_k|v_j) \leftarrow \dfrac{n^j_k + 1}{n_j + |vocabulary|}$

Classification phase

Input: Document being classified (*Doc*), a_i representing word occurring at i-th position

Output: The target value, *i.e.* category the document is classified to

- *position* $\leftarrow$ all positions of words in *Doc* occurring in *Vocabulary*
- Compute value of $v_{NB} = \arg\max_{v_j \in V} P(v_j) \prod_{i \in position} P(a_i \mid v_j)$

Practical implementation of NBCI classification algorithm is currently an issue of further research.

Modification of Naïve Bayes classifier with respect to itemsets is also described by Meretakis and Wuthrich [24] Large Bayes *classifier* proposed Meretakis and Wuthrich is reduced to Naive Bayes classifier when all itemsets are of size one only (*i.e.*, no feature space reduction takes place). Support of itemsets is determined with respect to their occurrence in the whole document collection (using *F* as a global set of all interesting and frequent itemsets), not a particular class (my suggestion). They work with the largest possible itemsets, leaving out shorter itemsets contained in larger ones. In my opinion, this idea does not work well in practice.

My draft if based on the concept of *characteristic itemsets*, likely with a fixed number of characteristic itemsets for each class. Feature space dimension is reduced significantly in all cases, leading to higher speed and lower memory requirements. Some combination with weight factors determined in itemsets classifier might also improve classification results.

Itemsets-Based Information Search and Retrieval

Discovering Interesting Web Sites

We can use itemsets-based classifier for looking for potentially interesting web pages, Classification engine can run in a background, trying to classify candidate web pages into topics of interest pre-defined by the user (thus representing user's profile). Threshold values must be properly set to prevent information overload. Short average length of web pages makes practical implementation of this idea quite interesting.

Classifier can be trained on a directory containing web pages downloaded by the user and designated as *interesting*. It is also possible for the classifier to browse through "Favorites" stored by the web browser, visit all pages in each category, get trained (*i.e.*, create sets of characteristic itemsets) and then look for additional pages that may fit into the corresponding category. Classifier could work in the background and notify the user of other potentially interesting web sites. Relevance ranking must be applied to prevent too many pages being offered to the user. Practical results of such a tool could be improved significantly by attaching user's rating of each web site visited by the user.

Output of the tool proposed herein would be represented by a web page containing links to recommended interesting web sites, sorted per relevance (a special web page per category in "favorites").

The tool could as well run permanently in the background while browsing on the Internet, highlighting HTML links recommended to the user, *i.e.*, recommending web sites deemed interesting based on previous training on favorite web pages.

Information Push

The classifier mentioned in discovering interesting websites could be as well trained on a single area of interest, boiling down to a simple binary classifier (*interesting/uninteresting*). Applying such a classifier on a scientific portal or a research digital library, we could filter out articles of user's interest only, pushing these to the user by e-mail. *InfoServis articles* considered relevant based on user's profile can be distributed to users by e-mail.

Searching for Similar Documents

We can also use itemsets classifier for finding similar documents. Let's have document *D* with the task to find similar documents in our collection. We will threat this document as an item to be classified using itemsets method. We will therefore find classes c_j... c_j (possibly one class only) based on characteristic itemsets occurring jointly in *D* and c_j ... c_j. We are then looking for "candidate similar documents", *i.e.*, we are looking for documents from c_j ... c_j. Containing itemsets occurring also in D. In the case we find any documents, we sort them according to pre-defined weight criteria and provide these to the user.

The above is based on hypothesis that similar documents can be found in the same semantic topic. Classification threshold must be sufficiently "liberal", so that c_j...c_j represent several classes, since documents can be classified into several topics, therefore similar documents can be stored in similar topics.

Querying

Let's create all possible k-itemsets from query *Q* entered by the user. These itemsets are then matched against characteristic itemsets associated with corresponding categories in document collection. If we find a match with a class, documents contained in this class are given higher priority for checking against *Q* – these documents will be assigned higher relevance. Maximum relevance corresponds to "match" over the largest *k-itemset.*

Topical Summariser

Automatic Document Summarisation is likely that itemsets-based approach could be also used for automatic document summarisation.

Let's suppose we have a trained itemsets classifier, i.e. we have a set of characteristic itemsets for each class of document collection.

We can regard all characteristic itemsets as phrases for a topical summariser. We also have a document to be summarized. We can make a sophisticated match of this document against characteristic itemsets of every single class. The class matching the highest number of summary sentences is the one to which document should be classified (elementary principle of itemsets classification). Topical summary is a by-product, consisting of summary sentences containing characteristic itemsets of that particular class. Proper thresholds must be defined for selecting sentences as summary or non-summary.

Itemsets Span Filter

Spam Filtering

The first spam filters were based on a simple principle-delete all messages containing pre-defined keywords. Obviously, such an approach leads to deleting many important messages at the higher than acceptable rate.

Modern spam filter is in fact a classifier trained on a single topic. By being classified into the "unsolicited mail" class, the incoming document is labeled as a spam; it is treated as a relevant message otherwise. Based on figures achieved by applying itemsets classifier on Reuters collection containing one topic only (nearly 100% precision and recall), we may anticipate successful filtering results when applying our classifier on incoming e-mail messages. We can train the classifier on a representative collection of unsolicited messages. Such a collection can be created ad hoc, or one of numerous existing spam collections can be used.

We can use the table below to assess quality of itemsets-based spam filter.

	Is it really a spam ?	
Identified as a spam ?	*Yes*	*No*
Yes → Delete	a^{OK}	b^{error}
No → Keep	c^{error}	d^{OK}

Relevance factor applicable to b must be several orders of magnitude (*e.g.* λ = 1000) higher than that of *c* (i.e. we desire to prevent deleting important messages). In other words, blocking legitimate message is λ-times more costly than misclassifying a spam message.

Classification accuracy (*i.e.*, filter accuracy) can be

defined as $\dfrac{a + d}{a + b + c + d}$

Precision $P = \dfrac{a}{a + b}$, Recall $R = \dfrac{a}{a + c}$

Results of a Preliminary Practical Implementation

Itemsets spam filter was tested on an "encrypted" collection of legitimate and spam messages, dubbed PUI corpus[27], which was made publicly available contributing to standard benchmarks. Also ten-fold cross validation was introduced to reduce random variations and an effect of attribute-set size, stemming and stop-list was taken into account.

PUI testing corpus[28] consists of 1099 messages: 481 spam messages in the English language, not containing duplicates; 618 legitimate messages. There are no more than five messages from each person because the reader usually saves the friend's address into the address book in the e-mail browser and in the future the messages from these people will not have to be examined.

Attachments and HTML tags were removed from all messages to respect privacy, in the publicly available version of PUI, fields other than "Subject:" were removed, and each token (word, number, punctuation mark, etc.) in the bodies or subjects of these messages was replaced by a unique number. For example:

```
From: spammer@spamcompany.com
To: spamtarget@provider.com
Subject: Get rich now !
Click here to get rich ! Try it now !
```

becomes:

```
Subject: 1 2 3 4
5 6 7 1 2 4 8 9 3 4
```

There are actually four "encrypted" versions of the publicly available of PUI corpus, one for each combination of enabled/disabled stop-list and stemmer.

PUI corpus statistics:

E-mail messages: 1099 (481 spam, 618 legitimate)
Classes: 2 (spam, legitimate)
Total length of e-mail messages: 849, 977 terms
Number of uniques significant terms; 24, 745

	Length of e-mail messages		
	Minimum	*Maximum*	*Average*
All terms	16	15677	773
Significant terms	12	14367	590

Impact of stemming:
Number of unique significant terms after stemming:
21,702 (87.70% of the original)

Impact of stop-list application:
The total length of the e-mail messages upon applying a stop-list : 6,48,414 (76.29% of the original)

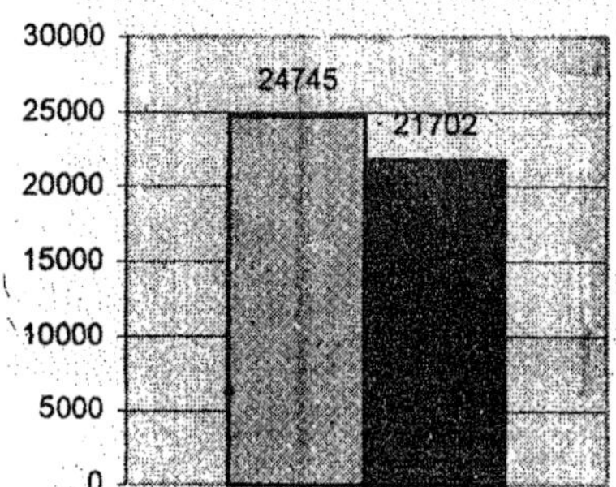

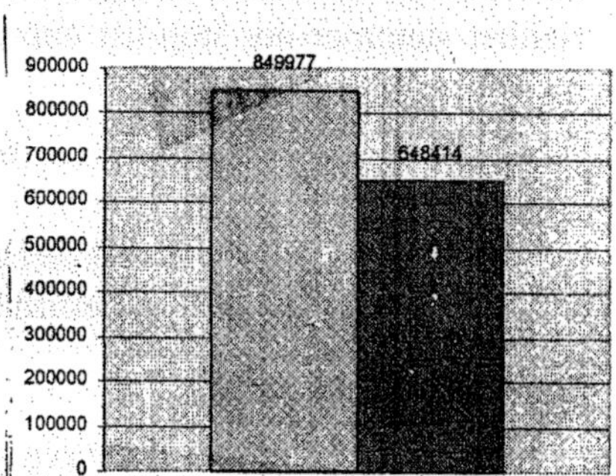

Testing

In all experiments with *itemsets* classifier, *ten-fold cross validation* was used to reduce random variations. That is, PUI was partitioned randomly into ten parts, and each experiment was repeated ten times, each time reserving a different part for testing, and using the remaining nine parts for training.

Results (applicable to 500 features) were then averaged over the ten runs.

Filter used	*(P+R)/2*
	%
(a) Itemsets	97.63
(b) Itemsets + stemmer	97.72
(c) Itemsets + stop-list	97.54
(d) Itemsets + stemmer and stop-list	97.81

We can also experiment with 2-itemsets, 3-itemsets, and 4-itemsets. In fact, this results in very little improvement, while increasing memory requirements and processing time enormously.

Implications

Practical implementation of an itemsets-based spam filter leads to very promising results. 2-itemsets, 3-itemsets, and 4-itemsets are not worth using because of significant time and memory requirements. Neither stemmer nor stop-list improved precision and recall of the filter significantly.

The following spam filters can be also considered for comparison purposes:

Spam Killer (www.spamkiller.com)
Anti Spam (securedisk.netfirms.com)

Conclusion

This report presents a survey of issues related to document classification, clustering, and summarisation. Practical implementation of a digital library is also presented. A survey of current text categorisation algorithms is provided, along with a preliminary idea of a new classification method, *itemsets classifier*, and its potential applications.

Further research will be focused namely on optimisation and ramifications of *itemsets* document categorisation, specifically the cross-collection and cross-method testing. Viability of its application on full-text document collections will be tested upon coming up with a suitable automatic document summeriser, which is an issue of yet another research.

Itemsets classifier will be optimized namely by improving the stemming algorithm, making detailed assessment of numerous input parameters and threshold values of the classifier, testing the impact of its sliding-window modification for various document collections, optimizing itemsets-generation phase for time and memory requirements.

Study will be devoted to other applications of *itemsets* method, such as spam filtering, document clustering, and modification of Naïve Bayes classifier. Any promising results achieved herein will result in integrating the applicable method into the real word digital library in order to back-up results by real-life use. Special attention will be paid to cross-cultural issues in the context of digital libraries, *i.e.*, significant differences between Czech and English document collections.

Itemsets classifier has already been subject to extensive testing (see author's publications below). Providing quite promising results (namely in the case of Reuters-21578 collection), comparable to those generated by SVM categorisation algorithm, in terms of precision, recall and storage/time requirements. Further work is needed to improve classification results on Czech documents, namely unabridged full-text files.

NOTES AND REFERENCES

1. Before we eliminate any terms from a query, we should define an irrelevance threshold based on the length of user query.
2. By using a more general (more specific) term from a thesaurus we can increase recall and reduce precision (increase precision and reduce recall).
3. Reuters-21578 is currently one of the most popular databases for evaluating text categorisation and clustering algorithms.
4. Publicly available at http://www.research.att.com/~lewis reuters21578.html
5. Topic spotting for newswire stories is one of the most commonly investigated application domains in text categorisation literature.

6. MEDLINE is available at: http://www.nlm.nih.gov/databases/databases_medline.html.
7. UCI Repository of Machine Learning databases, 1996, available at: http://www.cs.uci.edu/~mlearn/MLRepository.html.
8. Available at: http://uckn.ff.cuni.cz/CZ/cnc.
9. We have resorted to at least 50 positive training examples per category which testing itemsets classifier.
10. Description of the *Winnow* algorithm can be found at http://www.cs.kun.nl/doro
11. F_1 was initially introduced by van Rijsbergen [34]; it is defined as: $F_1(r.p) = 2rp/r+p)$
12. Herein below denoted as „characteristic itemsets".
13. In case of a shopping-basket transaction database, support provides a misleading picture of frequency in terms of the quantity of items sold. This is not the case of document collection, taking documents as transactions.
14. The *class support* is a variation of the usual support notion and estimated the probability that the itemset occurs under a certain class label.
15. A classifier is a function mapping a vector of document terms onto a set of topics (classes): $f(D)$ = {topics}
16. Categories are often represented in a hierarchical form. We are not considering this aspect in our research, although it would not be a problem – we might combine leaf topics into a single node, retraining the classifier on the adjusted structure.
17. K naturally depends on the size (in the number of terms) of document being classified. Needed to note that twice long a document does not mean twice longer the classification. We are working with significant terms only (leaving out stop words), also neglecting repeated occurrence of significant terms.
18. This is, of course, an ad-hoc approach. I have tried various formulae leading to various results. It is likely that I will come up with a different formula for the final version of this method.
19. Each topic is currently represented by a set of itemsets of fixed size.
20. When testing the classifier on training documents only, the average of P and R is 91.9%.
21. Short sentences tend not to be included in summaries.
22. Summary includes sentences containing any of cue phrases, such as „in

conclusion", „this letter", „as a result", „in summary", „to sum up", „the point is", etc.

23. Proper names, abbreviations and acronyms are often important, increasing score of a corresponding sentence. Special attention must be paid not to include abbreviations of units of measurement (Kg, MPa, F, C, etc.)
24. 80% of significant words occurring in the title correspond to the most frequent significant words in the document [22].
25. If an author-supplied abstract is present (heading containing the word *abstract*), subsequent paragraphs are used directly as the summary.
26. By defining a tree, we create a concept hierarchy. A digital library can be treated (not necessarily) as several trees, i.e. several concept hierarchies.
27. PUI corpus is publicly available from the publications section of http://www.iit.demokritos.gr/~ionandr
28. For detailed information on PUI corpus, see [23].

4

Building Infrastructures for Digital Libraries

We expect that Digital Libraries of the future will be comprised of a large number of heterogeneous services offered by various parties involved in the production, distribution, and archival of digital contents. For the user it becomes increasingly difficult to deal with a multitude of heterogeneous services with different user interfaces and access mechanisms, and requiring separate registrations. Hence the goal is to facilitate the interaction of the user with a Digital Library consisting of a set of heterogeneous services offered by independent providers. In particular, the user needs support in three fields: First, users have to locate and combine appropriate Digital Library services, including trading and negotiation of service properties such as prices, licenses etc. Second, users want to search and query over multiple information sources. Third, users want to stay up-to-date on relevant content of the Digital Library. In this paper, we present three projects that address these issues. These projects constitute the programme *Infrastructures for Digital Libraries* within the German Digital Library initiative *Global Info* [Glo01].

The *DEMETRIOS* federation service for bibliographical metadata is being developed at University of Magdeburg. It supports the flexible integration of bibliographical data from multiple information sources of various types. The unified query service offered by DEMETRIOS can be utilized by other Digital Library services such as HERMES.

The *HERMES* project at Free University Berlin has developed an alerting service for Digital Libraries [FFS+01]. Researchers who have entered their profile of interests into the HERMES system (http://hermes.inf.fu-berlin.de) are notified about matching bibliographical references harvested from a variety of heterogeneous underlying information sources. This means that researchers can delegate the tedious task of continuously scanning all available information sources for relevant publications to HERMES.

Within the *GIBRALTAR* project at the University of Hamburg, a comprehensive user-centered integration platform for electronic publication services is being created. The GIBRALTAR project provides fundamental infrastructure mechanisms comprising facilities for typing, trading, negotiation, and integration. These mechanisms constitute a broker for Digital Library services such as HERMES or DEMETRIOS, that are made available to the user through this portal [ZWBW01].

The developed functionalities may be used as infrastructures for various cases in the domain of digital libraries. Together, they constitute an integration environment for multiple aspects of information services. To give an introductive example, consider a scholar who needs information on a certain research topic. Entering the GIBRALTAR portal, (s)he decides to search catalogs and selects the service type catalogue. The portal suggests a set of various catalogs. Since a federated query service such as DEMETRIOS offers the functionality of a catalog, it is included as well. The researcher chooses DEMETRIOS because of its wide coverage and is thus forwarded to a search interface for DEMETRIOS. After posing his/her search requests and viewing the results of DEMETRIOS, the researcher finds a topic of interest about which (s)he wants to stay informed, so (s)he asks for an alerting service that covers the information sources relevant to this topic. The portal suggests the HERMES alerting system. After entering an appropriate search request, HERMES will start watching various sources for matching publications and will notify they researcher about positive results.

In the remainder, the interoperability issues within the projects DEMETRIOS, HERMES and GIBRALTAR arising from this scenario will be outlined.

Interoperability Issues

The domain of electronic publishing, as well as its sub-domain of virtual digital libraries, consists of many different application-level services including document repositories, catalogs, retrieval engines and alerting facilities. Today such types of services are mostly accessed via the Internet, where typically each one is offered by a different provider.

To constitute the functionality of a Digital Library in a multi-service environment, a specific set of service types has to be chosen, for which the best possible providers must be found and homogeneously integrated. While the identification of a set of interoperable services is done by the GIBRALTAR web portal, integration of different data sources is provided by services such as HERMES or DEMETRIOS.

Federating Bibliographical Databases

The DEMETRIOS federation service [EHS+00] mediates queries on various bibliographical data sources by offering extended query processing capabilities on a global view over the integrated data. It can be used to support simple search scenarios on publications, as well as other services requiring access to integrated, more complex data, like citation indexes [SES00].

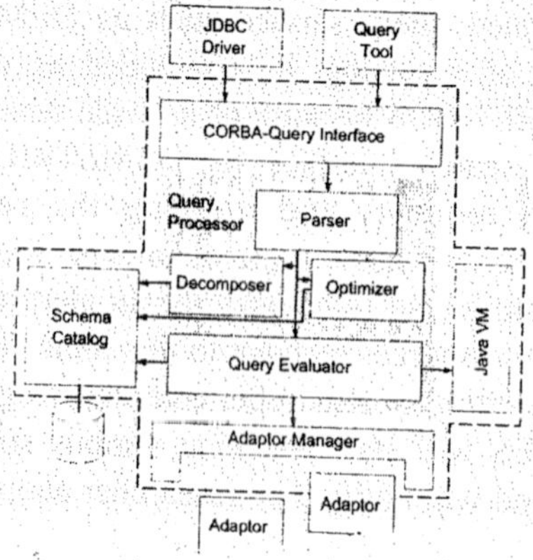

Figure 4.1: Architecture of the DEMETRIOS federation services

DEMETRIOS promotes the interoperability with its clients by offering a standard JDBC interface that allows to post standard SQL queries against the integrated data. For this purpose it deals with different data representations (model, schema) among the sources, data inconsistencies, like overlapping data sets, and possibly limited query capabilities of the source systems. These aspects are flexibly configured for a given application by describing the underlying sources and their interdependencies.

To achieve interoperability with the sources, easily configurable light-weight wrappers called adapters are used. Each adapter covers a class of data sources, *e.g.*, RDBMS, XML, HTML, Z39.50. For instance, we use the XML adapter to integrate the XML version of the DBLP bibliography [Ley01].

Harvesting Bibliographical Information

The main interoperability issue for the HERMES alerting system [FFS+01] depicted in Fig. 4.2 is to interface with various heterogeneous providers of bibliographical data by providing appropriate wrappers. We characterise providers along two dimensions: active vs. passive, and proprietary *vs.* standard. Active providers notify the alerting system on new available publications, typically by e-mail. Passive providers are monitored on a regular basis to detect new publications, for instance by using HyperView wrappers for their Web sites [FS00]. A promising standard for passive providers is the OAI metadata harvesting protocol. HERMES includes a generic wrapper for arbitrary OAI compliant information providers. Another HERMES wrapper is responsible for harvesting the bibliographic databases offered by the DEMETRIOS federation service, thus covering all bibliographic data sources integrated by this service. An example for a mixed type is our project partner Springer Verlag, who notifies via e-mail about new bibliographies becoming available at their FTP server.

Although most information providers use proprietary formats, some adhere to standards. For instance, the Majour SGML format [Eur91] is a quasi-standard used by publishers such as Springer to describe articles in scholarly journals. Internally, we use a slightly modified XML version of Majour to describe articles. HERMES uses various formal conversion techniques, ranging from ad-hoc implementations to rule-based methods such as XSLT and HyperView.

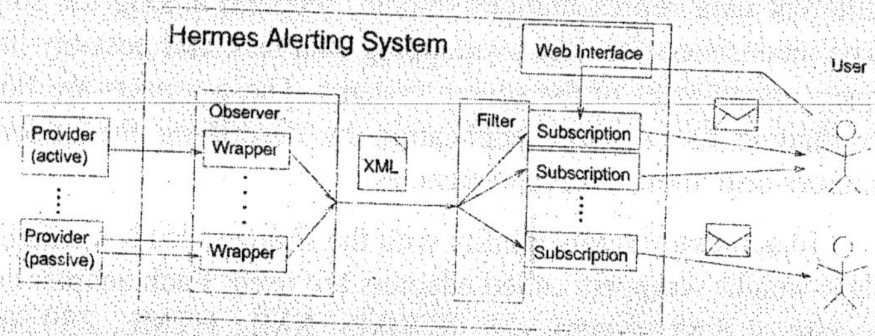

Figure 4.2: HERMES architecture

Brokering Digital Library Services

The GIBRALTAR project provides several system-support-mechanisms that dynamically broker electronic publishing services, as well as an advanced user interface in the form of a web portal (figure 4.3).

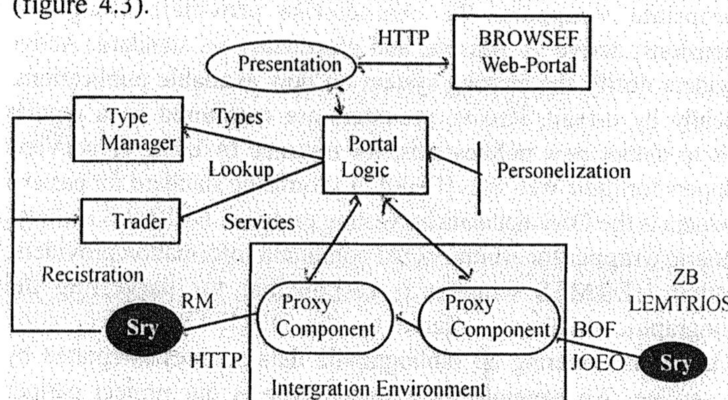

Figure 4.3: GIBRALTAR architecture

The fundamental infrastructure consists of a type manager and a trader component. Together they implement the system-level functions needed for service mediation. The type manager incorporates a sophisticated component-based type system [GZMW01] and allows for the handling of publication service specifications. The trader dynamically maintains a repository of current offers and matches requests for services in an optimizing fashion.

Services of remote providers are integrated through proxies, which are based on an extensible set of adapters for different communication protocols. The GIBRALTAR portal application uses the system-level components to provide orientation, mediation, combination and utilization to end users in a personalisable fashion.

Conclusion

We have presented the Digital Library services being developed in the *Global Info* programme *Infrastructures for Digital Libraries*. In particular, we have focused on the interoperability issues both within and among these projects.

Currently we are working on making HERMES and DEMETRIOS available through the GIBRALTAR portal. This includes specification of service descriptions and their implementation in form of APIs for a middleware such as CORBA.

Further open issues include a unified mechanism that transparently manages user accounts and preferences for multiple services, support for adding new services, and user assistance in combining services to a new customized services.

NOTES AND REFERENCES

1. M. Endig, M. Hoding, G. Saake, K. Sattler, and E. Schallehn. Federation Services for Heterogeneous Digital Libraries Accessing Cooperative and Non-cooperative Sources. In *Proceedings of Kyoto International Conference on Digital Libraries: Research and Practice*. IEEE Computer Society Press, 2000.

2. European Workgroup on SGML. *MAJOUR Header Manual*, 1.0 edition, 1991. Available at http://link.springer.de/author/sgml/help-sgml.html.

3. D. Faensen, L. Faulstich, H. Schweppe, A. Hinze, and A. Steidinger, Hermes – a notification service for digital libraries. In *ACM/IEEE Joint Conference on Digital Libraries*, Roanoke, Virginia, USA, June 24-28 2001.

4. Lukas C. Faulstich and Myra Spiliopoulou. Building HyperView wrappers for publisher web-sites. *International Journal on Digital Libraries*, 3(1):3-18, 2000.

5. Global Info Initiative. Globale Elektronische und Multimediale Information-Systeme fur Naturwissenschaft und Technik – Forder Programme des BMBF. http://www.global-info.org, 2001.

6. F. Griffel, C. Zirpins, and S. Muller-Wilken. Generative softwarekonstruktion auf basis typisierter komponenten. In U. Killat and W. Lamersdorf, editors, *Proceedings 12, Gl-Fachknonferenz Kommunikation in Verteilten System* (KiVS), Informatik aktuell, pages 325-338, Berlin Heidelberg New York, Feb 2001. Springer-Verlag.

7. Michael Ley. DBLP – Digital Bibliography & Library Project. http:/ /dblp.unitrier.de, 2001.

8. E. Schallehn, M. Endig, and K. Sattler. Citation Linking in Federated Digital Libraries. In M. Rantree, W. Hasselbring, and S. Contrad, editors, *Proc. 3rd Int. Workshop on Engineering Federated Information System, EFIS'00* Dublin, Ireland, June, pages 53-60, Berlin, 2000, Akadem. Verlagsgesellschaft.

9. C. Zirpins, H. Weinreich, A. Bartelt, and W. Lamersdorf, Advanced, concepts for next generation portals. In *Proc. First International Workshop on Web Based Collaboration WBC'01*. IEEE, 2001.

5

Principles for Digital Library Development

Want a library's content to persist and be accessible no matter which computer, browser, or digital format is used? Follow these principles and practices, as well as their implied promises.

Building a digital library is expensive and resource-intensive. Before embarking on such a venture, it is important to consider some basic principles underlying the design, implementation, and maintenance of any digital library. These principles apply not only to conversion projects in which analog objects are converted to digital form, but to digital libraries in which the objects have always been in digital form ("born digitally") and to "mixed" digital libraries in which the objects may be of both types. The principles are, in some sense, self evident, yet it is easy to lose sight of them when under pressure to build a system, despite limited resources and time.

Adhering to the following set of 10 principles as well as to the practices that evolve from them, benefits those responsible for the design and continued development of any digital library system and, perhaps, more important, continues to pay off over the long-term.

The principles are derived from our experience developing digital library systems over the past decade [7]. We migrated one digital library (created in the early 1990s, before any thought of serving its contents over the Internet) into a more recently created system called *Profiles in Science* (profiles.nlm.nih.gov/). Even though the original hardware and software in the two systems were completely different, the migration was successful, because each was designed with the same basic principles in mind.

Expect change. It may not be apparent why the changing technology landscape is such a thorny problem for digital library projects. Consider, for example, a conversion project in which documents are converted to some digital format. If the chosen format is part of a proprietary system, viewable only through a proprietary interface, when the company that markets the interface no longer supports the system and format, the digitized documents are all but lost. Consider, too, a scenario in which a document is created in a particular word processing programme and the document is attached to an email message sent to a notable person. Suppose the goal is to preserve all of that person's email messages for future generations. We are all too aware of our dependence on our email technology for reading such attachments. Imagine what today's platform limitations will mean to future generations, when the content of the attachments is likely no longer accessible.

Although the Internet, together with the Web, has made digital libraries possible, this fact may also contribute to unforeseen problems. If library designers depend too much on today's paradigms and tools. They might be tempted to create a Web-site with Hypertext Markup Language (HTML) pages and Web-accessible digital images of objects and documents—that may all be obsolete when HTML changes or is superseded by something else. Changing technologies can quickly outpace the ability of designers to maintain a particular digital library. An approach that anticipates and plans for change is needed to provide lasting access to its information.

Know your content. For users, content is the most interesting and valuable aspect of a digital library for a sample exhibit page in the *Profiles in Science system*). Creators of digital libraries need to manage and make decisions about their content, including selecting the objects to be included, digitizing items that exist only in analog form, possibly marking-up items using standard languages like the Standard Generalised Markup Language (SGML), and assigning metadata describing the content and other attributes of each object.

It is important for developers to decide on the nature and number of metadata elements early in a project. Although some elements may be added over time, significant costs might be associated with assigning metadata retroactively to already tagged and cataloged items in a collection. Some metadata elements describe the content of an item, including, say, its title, creator, date of publication, and subjects discussed. Other elements might be assigned for managing the collection; examples include scan status, quality-control status, and internal notes, as well as the technical aspects of the digital objects, such as file format and size.

Important, too, is deciding on the basic conceptual units, or objects, the system will include, such as individual document, photographs, videos, or lab notebooks. This decision affects the level at which metadata is assigned (for example, to an entire book or to each chapter in the book) and how the materials are organized, accessed, and archived. Sometimes overlooked is the practice of assigning each conceptual object its own unique identifier linking it to its metadata record and to other objects in the collection.

Involve the right people. Ideally, individuals from a variety of backgrounds and offering a variety of expertise contribute to building a digital library. In practice, this may not be the case, but even when it's not, knowing that building the system requires insight from a number of fields yields a better digital library.

The two fields involved most directly are computer science and library science. Computer scientists appreciate the possibilities, as well as the limitations, of technology and are generally the ones who actually build the system. Librarians, including catalogers, indexers, and archivists, have long been the custodians of information resources, understanding not only the information needs of diverse audiences but the issues involved in preserving materials for continued access and use. Digital library research and development have meant that each group has had to understand the other groups' perspectives.

Illustrating the importance of multiple perspective is the development of the Dublin Core metadata standard [8]. Computer scientists are concerned with the semantic interoperability a digital library metadata standard affords in the very large Internet information space; librarians already have deep experience indexing and cataloging and recognize the importance of these concepts for information retrieval. Moreover, because so much valuable data exists in a variety of metadata systems, including the Machine Readable Catalog (MARC 21) standard, methods to map the data between and among these systems using automated "crosswalks" have been developed [10].

Also important when embarking on a project within an organisation is whether its senior management supports the effort. Because most digital library projects are long-term efforts, they require the commitment of long-term financial and human resources. Beginning such as project involves an implicit, if not explicit, commitment to the continuation of the work and a promise that the digital materials will continue to be available. Lacking organisational commitment, it may not make sense to even begin a project.

Design usable systems. Most digital libraries are made available over the Internet through Web technology, though, strictly speaking, this is not a necessary attribute of a digital library. However, as the advantages of the Web are so great, most library systems today are designed to be Web-accessible. The most successful Web site designs account for a number of factors, including the technical difference among computers and browsers, including speed of access, and differences among users, including speed of access, and differences among users, including Web navigation preferences. Browsers differ in the way they display information, even though they use the same basic communication protocols (such as the Hypertext Transfer Protocol, or HTTP, and File Transfer Protocol, or FTP) and standard markup languages (such as HTML and perhaps the extensible Markup Language, or XML). Since users may change default settings, including font size and other parameters, it is always preferable to create as simple an interface as possible and avoid server-side control of the exact display of the data. Providing multiple access points not only makes a digital library more interesting, it also acknowledges the differences among its potential users.

Accessibility for users with a range of physical disabilities should also be a concern when developing the interface to a digital library. This includes user access to all content; documents that are clear and simple; user control of styles; the availability of context and orientation information; inclusion of clear navigation mechanisms; and standard markup.

Ensure open access. Ensuring open access is closely related to usability concerns, including access to the information in the digital library, as well as to the digital library itself. Christine Borgman defines access to information as "connectivity to a computer network and to available content, such that the technology is usable, the user has the requisite skills and knowledge, and the content itself is in a usable and useful form" [2]. Michael Lesk writes that open access to information raises a number of public policy issues, including whether or not all segments of society are given equal access to information [6].

One way to ensure open access to content is to avoid proprietary hardware and software solutions whenever possible. That is, while it may be reasonable to create content using commercially available systems and tools avoid requiring special software or hardware to access that content. A number of companies, while charging for the tools used to create digital images, make their interfaces available for free. As long as the software is easy to download and install, and the developers of the digital library make it clear which software is needed to view the images, the content will be accessible, as long as the interfaces are available. In all cases, however, for continued accessibility and use, open, nonproprietary systems are preferred.

Be (a)ware of data rights. A possible threat to open access to information arises because of intellectual property concerns. Existing intellectual property and copyright law provides economic and legal protection to publishers of physical artifacts. "Fair use" (allowing libraries to make, say, single copies of portions of books or journals) and "first-sale" rights (allowing individuals to, say, lend or resell copies of books they have purchased) have promoted greater access to physical artifacts than might be possible otherwise, but these notions are only indirectly applicable to networked information. A recent National Research Council report states: "The information infrastructure offers both promise and peril: promise in the form of extraordinary ease of access to a vast array of information, and peril from opportunities both for information to be reproduced inappropriately and for information access to be controlled in new and problematic ways" [3].

There are no straightforward answers to the enforcement of intellectual property rights for information available in digital form. The Internet and Web have emerged from communities that believe in sharing information, rather than restricting access to it. This has led to the perception, and perhaps even expectation, that anything available on the Web is freely available and may be redistributed at will. Some argue there will be a realignment in the way intellectual content is published and distributed worldwide (for example, so authors are the primary "publishers," largely replacing existing commercial publishers). Others argue for technical solutions to restrict illegal copying. Still others argue that copyright law needs to be strengthened to prevent unauthorised use of digital information. And still other argue that perhaps the legal protections should come from contract, rather than copyright, law, so data is licensed, rather than sold.

Some resolution to these problems, will undoubtedly arise in the coming decades. In the meantime, however, chose creating digital libraries need to be aware of the issues, participate in the public debates about their resolution, and establish procedures to manage them in order to protect their collections to the extent possible [1]. For example, in conversion projects, every attempt should be made to seek permission frcm the copyright owner for the materials that are to be digitized. Privacy issues should also be considered when, for example, the full papers of a prominent individual are being digitised. Ideally, the donor will have marked the items that are sensitive in some way and left instructions about how they should be handled. In all cases, however, careful tracking of permissions and privacy information ensures the collection will not be at risk at some future time.

Automate whenever possible. Because building a digital library requires significant intellectual effort on the part of the system's creators, the more automated tools that can be built and used, the better will be the use of precious human resources. These tools need to be easy to use and incorporate real-time aids, including data validation, pull-down lists, report generation, and other time-saving devices, thereby allowing the content expert to concentrate on the intellectual tasks at hand. Content experts use the metadata entry system to add metadata to a master database, entering the information only once. Subsequently, the information is extracted and combined as needed from the master database to generate HTML pages, search indexes, and reports. Entering the data only once saves human time and effort, reduces the error rate, and allows maximum flexibility. Nearly the entire Web interface is generated from the database, allowing regeneration whenever necessary, while adhering to the latest Web standards. The system is designed to be modular, allowing existing modules to be modified easily and new modules added for additional functionality. For example, we added the diagnostic server to provide a preliminary view of the master *Profiles in Science* Database, allowing content experts to discover and correct errors and inconsistencies before public release.

Figure outlines the relationship between the underlying master version of the system's data and its derivatives. High-quality loss less TIFF images, for example, serve as archival copies and as master copies for creating a variety of derivatives, such as PDF or JPEG files, for optimal use on Web sites. Then, as better compression algorithms are developed, it will be easy to discard the derivatives (precisely because they are derivatives) and generate a newer file format from the original master.

Adopt and adhere to standards. The use of standards in system building has many benefits. Applications are more readily scalable, interoperable, and portable [11]; these characteristics are all important for the design, implementation, and maintenance of digital libraries. Using standards is especially important for the aspects of digital libraries that are most labour intensive. Scanning, metadata entry, and document markup, all involving the evaluation and handling of individual items in a collection, are resource-intensive and best done carefully and only one. Data might still have to be migrated to other forms and formats in the future, but migration will be easier, because standards have been used consistently. Images scanned using standard file formats, such as TIFF, or texts saved in the open ASCII or Unicode formats will be more easily accessible in the future than images or texts encoded in proprietary formats.

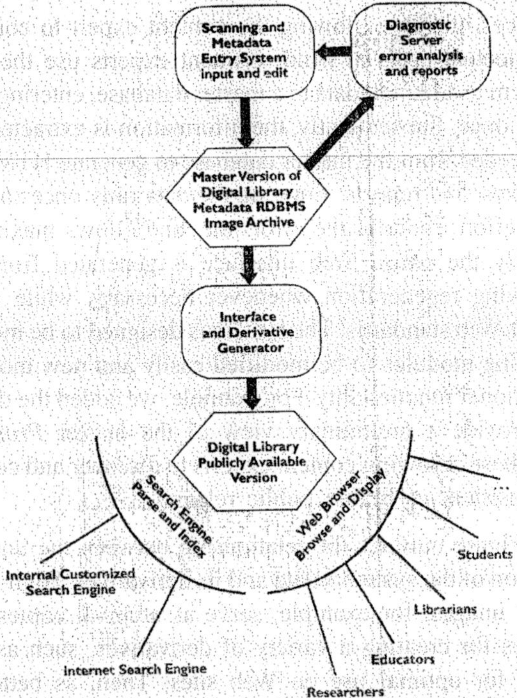

The benefits of using standards for interoperability should be clear to any developer. For example, if all finding aids for historical collections are marked-up in SGML, using the Encoded Archival Description document type definition, one can easily imagine distributed access to all the finding aids held by the members of a university library consortium. Delivering the contents of the digital library on the Web, using standard, valid, and current HTML including metadata tags, and other standard Web technology, increases the chances that other Web search engines will be able to find the library, as well as the specific items in it.

Because technology is changing so rapidly, it is important to question whether it will be possible to port an existing system to another platform, user interface or software. In principle, while porting should always, be possible, in practice it is much easier when the system's design and implementation adhere to certain standards. It's also possible that sometime in the future the entire digital library will be part of another more encompassing system, either within or outside the original institution. The transition will be smoother and more successful if the system is designed with open standards in mind.

Ensure quality. Quality metrics can be applied to all the processes and outcomes involved in creating a digital library. They are relevant to selection, metadata entry, image capture, and the overall usability of the system. Complete and correct metadata yields many benefits; incomplete or incorrect metadata affects the quality of the entire digital library. Metadata plays a vital role not only in resource discovery but in managing the collection. If, for example, subject codes are applied haphazardly or incorrectly, access could be more difficult, and attempts to generate browse hierarchies based on these codes could be foiled.

If scanning procedures and guidelines in conversion projects involve immediate review and evaluation of the scanned images for appearance, including orientation, resolution, colour, and tone, there will be fewer future problems. Images that are skewed, dark, or cut off are not welcome in a digital library. Digitized video and audio need to be reviewed periodically for adherence to evolving standards and for their ability to be viewed and heard using current tools.

Some quality-control metrics can be automated; others require careful human review. Digital library projects should define and then carry out quality-control methods as part of their normal procedures. Adhering to such methods ensures that quality assessment becomes an integral part of building and maintaining the digital library.

Be concerned about persistence. A recent article by Jeff Rothenberg describes a year-long effort to understand the issues of digital preservation, noting: "The conclusion reached by the impressive group of 21 experts was alarming; there is, at present no way to guarantee the preservation of digital information"[9]. While preservation has long been a concern of archives and libraries, it has only recently been of interest to a much larger community.

Anyone creating a digital library has a stake in the outcome of preservation approaches, yet only some address the problem directly. A survey of the member institutions of the Research Libraries Group, which is interested in the question of digital-object preservation,

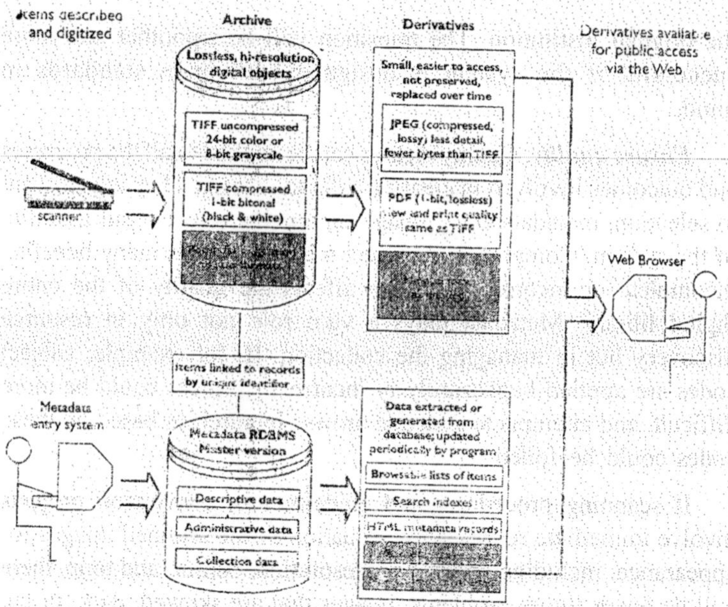

ranked "technological obsolescence as the greatest threat to digital collections" [5]. Several suggestions have been made by researchers to address preservation of digital objects. Perhaps the one discussed most often is the 'migration strategy," which entails the transformation of data from one file format to another, converting it from one software environment to another, or moving it from one physical medium to another. Migration implies a strong and enduring commitment on the part of an institution to continually refresh its collections to keep up with the technology. Another proposed method is the 'emulation strategy," which entailed the emulation of an entire software system so it runs on future unknown systems [9].

The Digital Library Federation, a consortium of libraries interested in electronic information technologies, draws an important distinction between preservation and persistence of digital objects [12]. Preservation refers to an objects technical longevity and quality; persistence is a much broader notion, encompassing preservation, but also referring to whether the object's would still exist in any form at all in the future. Persistence implies a commitment to both maintaining the object and keeping it accessible. It is even possible that entire digital libraries will disappear if efforts are not made to maintain them. Several years ago, an analysis of existing Web sites found the average lifetime of a URL was only 44 days [4]. This discouraging statistic may be accounted for in a number of ways, including that data has been moved, not deleted, but also that we, as a community, are right to be concerned about these issues.

Conclusion

When creating digital library systems containing valuable content, we are making important promises to both current and future users. Seriously attending to the principles discussed here and to the practices that evolve from them places us in a much better position to keep these promises. Valuable content should be handled with care and rendered in the highest quality possible. Valuable content should not disappear. We need to understand how to preserve and safeguard digital material, so it doesn't become obsolete simply because we didn't pay attention. Finally, we need to strive for continued open access to all knowledge. There is no better time to start than now and no better place to start then with our own valuable collections.

Accessibility guidelines

- Web Accessibility Initiative at W3C; www.w3.org/WAI/
- Federal Information Technology Accessibility Initiative; www.section508.gov/

Initiatives and resources

- Digital Libraries Initiative Phase 2: dli2nsf.gov/
- Open Archives Initiative; www.openarchives.org/
- Digital Library Standards at Berkeley SunSITE; sunsite. berkeley.edu/Info/standards.html
- Open Archival Information System (OAIS);www.ccsds.org/RP9905/ RP9905.html
- U.K. Interoperability Focus; www.ukoln.ac.uk/interop-focus/

Intellectual property

- Copyright, Intellectual Property Rights, and Licensing Issues; Sunsite. berkeley.edu/Copyright/
- U.S. Copyright Office; www.loc.gov/copyright/

Markup standards

- Hypertext Markup Language (HTML); www.w3.org/MarkUp/
- Extensible Markup Language (XML); www.w3.org/XML/
- Standard Generalised Markup Language (SGML); www.w3.org/MarkUp/SGML/

Metadata standards

- Dublin Core; dublincore.org
- MARC 21; lcweb loc.gov/matrc/
- Encoded Archival Description (EAD); lcweb.loc.gov/ead/
- International Federation of Library Associations and Institutions Metadata Resources; www.ifla.org/ll/metadata.htm.
- Metadata and Resource Description at W3C;www.w3.org/Metadata/

Network standards

- The Digital Object Identifier; www.dol.org/
- Hypertext Transfer Protocol (HTTP); www.w3.org/Protocols/
- Persistent URL Home page;purl.ocle.org/
- Uniform Resource Names (urn) Character; www.left.org/html.charters/urn-charter.html
- Z39.50; www loc.gov/z3950/agency/

Standards organisations

- Association for Computing Machinery (ACM) Technical Standards Committee; www.acm.org/tsc/
- American National Standards Institute (ANSI); www.ansi.org/
- Coalition for Networked Information (CNI); www.cnl.org/
- Digital Library Federation (DLF); www.clir.org/diglib/
- Institute of Electrical and Electronics Engineers, Inc. (IEEE) Standards Association; standards.ieee.org/
- International Organisation for Standardisation (ISO); www.iso.ch/
- Internet Engineering Task Force; www.letf.org/
- National Information Standards Organisation (NISO); www.niso.org/
- World Wide Web Consortium (W3C); www.w3.org/
- Unicode Consortium; www.unicode.org/

Subject access and control

- Medical Subject Headings (MeSH); www.nlm.nih.gov/mesh/meshhome.html.
- Getty Vocabulary Program; www.getty.edu/research/institute/vocabulary/introvocabs/
- Library of Congress Subject Headings (LCSH); lcweb.loc.gov/cds/lcsh.html.

— *Allexa T. McCray and Marie E. Gallagher*

NOTES AND REFERENCES

1. Arms, W. *Digital Libraries.* MIT Press, Cambridge, MA, 2000.
2. Borgman, C. From Gutenberg to the Global Information Infrastructure: *Access to Information in the Networked World.* MIT Press, Cambridge, MA, 2000.
3. Committee on Intellectual Property Rights and the Emerging Information Infrastructure. *The Digital Dilemma: Intellectual Property in the Information Age.* National Academy Press. Washington, DC, 2000.
4. Kahle. B. Preserving the Internet, *Sci. Am.* (Mar. 1997); see www.sciam.com/0397issue/0397 kahle.html.
5. Kenney, A. and Rieger, O. Moving Theory into Practice: Digital Imaging for Librarian and Archives. Research Libraries Group, Mountain View, CA, 2000.
6. Lesk, M. *Practional Digital Libraries: Books, Bytes, and Bucks* Morgan Kaufman Publishers, San Francisco, 1997.
7. McCray, A., Gallagher, M., and Flannick, M. Extending the role of metadata in a digital library system. In *Proceedings of the IEEE Forum on Research and Technology Advances in Digital Libraries* (Baltimore, May 19-21). IEEE Computer Society, Los Alamitos. CA, 1999, 190-199.
8. National Information Standards Organisation. *The Dublin Core Metadata Element Set: Draft Standard Z39:85*; see www. niso.org/Z3985.html.
9. Rothenberg. J. Avoiding Technological Quicks and: Finding a Viable Technical Foundation for Digital Preservation. Rep. to Council on Library and Information Resources, Jan. 1999; see www.dir.org/pubs/reports/rothenberg/pub77.pdf.

10. St. Pierre, M. and LaPlant, Jr., W. *Issues in Crosswalking: Content Metadata Standards*. National Information Standards Organisation, 1998; see www.niso.org/crsswalk.html.

11. Strand, E., Mehta, R., and Jairam, R. Applications thrive on open systems standards. *Standardview 2,3* (Sept. 1994), 148-154.

12. Waters, D. *The Digital Library Federation: Programme Agenda*. A Programme of the Council on Library and Information Resources, June 1998.

6

Integrating Harvesting into Digital Library Content

From its roots in the scientific e-print community, the Open Archives Initiative (OAI) has grown to hold a significant place in digital library interoperability efforts. By lowering the barrier for data providers to expose metadata, the OAI Metadata Harvesting Protocol provides a consistent tested for new service providers [6]. The OAI has thus successfully positioned itself between high-functionality, complex federation schemes and low-functionality, web crawled search services [1].

Harvesting document metadata has proved successful especially where documents are about a single topic and relatively short. Although these conditions hold for most scholarly articles in e-print archives, the primary data, for example, on which such articles are based are not as tractable.

First of all, primary sources are often quite long and amorphous and not about any single topic. (Is Stevenson's *Kidnapped* really *about* the 1745 uprising in Scotland?) Secondly, scholarly arguments often depend on citing specific passages, lines, or words in a source. Links from text span to text span –rather than document to document— are needed to follow many chains of reasoning. Finally, readers may want liking and visualization services while browsing.

Since its inception in 1987, the Perseus Project has worked on integrating services directly into reading environments and on searching and visualizing complex documents. In this paper, we describe first how our document management system extracts information from various structured documents and how we expose that information as a data provider. We then discuss our experiments with harvesting OAI repositories and integrating the harvested data into the Perseus Digital Library. We show how information extraction services can also be provided for content outside the digital library.

DL as Data Provider

In the past two years, we have been developing a document management system, the Hopper, for indexing and retrieving information in a variety of formats [7]. The Hopper is in production use on the Perseus web site (www.perseus.tufts.edu), which receives over nine million page views per month. Since the Hopper uses the Resource Description Framework as its metadata model and follows Dublin Core for most semantics, it was easy to become a registered data provider, as well as a founding member of the Open Language Archives Community. We expose metadata in OAI-standard unqualified Dublin Core and in the OLAC schema.

In addition to storing document level metadata, the Hopper extracts several kinds of information from document contents. First, it detects markup indicating subsections about particular topics. These divisions are most obviously useful for encyclopedias and dictionaries: our metadatabase is aware of an article about "coinage" in a classical encyclopaedia or one on "Fleet Street' in a survey of London. Second, the Hopper records citations in document content so that the cited documents can be linked back. Finally, the system identifies and disambiguates place names and dates to produce map and timeline visualisations of documents and corpora [2]. Since many documents contain tens of thousands of citations, place names, and dates, we do not currently expose these metadata through the OAI protocol. We are, however, experimentally exporting subdocument information for articles and chapters within large documents.

DL as Service Provider

The Hopper also functions as a service provider, integrating harvested metadata into searching and browsing. When a reader ventures into an unfamiliar discipline, unknown names and terminology can hinder comprehension. Users can also browse terms and named entities to discover documents covering similar topics [4]. The Hopper culls names and terms from the metadata of its documents and creates links in texts that use those words or phrases. Harvested metadata increases the set of terms to be linked to include the titles, authors, and subject keywords of dederated documents. When reading a speech by Demosthenes, for example, the user can click on the highlighted term "Areopagus" and link to pictures of the site of this law court in Athens and also to an article in the Stoa Consortium (www.stoa.org) about the history and procedures of the court.

As a member of the Open Language Archives Community, Perseus is interested in linking together disparate resources in linking together disparate resources for the study of historical and minority languages. Latin text in a Stoa publication, for example, can link each word to grammatical help and a dictionary in Perseus. Simply noting the presence of a Latin dictionary and linking all Latin words to it is not enough, however; the Renaissance Latin texts published by the Stoa contain many words not in the classical Lewis and Short dictionary in Perseus. Many links are thus made to non-existent dictionary entries. To give the user a better idea of what words can be successfully glossed, either the Perseus data provider would have to expose all dictionary headwords as metabata (68,000 entries for just one of Perseus' Latin dictionaries), or the Stoa would need some other mechanism to obtain this information.

Citation extraction is a service of interest to many digital libraries, as evidenced by the popularity of the ResearchIndex (CiteSeer) citation linking service [5]. While the links a document makes could be exposed as metadata, this has some disadvantages. The context in which a link is made can carry important information about its usefulness. A citation made in the body of a text may be more relevant to the main argument than a link in a footnote; a citation that also quotes a passage from a text or occurs in the abstract may indicate an even closer connection between source and target. Also, the citations in many heavily-used reference works take up more than half the space of the whole file.

The kinds of information that the Hopper extracts from documents are certainly not exhaustive. Also, as noted above, some types of metadata approach the size of the full content. In order to encourage new, more complex services, as well as for reasons of efficiency, we are experimenting with extracting information from full text in other digital libraries. Most OAI data providers, while they link to HTML displays, do not provide links from their metadata records to full content, even when a structured SGML/XML file underlies the data. While a full-text file is often available somewhere on the data provider's site, finding it would revive the need for web crawling, which the OAI is meant to obviate. Although we have demonstrated the Hopper's ability to manage content in disparate formats by the integration of SGML documents from the Library of Congress' "American Memory" and UNC's "Documenting the American South" and of PDF documents from the US Geological Survey, these will remain *ad hoc* examples without the ability to discover an acquire content through a standard protocol.

Even though we can seldom harvest full text for analysis, our service provider allows readers, once they have discovered OAI documents in our search interface, to browse them through a proxy service. The proxy inserts links to other Perseus and OAI resources into HTML and PDF documents. The system adds links anchored on the types of phrases mentioned above: subject labels, section headings, documents titles, etc. It is interesting to compare this systems to [3], which makes links based on existing links in other documents. Phrases are placed in a flat key-lookup database indexed by the first non-stopword of the phrase. As with documents in Perseus, remote documents are tokenized into markup and words. The system skips over text that is already linked and tries to match the longest possible phrase at each word position. Currently, the service allows users to restrict the set of phrases to be matched to terms from the whole digital library or from individual collections.

The proxy service only sends information in one direction. We are now experimenting with providing linking, term detection and name disambiguation as SOAP-based web services for content providers. By exposing full content to digital library services, data providers can create a richer testbed for services and greater enhancements for users.[1]

—David A. Smith, Anne Mahoney, Gregory Crane

NOTES AND REFERENCES

Arms, W.Y., D. Hillmann, C. Lagoze, D. Krafft, R. Marisn, J. Saylor, C. Terrizzi, and H. Van de Sompel. A spectrum of Interoperability: The Site for Science prototype of the NSDL. *D-Lib Magazine*, 8(1), January 2002.

Crane, G., D.A. Smith, and C.E. Wulfman. Building a hypertextual digital library in the humanities: A case study on London. In *Proceedings of the First ACM+IEEE Joint Conference on Digital Librarie*, pages 426-434, Roanoke, VA, 24-28 June 2001.

El-Beltagy, S.R., W. Hall, D.D. Roure, and L. Carr. Linking in context. In *Proceedings of the 12th ACM Conference on Hypertext and Hypermedia*, pages, 151-160, Arhus, Denmark, August 2001.

Gaizauskas, G., P. Herring, H Oakes, M. Beaulieu, P. Willett, H. Fowkes, and A. Jonsson. Intelligent access to text: Integrating information extraction technology into text browsers. In *Proceedings of HLT*, San Diego, CA, 2001.

Giles, C.L., K. Bollacker, and S. Lawrence. CiteSeer: An automatic citation indexing system, In *Proceedings of the 3rd ACM Conference on Digital Libraries*, pages 89—98, Pittsburgh, PA, 1998.

Lagoze, C. and H.V. de Sompel. The Open Archives Initiative: Building a low barrier interoperability framework. In *Proceedings of the First ACM+IEEE Joint Conference on Digital Libraries*, pages 54-62, 2001.

Smith, D.A., A. Mahoney, and J.A. Rydberg-Cox Management of XML documents in an integrated digital library. *Markby Languages: Theory and Practice* 2(3): 205-214, 2000.

7

Providing Social Interaction in the Digital Library

As we build the digital library, we need to be careful not to carelessly obliterate some of the important features of current libraries. Many proposals for digital libraries remove social exchange and interaction, focusing narrowly on the technical mechanisms of information access. This is not only unwise, it is unnecessary since we could provide mechanisms for social exchange and interaction within our systems. Simply put, we do not need to remove the social world from our systems. This paper discusses why such interaction is important, and then presents a toolkit, called the Café Construction Kit, that can provide computer-mediated communication support at low cost.

The Digital Library as Ideal

Clearly, the promise of the digital library is enormous [6]. In the ideal, an information seeker can have access to materials whenever and however he wants it. There will be no shortage of copies, retrieval can be instantaneous, and the materials will not decay or fade. One would never need to trudge in the snow to the library. In short, the idea of the "digital library" includes solving many of the technical and logistical issues in current libraries and information seeking.

Despite this promise, the digital library, if improperly considered, could lead to a problematic future. The scientist in the beginning quote inhabits such an environment. Many of the scientists at this research site have spoken with wistfulness about the pas, remembering themselves in a single physical room. They do not want to go back; they do not want to lose the independence of separate workstations. But, they do miss he camaraderie and social cohesion furthered by the interaction in that room.

Such interaction is too easily lost and regained only with great difficulty. Considering only the mechanical aspects of access can lead to ignoring the positive and useful social interactions in information seeking.

The Use of Social Interaction in Information Environments

Social interactions can be quite helpful to information seekers in four ways. First, one may need to know what to know. In general, it could be argued that as access to material becomes easier, emphasis will shift from the mechanical aspects to knowing what material to access. If we can have every book in the world, we will need to know what handful of books to read. *Help in selecting materials* can be alleviated through technical means (*e.g.*, better navigation methods, critical annotations by well-known scholars, and voting). Nonetheless, one may need to have the help of other people as well. For example, it is often easier to ask another person, since interaction can refine questions and tailor answers [1, 10].

Second, social interaction is helpful in providing mechanism for *seeking informal information*. Informal information includes unofficial information such as technical fixes, organisational work-arounds, and personal correspondence [11]. Because this information is often quite volatile and transitory, it seldom written down, let alone indexed. Other people are often the only source of informal information. Current libraries do not handle this type of information seeking, but digital libraries could [2].

Third, information seeking is often ad-hoc and highly contextual [8,12]. *Information seekers often have highly specific interests and needs*. It is often more simple and efficient to go to others for information than to written materials. Allen [3], in his classic study, noted that R&D engineers eschewed the formal literature, going instead to colleagues and the trade press for the information they considered necessary. Again digital libraries could provide this functionality.

Fourth, current libraries do have some important – and useful – social functions. For students, the university library can have an important *socialising function.* Students meet one another and talk in the hallways and canteens, and faculty members bump into colleagues in elevators and stacks. Libraries serve as a place to co-learn (*e.g.,* in study groups). Moreover, community libraries offer a number of social outreach and care programmes. Many of these useful social functions exist secondarily, as by-products of the library's information access goals. Nonetheless, they are not only useful functions, they also make life more pleasurable and rich.

There is some evidence that such exchanges and interactions provide a "glue" for communities Fischer [5], while examining people's sense of community in urban and small-town settings, found that the density and public-nature of social interaction may be a critical feature for people's perceptions. Certainly, there is little sense of community in sitting at one's workstation.

The above arguments – the need for help in selecting material, the desirability of informal information, the ad hoc and contextual nature of most information seeking, the personal enjoyability and community benefits from social interaction – all argue for the inclusion of some form of social interaction within the digital library. Such interaction should include not only libraries (or some human helper), but other users as well.

The Café ConstructionKit

The goal of the Café Construction Kit is to provide a generic interactive communications toolkit for supporting the easy construction of publications such as digital libraries and other CSCW projects. In short, the Cafe ConstructionKit provides a toolkit for sociality.

The Café ConstructionKit provides a set of reusable objects that include message transport for any asynchronous and synchronous communication, parsing for a variety of semi-structured protocols, private and public channels for narrowcast communication, message filters, and message retrieval by a variety of semi-structured methods. The Café ConstructionKit is programmable through the Tcl programming language [9]. By configuring the objects and providing the suitable Tcl programme, *any* application can include the functionality of bulletin boards, chat systems, and electronic mail filters. Additionally, we are actively working on providing the important construction facilities of MUDs [4], so that users can interactively and collectively construct information access methods and environments.

Because of this emphasis on providing building blocks for social interaction, the Café ConstructionKit can provide a range of social functionality to digital library applications. It can also serve as a platform for testing various heuristics for interactive information seeking, where users work together to find, create, maintain, and store new information and knowledge.

The current version of the Cafe ConstructionKit is still in prototype. An earlier version exists and was tested on small-scale problems. The first version showed that it was possible to provide a flexible, distributed construction set for interactive communications. However, informal user studies of the first version argued for a better command language (hence, Tcl), using a standard synchronous protocol (hence, the use of NCSA's Data Transfer Mechanism), user interface support for the interactive communication objects, and careful attention to scalability issues. The second and current version is under construction: The core objects (written in C++ and connected through the Tcl interpreter) exist and work, but more work is needed, primarily on the user interface components.

Conclusion and Future Work

This chapter has argued that the design of a digital library does not have (and should not try) to eliminate the social world. Quite simply, there are important elements of he social world, including a sense of community, that we do not want to lose from our notions of "library". Many social mechanisms are important and useful in information access, and social interaction provides an enjoyable and community-building function.

This chapter briefly presented a toolkit that makes it ways to add social functionality to applications such as digital libraries. The Café ConstructionKit provides auxiliary mechanisms for seeking and locating information without adding significant programming or computational overhead. Most importantly, using the social interaction capabilities of the Cafe ConstructionKit should make digital libraries and similar applications more pleasant to use – a worthwhile goal.

—Mark S. Ackerman

NOTES AND REFERENCES

1. Aaronson, A. And Carroll, J.M. 1987, Intelligent Help in a One-Shot Dialog: A Protocol Study. Proceedings of ACM Human Factors in Computing Systems and Graphics Interface (CHI + GI) '87, 163-168.
2. Ackerman, M.S. and Malone, T.W. 1990. Answer Garden: A Tool for Growing Organisational Memory. *Proceedings of ACM Conference on Office Information Systems*, 31-39.
3. Allen, T. 1977. *Managing the Flow of Technology*. MIT Press, Cambridge, MA.
4. Curtis, P. and Nichols, D.A. 1993. MUDs Grow Up: Social Virtual Reality in the Real World. Xerox PARC. Manuscript.
5. Fischer, C.S. 1982. *To dwell among friends: personal networks in town and city*. University of Chicago Press, Chicago.
6. Fox, E.A. 1993, Source Book on Digital Libraries. Virginia Tech, Department of Computer Science, TR 93-35.
7. Fox, E.A. and Lunin, L.F. 1993. Introduction and Overview. *Journal of the American Society for Information Science*, 44 (8), 441-446.
8. Hutchins, E. 1990. The Technology of Team Navigation. In J. Galegher and R. Kraut ed. *Intellectual Teamwork: Social and Technological Foundations of Cooperative Work*. Lawrence Erlbaum, Hillsdale, NJ.
9. Ousterhout, J.K. 1993. Tcl and the Tk Tookit. Book manuscript.
10. Pollack, M.E. 1985. Information Sought and Information Provided: An

Empirical Study of User/Expert Dialogues. *Proceedings of Human Factors in Computing Systems* (ACM CHI'85), 155-159.

11. Sproull, L. and Kiesler, S. 1991. *Connections: New Ways of Working in the Networked Organisation.* MIT Press, Cambridge, MA.

12. Suchman, L.A. 1987. *Plans and Situated Actions: The Problem of Human-Computer Communication.* Cambridge University Press, New York.

13. Swick, R.R. and Ackerman, M.S. 1988. The X Toolkit: More Bricks for Building User-Interfaces. *Proceedings of Winter 1988 Usenix*, 5-17.

8

The People in Digital Libraries: Multifaceted Approaches to Assessing Needs and Impact

Digital libraries (DL) serve communities of people and are created and maintained by and for people. People and their information needs are central to all libraries, digital or otherwise. *All efforts to design, implement, and evaluate digital libraries must be rooted in the information needs, characteristics, and contexts of the people who will or may use those libraries*. Like most principles, the devil is in the details—implementing and applying the principle to practical problems. Human-centered digital library design is particularly challenging because human information behaviour is complex and highly context dependent, and the digital library concept and technologies are rapidly evolving. Two important aspects of human-centered design are assessing human information needs and the tasks that arise from those needs and evaluating how the digital library affects subsequent human information behaviors. Given the evolving nature of digital library development, solutions to these challenges must be process-oriented and iterative rather than product-oriented and summative. Given the complexity of human information needs and the uncertainty about the effects of new systems, a multiplicity of data views is essential to guide design and understand the impact of digital libraries. This chapter focuses on two elements of design—assessing information needs and ongoing evaluation of impact.

Multifaceted approaches to needs assessment and evaluation of digital libraries are illustrated with three case studies, with particular emphasis on a users needs assessment conducted as part of a project to develop prototype interface designs for the Library of Congress National Digital Library Programme. The human-centered design principle above links three clusters of constructs: people and their needs, characteristics, and contexts; design, implementation, and evaluation; and digital libraries.

Human Information Needs, Characteristics, and Contexts

People is a term taken here to include the entire range of individuals, groups, and communities who have a stake in a digital library. The information needs of individuals have long been studied by researchers in marketing, education, and information science. There is a long history of studies of what types of information needs people bring to libraries (*e.g.*, Krikelas, 1983; Marchant, 1991; Paisley, 1980; and Wilson, 1981). Dervin & Nilan's (1986) review of the information needs literature dichotomizes system-oriented and user-oriented approaches to determining information needs. They criticize the system-oriented approach as too narrow to actually identify user needs and propose an approach that attempts to directly assess people's information needs. Needs assessment research in information science recognizes that there are different levels of needs (*e.g.*, Taylor, 1962, specified visceral, conscious, formalized, and compromised levels), that users may not be able to articulate their true needs (*e.g.*, Belkin, 1980, noted that users often bring anomalous states of knowledge to a search task), and that needs change as information seeking progresses. Highly personalised needs must eventually be translated into executable tasks. Practical design aims to support a common set of these tasks. A fundamental goal of needs assessment is to identify large numbers of specific needs and map these unique needs into common classes of needs that may be met with standardized task procedures. A related goal is to develop systems that assist/guide people in mapping their personal needs into the system-supported tasks. One of the reasons for the popularity of hypertext selection and browsing mechanisms available in the World Wide Web (www) is that people are able to personalize these mappings experimentally albeit laboriously.

That individuals vary on a host of physical, mental, and emotional characteristics is a defining condition of humanity. Much of psychology is devoted to identifying the essential dimensions of human behavior (*e.g.*, theories of multiple intelligence presented by Gardner, 1983; or Sternberg, 1985). A much-promoted but seldom realized aim of design in a democratic information society is universal access. It is axiomatic that designing for universal access is much more difficult than designing for specific populations because the entire range of human characteristics must be supported. Thus, assessing needs and designing a national digital library service requires examination of many communities and will likely lead to multiple system solutions.

In addition to the needs of individuals and group who make use of information in DLs, the needs of the providers and managers also influence design and evaluation. There are many groups and individuals *e.g.*, digital librarians, taxpapers, political leaders, philanthropists, etc.) who have needs that must also be taken into consideration in digital library design. Individuals are embedded in many different communities and communities are embedded in larger social and cultural contexts. When it comes to human behaviour, these contexts are inescapable and confound efforts to artificially isolate specific variables for assessment.

The variety of stakeholders and contexts exacerbates the inherent complexity of assessing human information needs and the impact of systems designed to meet them. Designers and evaluators who wish to take a human-centered approach are thus challenged to specify what people will be served, what levels and types of information needs will be supported, and what contextual influences will be at play. These challenges are summarised in Table 8.1 that expresses questions form the perspectives of designers and evaluators. Clearly, this is an overstated dichotomy—designers are concerned with evaluation questions and evaluators must consider the design questions. In practice, design team members collaborate to address these questions and in some cases, individuals serve in both roles.

Table 8.1: Human-Centered Design and Evaluation Questions

Designers	*Evaluators*
Who are the users?	Who is impacted?
Who are the potential users?	Who and what may influence impact?
What are the common needs?	What are the indicators of impact?
How can those needs be mapped onto tasks?	How can indicators be measured?
How will the new system change needs (and tasks)?	How do impacts influence future generations and systems?

Design, implementation and evaluation

Design, implementation, and evaluation are processes that marshal intellectual and physical capital to yield tangible, usable, and testable products. The design process is of primary concern to architects, engineers, and inventors and there is a significant body of literature devoted to theory (*e.g.*, Braha and Maimon, 1997; Simon, 1996), history (*e.g.*, Petroski, 1996), and practice (*e.g.*, Brooks, 1975; Norman, 1988). Computer system designers have begun to consider the human factors (physical and psychological) associated with system usage and there is a growing recognition of the importance of user-centered design for systems used by general populations. This approach is increasingly adopted by practicing software designers. Hix & Hartson (1993) offer many practical suggestions for assessing the tasks that users bring to computer systems and Shneiderman (1998) provides a rationale for mapping user tasks and needs onto the syntax and semantics of interface designs. Marchionini (1995) provides a framework for mapping users, tasks, and information need settings onto interface designs.

Implementation issues follow design and much of the work libraries do to digitise collections, provide access, and insure interoperation advances practice by demonstrating "how to" procedures. In the ideal, the design specifications are perfect, the work goes smoothly, and the project comes in on time, on cost, and includes all and only the functionality defined in the specifications. In practice, systems contain a variety of workarounds, add new features, and do not include all functions in the specifications. In spite of efforts to build a science of design, iterative design informed by evaluation feedback is more typical.

Evaluation may be a research genre aimed at assessing classes of techniques or methods (*e.g.*, Suchman, 1967 for social programs; Flagg, 1990 for educational technology), or a systematic assessment of a specific product for the purposes of improvement (*e.g.*, Nielsen, 1993). Summative product testing is another form of evaluation that is not applicable to complex and evolving concepts like digital libraries. A human-centered approach to design, implementation and evaluation is fundamentally complicated by the variability in human characteristics and behaviour. See Harter & Hert (1997) for a recent review of evaluation research in information retrieval.

Evaluation of a digital library my serve many purposes ranging from understanding basic phenomena (*e.g.*, human information-seeking behavior) to assessing the effectiveness of a specific design to insuring sufficient return on investment. Human -centered evaluation serves many stakeholders ranging from specific users and librarians to various groups to society in general. Additionally, evaluation may target different goals ranging from increased learning and improved research to improved dissemination to bottom line profits. Each of the evaluation goals may also have a set of measures and data collection methods. Finally, the evaluation must have a temporal component that can range from very short terms to generations. One approach to this evaluation complexity is presented in the Perseus DL case below.

Digital Libraries: Integrating People, Information, and Systems

Digital libraries are the logical extensions and augmentations of physical libraries in the electronic information society. Extensions ampiify existing resources and services and augmentations enable new kinds of human problem solving and expression. As such, digital libraries offer new levels of access to broader audiences of users and new opportunities for the information science field to advance both theory and practice (Marchionini, 1998). There is a substantial body of literature related to digital libraries including many conference proceedings (*e.g.*, Association of Computing Machinery annual DL series) and special issues of journals (*e.g.*,

Journal of the American Society for Information Science 1993, *IEEE Computer* 1995, *Communications of the ACM* 1995 and 1998. Information Processing & Management, 1999). Marchionini & Fox (in press) introduce one special issue by framing digital library design space with community, technology, service, and content dimensions and argue that most research and development to date have been devoted to the technology and context dimensions. Thus, the bulk of the work in DLs has been devoted to extending access beyond the physical walls of libraries and to extending citizen access to government-produced information. As extensions, we should be able to access more relevant information faster and with less expense. The augmentation of community and information services remain important challenges for the years ahead.

As DLs are actually developed, used, and improved, design guidelines will slowly evolve through experience and reflection. Needs assessment and evaluation offer several special challenges. An inherent limitation in directly assessing the human needs for an innovation is the fact that potential users must imagine what the innovation can and will do for them. This is very difficult to do and innovators often justify adopting a "build it and they will come" (BITWC) policy based on their own imaginations of needs and applications. If the engineering is good and the marketing successful, people will recognize the system's value and adopt it. Information technology history is filled with cases of top-down BITWC design success and failure. Alternatively, designers can study users continually and involve them at all stages of the design and evaluation process, thus insuring a ready-made market. This systematic, bottom-up approach can produce lowest-common denominator solutions, and in the worse cases may exhaust time and resources before any solution can be built. Clearly, some middle ground is needed for DL design. High-level visions guided by astute observations of human behavior coupled with systematic and iterative assessments seems the right approach.

Because digital libraries are extensions and augmentations of physical libraries, needs assessment and evaluation may be initially modeled generally on physical libraries. Starting with the general goals, stakeholders, methods, and outcomes of physical libraries and related information technology services, designers and evaluators must be alert to new applications and goals, new user communities that may emerge, changing needs and abilities of existing user communities, new technological developments, changing information processes and capabilities, and new possibilities for data collection and manipulation.

The design and evaluation of DLs is driven by high level visions but is mainly a bottom-up process that synthesises specific instances and cases based on systematic probes of authentic environments with results from controlled investigations in simulated environments (*e.g.*, laboratories). These approaches are equally expensive and mutually complementary. Authentic environments are context-rich but are therefore complex and not under the designers' control; additionally the environments must exist—there must be a working design to study. Thus, to design new environments, comparable built worlds must be investigated and results applied to new designs. Prototypes and laboratory studies offer good control over specific technical variables but only give glimpses of authentic environments. It seems clear that multifaceted approaches to determining user information needs and evaluating DLs must be used and the results integrated to inform design as an ongoing process. The integration is not algorithmic—it is, however, systematic, interpretive, and drive by the high level goals. This integration is analogous to medical imaging techniques (*e.g.*, CAT scan) that aggregate a plethora of data slices so that diagnosticians may interpret holistic organ status.Of course the data cases in DL design and evaluation are less precise and come from several different sources, making the interpretations and conclusions more time consuming and more dependent on inference. For complex phenomena such as DLs where the complexities of human characteristics, the world's knowledge, and sophisticated IT and social systems intersect, it is clear that principles and guidelines are synthesized over time rather than hypothesized and demonstrated.

Design and evaluation must be customized because every DL is situated in a context defined by community policies, human needs and characteristics, and technical constraints. Aristotle noted in his *Ethics*: "In practical science, so much depends on particular circumstances that only general rules can be given." To identify some of the general rules for DL design and evaluation and to demonstrate how multifaceted data streams can be synthesized, three cases are presented. One case (Perseus) is summarized to illustrate an iterative, longitudinal, and multifaceted approach to evaluation of DLs. The case illustrates how a community develop, how usage patterns evolve with technology, and what long-term impacts DLs can have on a multiplicity of stakeholders. The second case (Baltimore Learning Community) is described briefly to highlight specific high-level goals that drive design decisions and illustrate that good design in not sufficient to community building. The third case (Library of Congress) is discussed in detail to illustrate the multifaceted approach to user needs assessment when the user community is ill-defined and there are no precedents for the system.

The Perseus Project Evaluation

The Perseus Project began developing a corpus of multimedia materials and tools related to the ancient Greek world in 1987. The mission of this project was driven by the perceived needs of students and faculty to have improved access to primary source materials and to have juxtaposed linguistic and visual resources to better learn and understand culture. This evolving digital library (www.perseus.tufts.edu) began as a HyperCard-based CD-ROM library of Greek texts and English translations, images of vases, sculpture, and sites, maps and drawings of Greek sites, and a variety of retrieval and philological tools. The DL transitioned to the WWW in 1995. From the first days of the project, an evaluation team worked to address a set of research questions related to learning, teaching, scholarly research in the humanities, and electronic publishing. The evaluation effort has continued for more than a decade and there are many published reports on the project as well as the evaluation (several evaluation reports are able at http://www.perseus.tuffts.edu/FIPSE/ see also, Marchionini & Crane, 1994). The purpose here is to provide an overview of how the evaluation was initially framed and how it evolved over the years as the digital library was developed, used, and expanded.

In the original four-year evaluation plan, four evaluation goal sets were identified: learning, teaching, system (performance, interface, electronic publishing), and content (scope, accuracy). Three characteristics of the computational medium that we believed would add particular values were identified for particular emphasis: access, learner control, and collaboration. Based on these goal sets and media characteristics, a hierarchical set of 94 questions was developed to guide the overall evaluation.[1] Four sets of stakeholders were identified for study: students, instructors, project staff, and classics researchers. Based upon these goals and stakeholders, a set of data collection methods were adopted. These methods fell into three general classes: observations, interviews, and document analysis. Observations included baseline notes made by evaluators during classes or in laboratories, structured checklists and forms completed in these same settings, audiorecordings of people thinking aloud while using the system, and transactions logs of Perseus usage. Interviews included one-on-one and group interviews and discussions that were audiotaped and transcribed, and various written questionnaires completed by students, instructors, and scholars. Document analysis included examination of the system software and documentation; syllabi and assignments created by instructors and student responses to assignments (essays, journals, and hypermedia paths). Observations and interviews were done at a variety of university sites that included major research universities (both public and private) and small liberal arts schools, and in selected high schools and museums.

Over the first few years of the evaluation the scope of work and resources available caused the evaluation team to decide to invest most efforts in the learning and teaching goals and on students and instructors as stakeholders. This is a practical example of prioritizing evaluation goals. Additionally, additional data collection techniques were added (*e.g.*, written comments of visitors to a museum exhibit at the National Gallery of Art in Washington where Perseus was available as an adjunct to a sculpture exhibit). As the Perseus corpus grew in size and especially as it migrated to the www, the evaluation team was able to examine more longitudinal effects. By the late 1990's evidence was gathered to support the notion that Perseus was having systemic effects on the field of classical studies.

The main findings over the first eight years of evaluation can be summarized in four categories: amplification and augmentation, physical infrastructure, conceptual infrastructure, and systemic change.

Amplification and Augmentation. The Perseus DL amplifies and augments teaching and learning. Amplification takes two forms: (a) more texts (including some not available for students in print forms) and more images and maps than most department slide and map libraries offer; and (b) an integrated corpus that allows text-oriented courses to easily add image-based context and vice versa. Another type of amplification often noted is that content may be accessed more quickly and easily than physical versions in libraries (a kind of mechanical advantage). Augmentation is evidenced by instructors who introduce new activities that are otherwise impossible. For example, the philological tools allow instructors in class to illustrate points with word analyses or to visually and easily correlate geographic characteristics and textual passages. In addition, entirely new courses were created that integrated the varied and multiple resources in the DL. More importantly, Perseus empowered new kinds of student learning such as sophisticated philological investigations by students who knew no Greek, visual investigations of vase painting themes, and new discoveries by students alone or as part of a class.

Physical Infrastructure. Using the Perseus DL requires substantial physical infrastructure investment. At every site evaluated, hardware and network problems caused frustration for faculty and students, substantial economic and human resources were necessary to make Perseus available in classrooms and laboratories, and laboratory staff had to be trained to support faculty and student access. These challenges are faced by all educational institutions introducing technology into instruction and reflect the larger learning curve investments taking place in all disciplines at the close of the twentieth century. One important effect apparent when Perseus was used through the WWW was the relative ease of use when compared to the HyperCard-based version—students did not have to learn a new system but used the mostly familiar interfaces of web browsers. Thus, the common infrastructure of the WWW, especially the general purpose client-side browsers that faculty and students use for many different courses and purposes, mitigated some of the technical requirements for Perseus use. One result that recurred over the years is that-self-reports on the system interface and learning effects are highly correlated, whereas demographics, computer experience, and frequency of Perseus use are not statistically correlated with self-reported learning effects.

Conceptual Infrastructure. The Perseus DL demands new conceptual infrastructures for teaching and learning. Instructors must learn to teach with the DL and students must learn how to learn with it, and both these requirements involve substantial amounts of time. Many instructors noted the large investments in time required to create assignment and Perseus-augmented lecturers. Likewise, some students complained about the amounts of time it took to learn to use and access the system and to find the information needed. Several instructors noted that students took longer to complete assignments than anticipated and that classroom use often took longer than planned since interesting alternatives or additional examples could easily be pursued with the system. Instructors should take into consideration that the novelty and amount of work an innovation demands may lower student course evaluation results during the early years of adoption. Several instructors noted that Perseus raised their levels of expectations about the scope of material accessible to students. Likewise, students at schools where Perseus was used in multiple course came to expect that such resources would always be available for use in their courses.

A number of opportunities and challenges related to teaching emerged. The traditional dilemma of how best to mix open-ended and guided instructional activities is exacerbated by the many possible uses that Perseus offers. Likewise, how to best use class time and what content is displaced when Perseus-based content is introduced into a course or curriculum must be considered? Perseus allowed instructors to model how they do their own research and the risks and time required to model research should be considered. Instructors must learn to evaluate electronic assignments. One instructor noted that more extensive feedback was made possible by having assignments and his comments in electronic form since he could leverage all the advantages of word processing while grading. Certainly, instructors and administrators must understand that iterative planning and implementation cycles are required over years rather than weeks or semesters, and appropriate allowances, resources, and rewards must be available.

Opportunities and challenges related to learning were also varied. Students are certainly motivated by Perseus, especially by the images. Students were observed to work harder and better when their assignments were put on the web—the persistence of the assignment beyond the end of the course and the "publication" of the work are likely explanatory factors in this regard. Some students reported being overloaded by the amount of content available. Likewise, some students wee overwhelmed in lectures that included many Perseus examples and multiple verbal themes. The learning curve necessary to use Perseus tended to be more problematic in large, general studies courses than in advanced courses for classics majors who tended to recognize the time it took to learn to use the tool as an investment to be amortized over multiple courses.

Systemic Change. Perseus is bringing systemic changes to fields of classics. In 1998 there were more than 50 courses included on the Perseus web site representing more than a dozen colleges and two dozen instructors. These courses use Perseus in a variety of ways and illustrate the penetration of Perseus into the classics curriculum internationally. In some universities, multiple instructors use Perseus for several of their courses. Several instructors noted that Perseus use has led students, faculty, and administrators to see classics as technologically "plugged-in" leading to more recognition and resources on campus. While it is too soon to generalize, the new courses created based on Perseus tend to integrate textual and visual materials and illustrate ways to break down barriers between distinct areas such as philology and art history. New classics faculty position announcements list computer experience as requisites. Popular textbooks now include Perseus companion paths, and a Spin-off company: Classical Technology Systems provides training and support. The Perseus project continues to attract funding for expanded work, and workshops and papers related to Perseus are standard fare at professional conferences in the multiple fields of classics as well as education. By 1998, the Perseus DL was responding to approximately 25,000 hits per day (unique requests excluding GIFs) and has become an electronic gateway to a suite of electronic resources well beyond the original ancient Greek culture corpus and tools. Many of the tools and techniques have been integrated into new projects at Tufts University (*e.g.*, Rome, ancient science) as well as in other projects. The Perseus DL impacts a large and diverse community beyond university classics courses. It serves as a stable and authoritative resource for other publications (*e.g.*, several commercial online encyclopaedias refer to the Perseus DL) as well as for distance education and other non-traditional education venues.

These results address many of the high level goals related to teaching and learning that were set out in the original evaluation plan more than ten years ago. The evaluation adapted to new technologies and content and to the new ways that instructors and learners found to apply this DL to their needs. It was opportunities in that it took advantage of new venues (museums and high schools) and new data collection techniques (*e.g.*, the transaction logging scripts built for HyperCard version and the less user-specific but more broad-based transaction logs of the WWW). It took a multifaceted approach to evaluation that was botton up in that it integrated many specific data collection efforts guided by the high-level general questions that guided it. The longitudinal dimension allows the evaluation team to extent that evaluation space to a temporal dimension. Figure 8.1 illustrates this expansion by framing a wide range of stakeholders across time (Marchionini, 1995). Such a framework gives a "big picture" flavour to digital library evaluation research and can easily be adapted for other stakeholder sets or evaluation goals. In the figure, time intervals are: immediate (days or weeks), annual (year), short term (two-five years), mid term (five-fifteen years), generational (20-30 years), and very long term (50+ years). The icons in each cell are balance beams that represent tradeoff balances between tangible and intangible costs and added values of the DL. In the figure, all balance beams are equivalent. Specific DL evaluation efforts can aim at determining what cost-benefit tradeoffs are evident for any stakeholder/time subset. In the Perseus example, we might depict the immediate benefits to learners and instructors as more costly than traditional resources but show better payoffs in the short or mid-term rows. Such situations would be visualised by balance beams tipped in opposite directions in different rows and columns.

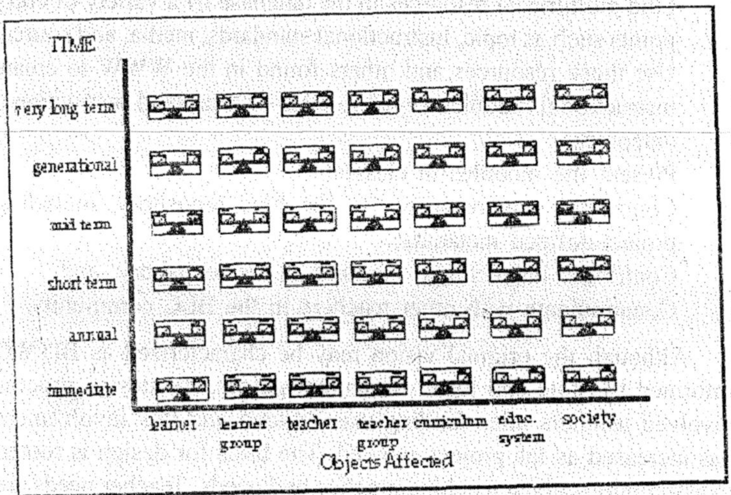

Fig. 8.1: Temporal Framework for Evaluating DL Effects on Educational Stakeholder

Baltimore Learning Community

The Baltimore Learning Community (BLC) Project aims to leverage DL resources and technology to facilitate a community of teachers who create and share outcome-oriented instructional modules. Beginning with a seed collection of video material from Discovery Communications Inc., the BLC project team worked with teachers to create a small repository of multimedia materials, and tools for accessing those materials and building and using instructional modules. Teachers are encouraged to share the modules they create, together with reflections on how the modules were used in classes. Additionally, teacher may contribute specific resources to the BLC repository.

Together with face-to-face meetings, requiring multiple participants in each school, and Internet communication facilities, this sharing of ideas, raw materials and modules were central components for the vision of community building and sustainability. The BLC DL provides support for teachers to:

Find multimedia resources in the database by a variety of entry points such as topic, instructional standards, media, and source;
Use those resources and others found in the WWW to create instructional modules keyed to state of Maryland instructional outcomes;
Present the modules in classes;
Contribute new resources to the bloc repository, including project-defined metadata;
Contribute instructional modules to the repository; and
Communicate with other teachers in the BLC community.

Although the original vision may be characterized as BITWC informed by state and local curriculum guides, the design process involved teachers after funding was secured and this involvement has increased as the project evolved. The basis for design is rooted in assumptions about teaching practice and needs. Teacher needs are actualized in curriculum standards and guidelines—it is unmistakable that teachers in public schools are strongly influenced by local and state curriculum guidelines and assessment procedures. Our intention from the start was to assist teachers in addressing these needs. The mechanism was providing teachers with access to high-quality multimedia materials tied to curriculum rubrics and encouraging them to leverage these materials to build community where teaching practice and lessons are shared to everyone's benefit. This approach to meeting common needs through shared resources and experiences is the basis for the sharium concept—a distributed electronic problem solving space with rich information resources and tools where people can work independently or collaboratively to solve problems (www.ils.unc.edu/~march/sharium/shariuml.l.html).

The BLC evaluation plan aims to document how teaching practice evolves in such an environment and eventually how student learning is affected. See www.learn.umd.edu for background on the BLC, including a demonstration of selected system components and a set of reports on the project. See Enomoto, Nolet, & Marchionini (1998) for preliminary evaluation results.

The system design used a selection and form based approach to lesson construction, alternative interface options for teachers to facilitate personal styles as well as working at home or at school, a dynamic query interface style to facilitate resource exploration, and different video surrogates to save teacher preview time. The system design evolved as teachers expressed their needs more sharply as they gained experience. Based on teacher feedback, several changes to the design have been made:

a simple slide-show presentation component was added to the original presentation component that included details on pedagogy (*e.g.*, objectives, groupings, instructional strategy, etc.):

the full Maryland School Performance Assessment Programem Outcomes Model and Content Indicators for social studies and science were made available from the module construction tool:

a feature for printing locally-required lesson plan formats from the modules was added; and

the resource explorer tools were embedded in the module construction tool rather than remaining separate functions.

In the fourth year of acquisition, indexing, interaction, and use, the system continues to evolve and there are a few indicators that a community is forming. Overall, progress has been slow and arduous.

a few teachers have contributed original materials (*e.g.*, photographs of the Baltimore harbor were taken, indexed, and contributed);

more than 100 modules have been created and added to the repository although teacher reflections and commentaries on usage have seldom been included;

most teachers have made significant strides incorporating the Internet into their classrooms, in most cases without using the BLC repository directly (although they often add create modules that incorporate WWW materials they find); and

a fourth middle school and group of more than a dozen teachers have joined the project.

On the research and development side, the advanced interfaces have been incorporated into web-based application and a series of empirical studies of video surrogates have been conducted (*e.g.*, Ding et al., 1997; Komlodi & Marchionini, 1998; Slaughter *et al*, 1997). It is clear that the process of community building in schools and across schools is a very low process. Building the DL has proven to be much easier than building a community of instructional practice. Although some of the difficulties teachers have in creating and sharing materials are due to technical issues (*e.g.*, slow access, system crashes, multiple platform incompatibilities), the challenges of teaching in inner –city middle schools, administrative pressures to raise test scores, and lack of incentive for out-of-class time investments deter forward progress. Few teachers have actually used the modules created by other teachers, there is a flurry of activity immediately after the annual summer institute and less activity through the school year. With the exception of a few teachers who are actively creating and using modules, most teachers ignore email and choose not to attend after–school development sessions (small stipends are provided).

It seems clear that the demands of students, administrators, and the school system climate get much more attention than the project. It is likely this is as it should be—DLs and technology are not panaceas to solve the problems of public education. I will take time for communities to form around the resources and tools the DL research and development community provide. This case illustrates that content and technologies are not sufficient to create sustainable communities in highly structured environments such as public schools. Funding bodies and designers must show good patience in assessing impact in such environments. Designers and evaluators must exhibit reasonable expectations in such settings, recognizing that the people who use the DL are concerned with the immediate value to their work rather than with the design and evaluation.

Library of Congress National Digital Library Programme

This case study reports on the Users Needs Assessment conducted for the Library of Congress National Digital Library Programme in order to develop prototype user interfaces for the National Digital Library (NDL). The design process and the various prototypes are described in Plaisant. Marchionini, Bruns, Komlodi, and Campbell

(1997), and Marchionini, Plaisant & Komlodi (1998). The focus here is on the extensive information needs assessment that was undertaken before designs were begun. Based on the perceived needs of the populace to have better access to the Library of Congress' (LC) treasures, a multifaceted and flexible approach to estimating the needs of the citizenry was taken.

This users needs assessment of the LC NDL was conducted over a relatively short period of time (four months) so the flexibility proved especially important in identifying potential users and tasks using techniques that were practical in the allotted time period. For example online surveys of users of the existing NDL web interface were not used for two reasons: first they only reach self selected users who have already found the NDL and chose to fill the questionnaire, and second they required a long process of authorisation, review and implementation which was prohibitive in this case.

As we collected information about user characteristics and their needs, were examined corresponding user interface challenges. A taxonomy of users and tasks was proposed. It is highly likely that this taxonomy will change as the NDL evolves since it is rooted in data that come from a mix of current users of the physical LC, early adopters of the nascent implementation, and non-users asked to speculate about using it. This taxonomy and a general list of interface challenges became important reference materials for the team designing the prototypes for the NDL.

The LC NDL Context and High Level Goals

The Library of Congress has taken a leadership role in the development of a National Digital Library. LC's role in this effort is to digitize 5 million items from 200 Americana collections over a five year period (http://memory.loc.gov/ammem/amabout.html). As part of this initiative the NDL Programme planned activities for preparing, digitising archiving, and providing access to these historical and contemporary materials and for managing the overall project and collaboration with other institutional partners. The challenges of providing access are addressed by efforts to develop an easy to use yet powerful human-computer interface. It is our view that a poor user interface is actually worse than denying equitable access since it frustrates people and wastes their time. To guide the development of the interface, a user needs assessment was undertaken to determine what tasks and search strategies users bring to the Library today, what new types of users, tasks, and strategies the NDL will attract, and how these user needs may best be served by the NDL interface. Because the NDL Programme was new, there was no extract user community. To assess the needs of potential user a variety of data collection approaches were taken and a flexible approach to integrating and interpreting data was adopted.

Needs Assessment Stakeholders

Three general user communities were considered at the beginning of the project and others emerged as the needs assessment progressed. The three original groups were:

LC staff. This community is characterized as experts in both library system and content, as heavy users of the existing systems, as knowledgeable about articulated (formalized) user needs, and able to devote short (usually less than two hours) amounts of time to individual's needs.

Scholars and other visitors to LC. This community is characterized as having high levels of domain expertise and knowledge of library systems. They are also able to devote large but specific amounts of time (days or weeks) to their individual information needs.

Visitors/Prospective users. This community is characterized as having varied levels of domain expertise and low levels of library systems knowledge. They are able to devote only short periods of time to their information needs or explorations.

Data Collection Procedure

Three types of data collection were undertaken: selected LC Reading Rooms were visited and staff hosts were interviewed; written questionnaires were created and distributed to important prospective user communities; and LC documents were examined.

Reading Room Visits and Interviews. This was considered to be the most informative component of the assessment since the librarians in the reading rooms are not only themselves important users of the existing system but also have extensive knowledge about current user needs at LC. In addition, many of these staff members are either directly or indirectly involved in the development and maintenance of the NDL and have stakeholder needs that must be captured. Two or more project team members participated in visits to nine different reading rooms. For each visit, information was gathered with regards to the three facets of the user needs assessment and a fourth category was added for miscellaneous data. These facets were:

Content: What materials are housed in the reading room, what indexes or finding aids exist, and which materials were scheduled for inclusion or possible inclusion in the NDL.

Users: The types of users who typically used the reading room, what types of information needs they brought to the Library, what levels of searching skill they typically have, how these users might benefit from the NDL, and what new users might be attracted by the NDL.

Strategies: how do users conduct searches, what types of search tools are available in the reading room, and how does the reading room staff assist users.

Other: Any notes on interface implications, additional notes specific to that reading room.

The notes were transcribed by one of the interviewers and sent via email to the other team members who participated in the visit. These team members augmented and edited the electronic notes based on their own written notes and the final electronic version was sent for comment (member checking) via email to the reading room staff member who had hosted the visit. After staff had made comments, corrections, or addition, a final set of notes was prepared.

Questionnaires for Potential Users. Because K-12 teachers and students are featured prominently in plans for the NDL, a limited survey of educators was conducted. Rather than an expensive and time-consuming random sample, we took advantage of existing contacts to survey a convenience sample of educators. There were two groups so selected. The first group was a set of 24 teachers from different areas of the U.S. who participated in NDL orientation sessions. The second group of educators was the set of 27 school library media specialist supervisors in the state of Maryland. Both of these groups were administered a questionnaire including questions on types of materials used, search strategies applied, system characteristics preferred and possible future applications of a NDL collection. The difficult task of assessing the needs of the general citizen was addressed by a survey of parents and workers in a large daycare center. This facility serves a large and diverse community of blue-collar and white-collar workers in the Midwestern U.S. city.

Document Analysis. Documents represent an institution's expression of procedures, policies, and responses to user needs. Three types of LC documents were examined as part of the needs assessment to better understand user and system needs:

Reading Room handouts and brochures. During reading room visits, many handouts were obtained and these handouts reinforced the notes taken during visits in that in some cases they illustrate user needs that are so pervasive that special publications or finding aids are created.

User study reports prepared by LC staff. These two studies reported on the experiences of different user groups in different environments with the pilot American Memory project, a precursor to the NDL using similar materials. These reports identified many interface issues.

User email commentaries or inquiries about the NDL sent by early users of the infant NDL, as well as staff responses, were analysed and categorized.

Results of Reading Room Visits and Interviews

Results are organized by content and by users and strategies.

Content. The NDL is not an academic exercise that begins with well-articulated user needs and then adds content that is tailored and organized to meet those needs. Instead it is a large, real-world effort that is rooted in a complex cultural context. Content for the NDL is selected based on a variety of economic, legal, social, and political exigencies. As the digitization plan continues to evolve, we can anticipate that materials added to the NDL will be as varied as the holdings of the Library itself. This implies that interfaces to the NDL must be driven by content decisions as well as users' needs.

Table 8.2: Samples from reading room notes related to the "content" facet of the assessment, and corresponding interface challenges

Examples of Visits	*Extracts from Notes*	*Interface Challenge Examples*
American Folklife Centre	The collection is largely uncatalogued, must of it is unpublished. Originally consisting of folk songs, it now includes cultural documentation in various media. Most collections are multi-format. Most include recorded sound.	Browsing of materials will be more important than catalog search. Accessing audio (searching capability as well as download times); showing between to multi-format items (*i.e.*, coordinating a sound tack and textual field notes)
Map Reading Room	Items include panoramic maps (cataloged), county atlases (cataloged), railroad maps, East European maps (not cataloged, heavily used by genealogists), Civil War maps, Sanborn fire insurance maps (about 7,00,000 items), and selected maps of American history.	Very large maps to be seen at varying resolutions. Specification of areas/ regions on maps; Problem of place name ambiguity.
Prints and Photographs Room	Items for NDL include: Washington, Lincoln, Jefferson, papers; WPA life histories; Whitman notebooks; Margaret Mead collection; some finding aids for other collections. Finding aids very important, but vary in detail.	Full-text search. Specification of limits of search within a manuscript, across a collection, etc.; Important to distinguish finding aids levels and primary materials.

Challenges are posed by the variety of content digitized from the collections of the different reading rooms. For each visit we used the notes to compile a list of content-related interface challenges to be addressed in the prototypes. Table 8.2 gives samples extracted from notes and lists of challenges:

Next all challenges were summarised into a set of general content-related interface challenges. First, there are a variety of materials that will become part of the NDL. Not only do the materials vary by topic, size, and format, but also by degree of cataloging. Some materials are cataloged at the item level, some are cataloged only at the collection level, and some are uncataloged. This state of affairs presents huge challenges to LC staff as they work to serve user needs and challenges to users who are trying to find information in the NDL. It is highly unlikely that new cataloging efforts can be undertaken to catalog those items not current cataloged (*e.g.*, in the Geography and Map Reading Room alone, only about one-quarter million items are cataloged out of 4 million). It is also unliked that catalog records for specific items in collection cataloged at the aggregate level can be created, or that existing catalog records can be edited to reflect any special requirements of the NDL (*e.g.*, geo-referencing for maps). Thus, the first challenge is to develop a conceptual interface design—an organisational framework with appropriate rules for applying the framework. This framework must characterized for users the granularity, size, and nature of objects in the NDL. This challenge cuts across all the reading rooms and has several facets. The interface must communicate to the user the following:

- What is contained in the entire NDL,
- The level of representation for a displayed object (bibliographic record to collection, series, or item).
- The alternative levels of representation available for a displayed object (bibliographic record only, thumbnail or other extract, primary object),
- The nature of a displayed object (secondary or primary; format(s); concomitant or linked objects).

This challenge must be met within the current levels of indexing. However, just as the Library takes advantage of user browsing behaviour in uncataloged collections or in collections that are described only at a group level to create records subsequently for individual items selected by patrons and therefore presumed to be "high demand" (*e.g.*, photographs found and copied by patrons in Prints and Photographs), the NDL presents an opportunity to add additional cataloging information to items that users find while browsing the digital collection. Another element of this challenge is to integrate searching of catalog records with searching of SGML finding aids available for some objects such as manuscripts.

A second challenge is to communicate to the user what items are NOT in the NDL. At one level this places the NDL within the context of the entire LC itself (*e.g.*, copyrighted materials, 3-D objects, etc.), and in the context of the world of information available in other institutions and on the entire Internet. On another level this assists users in planning for visits or becoming aware of related information at LC or other institutions.

A third challenge is to support users in the NDL without human intervention. Although some level of reference service will be necessary in the NDL, every patron cannot expect the level of human support current visitors to LC need, receive, and expect.

A fourth challenge is to create an interface that is accessible to user with state-of-the-market technology. The interface (and underlying retrieval system) cannot be based on assumptions about state-of-the—art hardware (*e.g.*, in 1995 terms: 20 inch high-resolution displays, very high-speed connections, huge RAMs, specialized I/O devices) or software (*e.g.*, the latest operating system or web browser).[2] Just as the overall system must leverage compression/decompression and advanced retrieval algorithms, the interface must inform the user about temporal demands for data transfer, provide posting information about result set sizes, and provides some level of explanation for ranked results. In addition, the interface must be "growable" to keep pace with the evolution of hardware and software.

A fifth challenge is to invent new techniques to search for multimedia objects and to integrate those techniques into the interface (*e.g.*, visual and audio query languages, surrogate viewers).

Together with the specific interface challenges listed in the reading room summaries above, the NDL content begins to define both a development and a research agenda for more general digital library interface design. Although these challenges were addressed at preliminary levels in the resulting prototypes, they all will remain-

Table 8.3: Samples from reading room notes related to the "Users and strategies" facets of the assessment, and sample interface challenges

Examples of Visits	*Extracts from Notes*	*InterfaceChallenge Examples*
Geography and Map Reading Room	One-third of users (estimate) looking for genealogical information. Estimate one-forth of users are contractors looking for environmental information. Specialised maps are often sought (e.g., railroads, land use, hot topics) Users rely heavily on reference librarians to get started, and are often not cartographically nor geographi-cally literate.	Specifying areas; awareness of the potentially huge files to transfer and display.
Newspaper and Current Periodical Reading Room	Many users are first-time visitors to LC; about 20% are regular users who come for sustained scholarly visits. Reference interviews are important. Since much of collection is copyrighted, finding aids and a few specialized items will be in NDL. Holdings information is as important as pointer information.	Helping NDL users quickly understand that few of the primary materials are online.
Law Library	Primary users are Congressional staff. People in the wrong place are directed to their local libraries; there are good law materials on the Internet so an analogues strategy can be used in NDL.	Determining when to point users elsewhere

	Novices pointed to law encyclopaedias. Main entry points are time, country, type of material (law, court decision).	
Manuscript Reading Room	80-90% are academics visiting for a few days to more than a month. When visiting, part of the entry registration process is a reference interview with a librarian. Most users have to work through multiple levels of guides to get to primary materials and are heavily dependent on librarian assistance. Entry points are mainly name of person, some subject access that point to finding aids.	Helping NDL users quickly understand the few of the primary materials are online and that there are many levels of search to work through.

long-term problems for the DL research and development field for many years to come (see http://www.cs.umd.edu/projects/hcil/ndl/index.html for reports and various prototypes).

Users and Strategies Facet. The Library of Congress is mandated to first serve Congress and its staff. It has traditionally been a library of last resort for other citizens in that its collections are so large and specialised that only well-prepared researchers can take full advantage of the Library. Although many casual visitors come to LC to see and experience it as an institution, it is a research library and operates to serve those prepared to work in a complex and scholarly environment (*e.g.*, citizens under the age of 16 are not permitted to use the Library). The NDL is a fundamental change in the service mission of LC in that a much broader user community is addressed. Table 8.3 below gives samples from notes and interface challenges.

There are many interface challenges posed by the assessment of users and the strategies used in the reading rooms. The most fundamental challenge is: How to serve a wide range of users who will visit the NDL? This general problem has several facets.

The entire range of the U.S. citizenry

- User of different ages
- Users with the entire range of educational level
- Users with a range of cultural and ethnic perspectives
- Users with special physical and cognitive needs
- Users who vary in their experience with computer technology
- The entire range of experience specific to their visit to the NDL
- Users who vary in experience in the domain of the information problem they bring to the NDL
- Users who vary in their experience with libraries and research collections.

In addition to the challenge of individual user characteristics, the interface must support a wide variety of information needs that users bring to the NDL. Because we are focused on formalized and compromised needs, we use the term task in the following. From a user's need perspective, these tasks vary on five non-orthogonal dimensions.

- Complexity
- The number of concepts involved
- How abstract are the concepts
- Specificity (ranging from a particular fact to interpretations)
- Quantity (the amount of information required or expected to meet the need)
- Criticality (how important it is to the user to meet the need)
- Timeliness (how long users are willing to spend or expect to spend in meeting the need.

The NDL interface must help users easily communicate some of these characteristics of their task to the system. Other general challenges echo the content challenges above.

- The interface should help users distinguish primary and secondary materials (including multiple layers of each).
- The interface should help users make links among items across different collections and reading rooms.
- The interface must capture the essential elements of the reference

interview so that users can find what they need without human intervention.

In sum, the reading room interviews reinforced well-known general challenges for interface design but also raised concrete cases specific to multimedia DLs aiming to serve general populations. They also served to introduce the project team to the rich culture and collections of LC.

Questionnaire Results

Teachers and School Library Media Specialists. Responses from the teachers and school library media specialists were very similar and provide insight into the great diversity of technology penetration in U.S. schools in 1995. Thirteen of the 24 questionnaires (54%) sent to teachers were returned and eleven of the 27 questionnaires (41%) sent to school library media specialist supervisors in the state of Maryland were returned. The two-page teacher questionnaire had four general demographic questions, three scaled questions (Likert) on types of materials, five scaled questions on search strategies, five scaled questions on student search strategies, five scaled questions on computer system characteristics, three scaled questions on access to LC NDL, and one open ended question about desired useful materials for teaching. The school media specialist questionnaire was the same but media centre was substituted for classroom and teachers in your school for students.

The data for the two groups showed very similar patterns. For preferred information-seeking patterns both groups reported using all the strategies listed in the questionnaire often: browse list of potential terms; browse items with embedded links; navigate a hierarchical set of menus; search using controlled vocabulary; search using natural language. Both groups were similarly generous in estimating students' use of the entire variety of information-seeking strategies. Likewise, teachers and school library media specialists were unified in demanding a system that could be used in school and home, and is easy to learn and use. There was less unanimity within or across the groups about the need for access to large amounts of primary materials. Even less agreement was reported for the need for access to multimedia materials, perhaps reflecting concerns about the computing infrastructure in schools at that time. Both groups were far more concerned about professional use of the NDL than they were about personal uses.

Although both groups rated primary documents as important, teachers were more uniformly consensual in rating them as extremely important. Teachers rated finding aids as somewhat less important than school library media specialists (most of whom are trained as librarians). It is interesting to note that teachers rated teacher guides as somewhat less important than did the school library media specialists.

At the time of the survey (Fall (1995), there was a wide range of equipment available in these schools ranging from DOS and Apple II machines to Windows and Macintosh machines. This wide range of equipment was problematic, as significant numbers of work stations in these schools were not be capable of using the NDL. It was somewhat surprising that all but two respondents said that there was some kind of Internet access in their schools, most often in the school library media center. Perhaps even more surprising, eight of the thirteen teachers and six of the eleven school library media specialist supervisors reported having Internet access at home. Although Internet access was not defined as a IP-capable connection, some type of remote access capabilities is available either in school or at home to most of this very select group of educators.

The final open-ended question asked what types of materials respondents would find most useful for themselves or their teachers. Not surprisingly, the teachers were more verbose in describing specific materials they could use in class, in many cases citing very specific NDL collections that presumably they had encountered in their LC training.

Examples of Teacher Suggestions:

> Images of the past & current interest linked to curriculum & interesting primary sources and documents; sounds of historical events and music.
>
> Major American figures from all areas of life—pictures, writing, inventions, personal items (diaries)
>
> Life in other times (Edison film of NY harbor, sharecroppers, immigrants, farm life, etc.) Documents that helped shape

our nation.

Links to related sites (archives, Smithsonian, etc.)

Include photos of Depression, American Indian, Black studies, popular culture, World Wars

Ease of access is vital.

Examples of School Library Media Specialist Supervisor suggestions:

Donwload public domain information; indexes finding guides, etc.

Lesson plans for all subjects areas; support materials for lessons (text, sound, images); text will accompany images (that can be printed and used away from terminal)

Social studies, American history documents, text, visual, census statistics

Source information on specific subject area topics, teaching strategies & techniques for given objectives/outcomes.

Day Care Centre. The results of the day care centre questionnaire stand in somewhat sharp contrast to the school-based data. The two-page questionnaire was administered in the fall of 1995, and had five demographic questions, five questions on computer usage, three questions of library usage, and twelve questions on expectations about the NDL. Eighty-five questionnaires were returned and provide a 1995 snapshot of the views of citizens remotely located from the Library of Congress. About two-thirds of the respondents were female

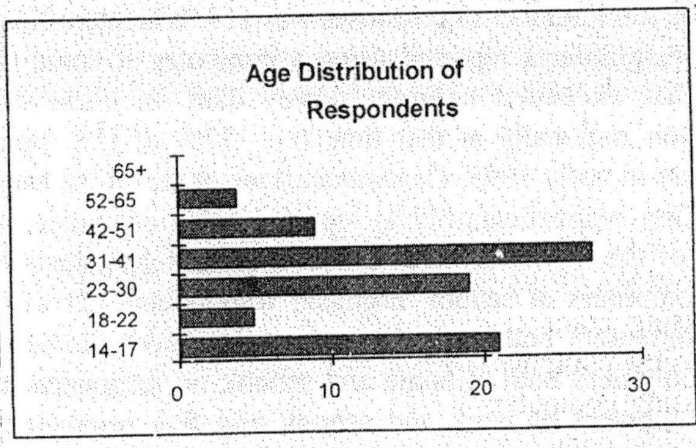

Figure 8.2: Age Distribution (N= 85)

and the largest number were in the 23-41 age group (another large group was composed of high school students who worked at the center). Figures 8.2 and 8.3 illustrate these data. This distribution is representative of working parents with day-care age children.

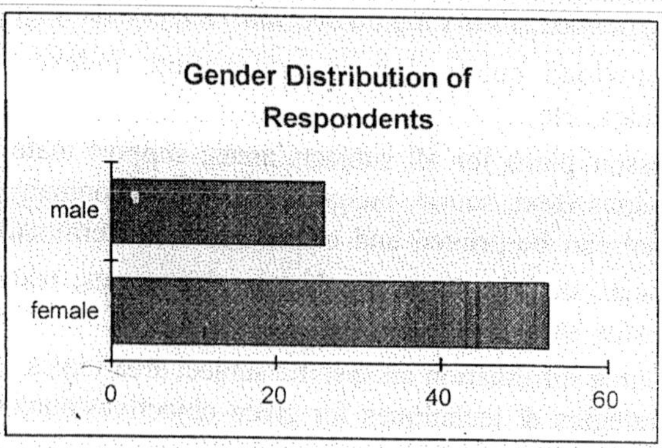

Figure 8.3: Gender Distribution (N=79)

There was a wide range of educational completion levels in the group, and most respondents expressed an interest in learning more about computers. The responses to computer usage questions illustrate the gap between interest to learn and actual experience. Figure 8.4 shows where respondents accessed computers. Ten participants did not respond to this question. As they were asked to check all that apply, the total number of responses was 117. It is interesting to note that 51 respondents reported using a computer at home (60%), a figure that exceeded national survey data on home computer penetration nationally at that time (*i.e.*, 37% of U.S. homes had computers in early 1995, *Communications of the ACM*, May, 1995, p. 9). Forty respondents (47%) reported using computers at work. Twelve of the 18 (67%) high school student respondents reported using computers at school. Eighteen respondents (21%) reported using computers both at home and work; eleven (13%) reported using computers both at home and school; no respondent reported using computers at work and school; and five respondents (6%) reported using computers in all three locations.

Figure 8.5 depicts how often respondents use computers. Twenty-nine (35%) of the respondents reported using computers on a daily

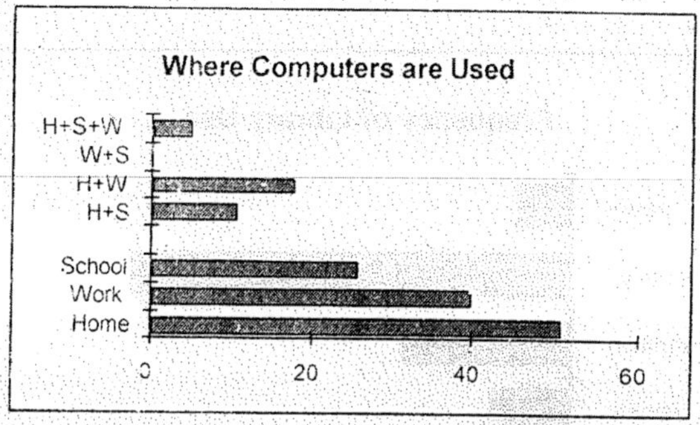

Figure 8.4: Where Computers are Used

basis; 20 (24%) reported using computers several times a week; 15 (18%) reported using computers several times a month: 14 (16%) reported using computers once in a while, and seven (8%) did not respond to this question. Seventeen respondents selected reasons for not using computers, with access (6 respondents) and knowledge (5 respondents) the most frequent selections. Twenty-five (29%) of the respondents reported having access to some online service. These data suggest that computer usage was pervasive with well over half of the respondents in this survey using computers in a variety of

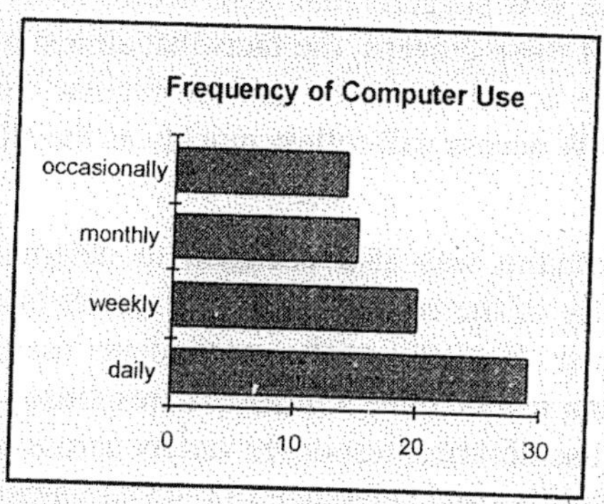

Figure 8.5: Frequency of Computer Use

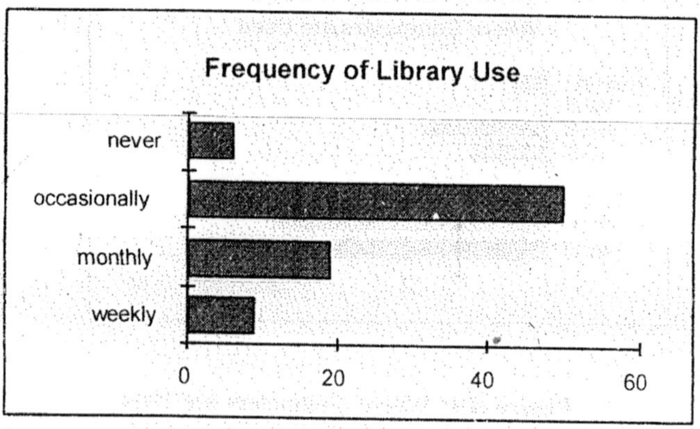

Figure 8.6: Frequency of LibraryUse.(N=840

settings multiple times per week and that almost one-third had some type of online access.

A very different portrait emerged from the responses related to the World Wide Web (WWW). Although 32 (38%) of the respondents had heard of the WWW, only nine (11%) had actually used it. Of those who did use it, only three were high school students so the adult users were beginning to use the WWW. Although this very low penetration of the WW suggests that NDL access today would reach a small portion of these citizens, the facts that almost one-third now have some online access and over half are regular computer users suggest that WWW access will follow quickly as the NDL continues to evolve.

The questionnaire was also designed to determine the basic library use facility of the respondents. The results (see Figure 8.6) illustrate that most (50=59%) of the respondents use the library on occasion (less than several times a month). In response to the question about why they use libraries, responses variety across the categories, with school (40=47%) and reference (38=45%) garnering the most frequent usages (see Figure 8.7). It is interesting that 33 respondents

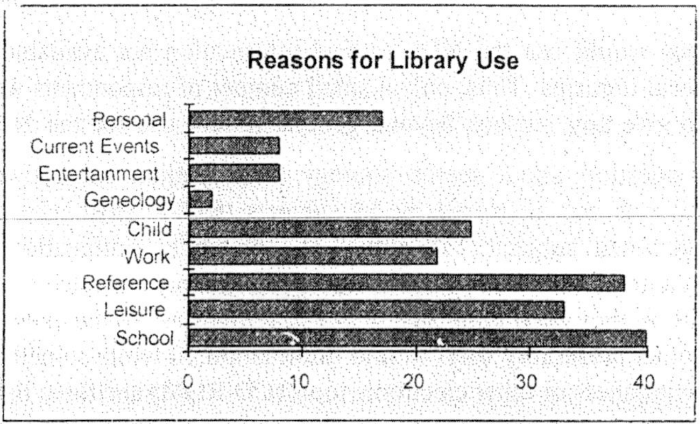

Figure 8.7: Reasons for Library Use

(39%) selected leisure reading as a usage. Of all these usages, perhaps leisure reading is least likely to be affected by NDL availability.

The main objective of the questionnaire was to determine what needs exist or may evolve for the NDL. This was also the most difficult objective to achieve since subjects were asked to articulate needs related to a new entity about which they knew very little if anything. Thirty-six (42%) of the respondents said they expected to use the NDL for the same reasons they currently use libraries, however, the fact that 41 (48%) selected don't know illustrates the lack of knowledge about the NDL. To address the difficulty of eliciting information about an unknown entity, the questionnaire was designed to be open ended in this section. Although, we recognised that this would make responses more difficult and many participants would skip these questions, we wanted to provide the broadest possible scope of responses. For the question about why subjects would like to use the NDL, most respondents (54-64%) wrote nothing or NA/ none. Several of the respondents made generic comments about easy, fast access to information or about gaining more information or knowledge. A few made general comments about using it for school and a few noted the importance for children. Five respondents gave specific information topics or types of information (World War II, genealogy, history from a different perspective, educational materials for teachers, and maps and photographs). Two respondents noted that they would use the NDL to find information not available in their local libraries. Thus, only a small number of respondents were able to give any reasons beyond generic library use for the NDL.

A question about search strategy (title, author, subject, and browse) was not answered by 53 subjects (62%). Most who did respond noted subject (11), author (5), or some combination of subject/author/title (11 Thus, the respondents mainly expected to use the NDL as they do finding aids in physical libraries. To the question about other preferably ways to find information.10 wrote something about computers or other electronic tools (CD-ROM) and three listed a librarian.

To the question asking if they thought they could find information easier if were available electronically, most respondents (84%) answered yes, showing confidence about their ability to use computers to find information and high expectations of the use of computers in searching for information.

Faster and easier access to information was given as an example in the questionnaire items on expected advantages and disadvantages of DLs.[3] Forty-seven (55%) of the respondents indicated one or both of these reasons. Two of those respondents also noted that there could be more information, another noted that it would be faster since they could send information to their local printer, and another noted that there could also be many more cross references. Twenty-two (26%) gave no response. Five respondents said there would be more information; six said they could do work from home or work: two noted that they could find information beyond that available in their local libraries; two thought that they could get more precise (exactly what I want) information; and one noted that it would have no advantages since the computers in libraries were too confusing to use already.

The disadvantage question gave "slower more difficult access to information" as an example. Six respondents noted that access might be slower; seven said that it might be difficult to use the technology, three noted generic difficulty, and three noted difficulties related to finding information. Forty-five (53%) of the respondents did not answer or said no disadvantages. Two respondents were concerned with access to terminals; five noted potential problems with technology failure; three noted concerns about system overload (busy lines); one noted potential information overload; one was concerned that not everything needed would be available; three were concerned about costs; one noted that no librarian would be available to help; and one thought the entire idea was a waste of tax dollars.

The final open-ended question asked participants to list ways that they might use NDL materials. Thirty-eight (45%) of the respondents did not write anything or wrote NA. Fifteen (18%) specifically noted schoolwork or projects; seven (8%) noted to help children (one said younger brother); eight (9%) said reports, presentations, or projects; and four said for general reference. The remaining responses related to some sort of personal knowledge: five noted general personal information; five noted travel or vacation information; three noted general knowledge acquisition; two said knowledge of history; two said genealogy; and one each noted music/ literature, multiple sclerosis, and art inspiration. One other respondent said for entertainment, and one said "just like a library."

Although it was difficult for the respondents to speculate about the pros and cons of the NDL they knew little about, the comments given do cover the commonly expressed advantages of digital libraries and provide a wide range of concerns about technical and intellectual challenges to the NDL.

Summary of Questionnaire Analyses. At the time of the assessment, the general populace showed interest in computers and the information resources networks offer but had limited first-hand experience with the WWW. Home computer use was high with some sort of online access becoming more common. Schools used a wider range of computers and many have some type of online capacity in the building but few had it in classrooms. The day care results show that few respondents gave specific reasons for using the NDL and cited no specific collections. The media specialists gave some specific reasons but no specific collections. The teacher respondents who had participated in LC training cited specific materials. These results reinforce the theme of diversity in users, needs, and computational settings and suggests that the NDL must be purposefully introduced to potential users.

LC Document Analysis

Reading Room Handouts. The first documents examined were those available in the reading rooms as handouts for visitors. There is a rich set of knowledge captured in these handouts and the NDL interface must provide some of their functionality. Some of the handouts related to physical space and working hours – functions less critical in the NDL but still needed in terms of services and the interplay between digital and physical collections. Others provided descriptions of the collection and policies for using the collection and are clearly applicable to the NDL. A challenge is finding ways to integrate the many different reading room descriptions into a common introduction for the integrated NDL. Documents that help users actually use the collection or conduct research in the field will also be as valuable for NDL users as they currently are for LC reading room users. Finally, the reading rooms have created specialized documents related to particular user needs or hot topics (*e.g.* current events, anniversaries). The existence of these documents illustrates the need for some similar service in the NDL interface.

All these documents reinforce the complex nature of the individual reading rooms, let alone the complexity of the aggregate LC. Preliminary versions of the interface can simply point to electronic versions for these documents, however, specialized electronic versions will emerge over time and be integrated into the system help and guided tour components.

LC User Studies. The two LC user studies we used offer a rich set of specific interface recommendations. Some of the impressions and commentary at the early American Memory test sites strictly reflect individual preferences, however some trends were common across many sites, for example:

- Students preferred buttons to pull-down menus,
- There were many instances of poor understanding of search strategy (*e.g.*, misunderstanding Boolean AND, lack of systematic reformulations or use of results).
- Complaints about time to use the system (both physical access due to a single workstation and response time).

- Teachers noted that linkages between the primary material and their curricula would be beneficial (a common use for the content and system was as an enrichment adjunct rather than an integral part of the course), and several noted that it is essential that materials can be printed and/or saved to disk.
- The Prints and Photographs WWW Public User Interviews identified a variety of navigational problems. For example the lack of basic graphical user interface literacy made it difficult to use a mouse, scroll, use pull-down menus. Moving among levels of representation was also difficult (*e.g.*, between a full image, thumbnail, and brief display), and losing buttons after scrolling was frustrating.

The search strategy problems identified included:

- Confusion regarding relevance ranking of results.
- Need for easy-to-use alphabetical subject headings,
- Limiting hit lists to 100, or having too much to look through, and
- Need for posting data (frequency of occurrence) after all moves.

Both of these sets of results highlight challenges for the NDL interface. In addition to reinforcing the importance of computer experience, these findings illustrate: the need for crisp and intuitive dynamics between screens/windows so that users can focus on different levels of representation easily or possibly juxtapose them; judicious use of any scrolling functions; and the need for clear yet powerful search articulation and results display.

Email Messages. The sample of representative electronic mail messages answered by LC staff provides an interesting mosaic of users who are actually using the infant NDL and the types of information needs and problems they bring to the Library. Based upon a content analysis of user messages, staff responses, and a brief classificatory commentary provided by staff for the exchanges, the messages fall into three broad categories: system, user needs, and miscellaneous.

The "system" category includes the following types of messages:

- Praise (compliments about the NDL)
- Crashes (complaints or inquiries about server or telecommunications problems)
- Technical questions or suggestions (difficulty launching video players on client, suggestions for alternative data formats)
- Suggestions to add
  - Content (add specific collections)
  - Indexes or services (one interesting request was for a zipped index of the NDL that could be downloaded and used locally to save connect charges)
- Corrections (*e.g.*, mislabeled photograph).

The "user needs" category includes the following types of messages:

- Reference questions (*e.g.*, census data for NY state 1600-1900 and how to find it)
- Requests for special collections

  Requests for specialised services (*e.g.*, photograph copy requests online)
- Requests for help (some have done searches and want help in narrowing: others confused about what to ask, where the mail is going).

The "miscellaneous" category includes the following types of messages:

- Contributions of two types
- Specific items (*e.g.*, want to donate a photograph) URLs (requesting LC to link to their web sites)
- Job seeking (to work on NDL)
- General communication (some users reply with thanks and commentary to a reply to their earlier message-want to maintain dialogue).

Taken together, these documents capture a wide range of knowledge about the LC, the users who use it, and the types of information needs they bring to it. The existing documents must be captured and integrated into the NDL Analysis of future email will surely contribute important data as the system evolves and new, systematically scheduled user studies are highly recommended.

User Type/Task Taxonomy

A central theme emerging from this investigation is diversity. There were wide ranges in users, the tasks they bring to the NDL as manifestations of their needs, the technological settings they work in, and in the wide variety of content that makes up the NDL. To integrate the results from the different components of the investigation we revisited the nature of users and needs in light of the types of user communities identified before data collection began. It was clear that the three communities (LC staff, current scholars, and prospective NDL users) were too broad to capture the diversity or to fully guide the interface design.

A more fine-grained classification is possible by combining the analytical framework of users and tasks (Marchionini, 1995) with the empirical data from this investigation. The analytical framework crosses users, tasks, and the personal situation that motivates the search.

Users have a host of individual characteristics, preferences, and experiences, which are not orthogonal:

- Personal attributes (physical, cognitive, social).
- Experience in the domain of knowledge related to the information need.
- Experience in using library systems (including information technology) and research techniques.

Five non-orthogonal dimensions of the information-seeking task are:

- Complexity (both the number of facets involved and the level of abstraction).
- Specificity (how confident the user is to determine the accuracy and completeness of results).
- Quantity (the amount of information expected).
- Criticality (how important it is that the need be met).

- Timelines (how much time the user is willing or expects to invest).

Analytically, we would define scales for each dimension (*e.g.*, low, average, high) and population the resulting matrix with examples or cases. Assuming three points per dimensions, we would have 27 cells for user characteristics and 243 cells for tasks. Crossing the two matrices would yield 6561 cells to fill. Adding the many types of motivations and situations that contextualize specific instances of information seeking similarly expands the theoretical possibilities. Clearly, this approach is a) impractical due to the large number of variations for which interface features are considered, and (b) minimal and simplistic on the user characteristics side.

A more realistic approach is to collapse some of the dimensions in light of the empirical evidence collected in the reading rooms, surveys, and document examinations. Based on the evidence, factors that characterize users are:

- Motivation (the personal situation that brings one to the Library, including quantity, criticality, and timeliness)
- Domain knowledge (related to the particular need)
- Library system knowledge (including information technology)
- Focus (a combination of complexity, quantity, and specificity) and
- Time allocated (combining timeliness and criticality).

These factors were applied to the different types of users and user needs described in the reading room visits. Such an approach yielded nine user classes listed in Table 8.4. These classes are not exhaustive, nor are they mutually exclusive. Moreover, any individual belongs to a class for each information need (*i.e.*, in different visits or sessions users may fall into different classes). It is highly likely that this taxonomy will change as the NDL evolves since it is rooted in data that come from a mix of current users of the physical LC, early adopters of the nascent implementation, and non-users asked to speculate about using it.

Table 8.4: User Taxonomy

1. LC staff, high motivation, medium domain knowledge, high library system knowledge, high focus, and limited time allocations
2. Hobbyists (*e.g.*, genealogy, Civil War, railroads, other examples), high motivation, typically high domain knowledge, a range of library system knowledge, high focus, and high time allocations
3. Scholars (*e.g.*, historians, sociologists, anthropologists, authors), high motivation, high domain knowledge, high library system knowledge, high focus, and high time allocations.
4. Professional researchers (*e.g.*, picture researchers), high motivation, medium domain knowledge, average to high library system knowledge, very high focus, and medium time allocations.
5. Rummagers (browers) (*e.g.*, PhD students looking for topics; scholars looking for new directions, topics), high motivation, medium domain knowledge, range of library system knowledge, low focus, and medium to high time allocations.
6. Object seekers (*e.g.*, some authors, CD-ROM/multimedia developers, TV/video producers, and instructional materials developers), high motivation, range of domain knowledge, low library system knowledge, high focus, and low to medium time allocations.
7. Surfers (*e.g.*, those who are curious those who bump into the NDL, etc.), low motivation, low domain knowledge, low library system knowledge (but may be high computing system knowledge), low focus, and very low time allocations.
8. Teachers K-16 medium motivation, medium to high domain knowledge, low to medium library system knowledge, medium focus, and low time allocations
9. Students K-16 low to medium motivation, low domain knowledge, low library system knowledge, low to medium focus, and low to medium time allocations.

This taxonomy was very useful to the prototyping phase of the project by providing detail to the general design vision and acting as a "reality check" for design discussions. Three additional uses are apparent for continued development of DL interfaces. First, it can guide the development of features that substitute for the reference interview. Since a human resource will not be readily available, the system must provide ways for users to articulate specific needs (*e.g.*, queries) as well as contextual information (*e.g.*, granularity and scope of need). A set of user templates varying according to the parameters above was sketched early in the prototyping phase of work. That work was not pursued as other features with higher priority were addressed. Second, the taxonomy can provide the basis for variations in discussions of interface features such as help, tours, and tutorials. Third, the taxonomy can provide the basis for testing prototypes with scenarios and representative tasks.

Design Implications

This needs assessment identified many design challenges specific to LC. Table 8.5 summarises these challenges. As the design process proceeded, these challenges were prioritized and specific prototype features were created. We chose to address the general challenges of content and strategies in the prototypes we implemented.

The needs assessment identified a wide range of users and needs and corresponding interface design challenges. The interface must communicate to users what the NDL is and is not, *i.e.*, is composed of multiple but not uniform data types (both formats and levels of representation) and is not the entire LC let alone the entire Internet. The interface must help users see that the NDL has multiple but not uniform access points (entry points are useful for some objects but not others). It must support a range of search strategies from hierarchical selections to formal and comprehensive queries so that novices and experts are all well served. It must provide help and guidance and emulate the reference interview. It must be usable on a variety of platforms and sensitive to a variety of physical infrastructures. The interface must allow users to meet their needs without the benefit of a human intermediary and for casual users it must do so without long processing delays.

These are strong requirements and the degrees of success varied according to how prioritized the challenges. The general user needs identified in this assessment oriented the design team in understanding both the needs of potential users and the characteristics of the rich and varied collections of materials scheduled for the NDL. In addition to contributing to the eventual prototypes, the multifaceted approach to assessing needs was applied and extended in other projects in different public access settings. Hert and Marchionini built upon these methods to develop a user-task taxonomy for federal government statistical web sites (Hert & Marchionini, 1998: http://ils.unc.edu/~march/blsreport/mainbls.html).

Table 8.5: Interface Challenges identified the users need assessment and to be addressed by the prototypes

Content-interface challenges
General interface challenges across reading rooms
developing a framework characterizing for users the granularity, size, and nature of objects in the NDL across all the reading rooms
communicating to the user what items are NOT in the NDL
supporting users in the NDL without human intervention
creating an interface that is accessible to users with state-of-the-market technology
inventing new techniques to search for multimedia objects and to integrate those techniques into the interface (*e.g.*, visual and audio query languages).
Specific interface challenges from different reading rooms
audio access (searching as well as download times)
access to multi-format items (*i.e.*, a sound track and textual fieldnotes)
user specification of areas/regions on maps
place name ambiguity
identifying and representing links
distinguishing documents that help one do genealogical research from the primary materials
integrating full-text and controlled vocabulary searching both across and within collections
distinguishing finding aids levels and primary material need for linkages from browsable covers to bibliographic records and microfilm text available at LC
image searching(including displaying series of related images and images in challenging formats such as panoramas and oversized posters)—possible user of P&P

thesaurus;
enabling researchers to absorb enough of the context for historical images and captions (why images were made) to deal sensitively with content that might otherwise be deemed offensive.

Users and strategies – interface challenges

General interface challenges across reading rooms

serving a wide range of users
serving a wide variety of information needs
helping users distinguish primary and secondary materials (including multiple layers of each)
helping users make links among items across different collections and reading rooms
capturing the essential elements of the reference interview so that users can find what they need without human intervention.

Specific interface challenges from different reading rooms.

specifying geographical areas
potentially huge files to transfer and display
determining when to point users elsewhere
helping LC NDL users to quickly understand that few of the primary materials are online
helping LC NDL users to quickly understand that there are many levels of search to work through
identifying copyrighted materials (so patrons do not find pointers to them and expect they can come and copy them at LC)
supporting hot topics, specialized exhibits

Overcoming patrons lack of knowledge about media (*e.g.*, how pictures were produced at different times)

Conclusion

These case studies are meant to illustrate three different DL situations in which multifaceted and flexible approaches to human-centered DL design and evaluation were taken. They are juxtaposed to highlight some of the general approaches to DL design and evaluation while demonstrating the unique challenges of each setting. Practical design is a compromise between the top-down BITWC and bottom-up, organically grown system. Our central assumption is that practical designs guided by general design visions that are informed by multifaceted approaches to ongoing assessments of user needs and system impact.

The Perseus DL evaluation illustrates how multifaceted approaches can over time yield evidence of significant effects across a broad community of users. In this case, the user needs were perceived by the DL designers, the primary user populations are university students and professors, and the primary design goals were to provide large quantities of primary text and image materials with little or no interpretation. The evaluation effort was begun at the inception of the project, used a multiplicity of methods to collect data on a large set of evaluation questions tied to a matrix of stakeholder, DL mission, and technical dimensions. Early results demonstrated typical effects of mechanical advantage, the difficulties of learning to teach with technology, and some examples of new kinds of learning but it was only through the longitudinal results that systemic change in larger sets of stakeholders (the field of classics) began to emerge. Without a steady and varied stream of data, these larger effects would likely not have been demonstrated except through some future historical efforts.

The Baltimore Learning Community case illustrates the difficulty of influencing complex human behaviour (teaching) through external interventions regardless of the informational or technical innovation. In this case, user needs were determined by state and local administrative curricula and assessment programmes, the primary user population is middle school science and social studies teachers and their students. The primary design goals were to provide relatively small quantities of multimedia materials that teachers could map to well-defined curriculum guidelines in creating lesson plans. The experience of this case demonstrates that advanced technical solutions and high-quality content are not sufficient to initiate or sustain community in settings where day-to-day practice is strongly determined by personal, social and political constraints.

The Library of Congress NDL case details how one multifaceted user needs assessment was conducted and used to guide user interface prototypes. User needs were largely unknown and the first phase of the design project was devoted to investigating potential needs in a variety of settings. This DL aims to serve the entire US population and the design goals were to provide universal access to historical materials in a variety of formats and at the entire range of granularities from bibliographic records and finding aids to full manuscripts and images. The user needs assessment yielded as set of user types and interface design challenges that guided the eventual prototypes and may find use in other DL settings.

Although these three DLs aim to serve different user populations and had distinct design goals, there are several general design and evaluation principles that resonate across the cases. First, DL designers and evaluators must know the user(s). This general rule is followed through needs assessments and the different cases illustrate that needs may be externally or internally motivated, well-defined or ill-defined, and narrow or wide-ranging. The three cases demonstrate the benefits of using direct methods such as interviews and observations and indirect methods such as document analyses or interviews with intermediaries. It is only through understanding user characteristics and needs that DL designers can build tools to help users map information needs onto DL tasks and evaluators can develop a good set of questions to guide research.

Second, it should be clear that DL design and evaluation are processes that aim to create and understand complex products. As such, they proceed in stages over multiple iterations. DLs are constantly evolving to meet the needs of users who grow and learn and technologies that advance exponentially. Design and evaluation efforts must be embedded into the overall DL management culture and applied on an ongoing basis.

Third, in addition to the complexities of change above, DLs must serve people with a wide range of characteristics and needs. To do so requires that designers and evaluators create and use multiple and flexible systems and tools. Designers must create overviews that allow DL patrons to quickly understand what is and is not available in the collection. We must provide alternative entry points and search tools so that diverse user needs and experiences can be accommodated. Evaluators must seek data from all fronts and create ways to integrate those data streams to make judgements about progress and next steps. Just as the blind men could only understand parts of the elephant they experienced first hand, our understanding of DL design and evaluation processes will require us to examine multiple views through multiple lens.'

NOTES AND REFERENCES

1. The number of questions were as follows: learning had four general questions, twenty four sub-questions, and two more specific questions, teaching had three general questions and nine sub-questions, system had three general questions, thirteen sub-questions, and twenty-six more specific questions, and content had three general questions and twelve sub-questions. As an example, the first general learning question was: What tactics and strategies do students employ at particular junctures in the Perseus environment? A sub-question under that question was: What proportion of time do students spend in the primary text?
2. A more parsimonious position is to assume a state-of-the-installed-base which seems entirely too constraining for an evolving, forward-looking project like the NDL.
3. In asking open-ended questions about phenomena that respondents may have little experience with, a questionnaire design decision is whether to give examples or not. Examples explicate and focus the question but also may lead and bias responses. We decided to use speed and ease attributes as examples of both possible advantages and disadvantages of DLs. Participants were asked to speculate on advantages and disadvantages that might be expected with NDL use.

9

Knowledge Organisation Systems: An Overview

The term *knowledge organisation systems* is intended to encompass all types of schemes for organising information and promoting knowledge management.[1] Knowledge organisation systems include classification schemes that organise materials at a general level (such as books on a shelf), subject headings that provide more detailed access, and authority files that control variant versions of key information (such as geographic names and personal names). They also include less-traditional schemes, such as semantic networks and ontologies. Because knowledge organisation systems are mechanisms for organising information, they are at the heart of every library, museum, and archive.

Knowledge organisation systems are used to organise materials for the purpose of retrieval and to manage a collection. A KOS serves as a bridge between the user's information need and the material in the collection. With it, the user should be able to identify an object of interest without prior knowledge of its existence. Whether through browsing or direct searching, whether through themes on a Web page or a site search engine, the KOS guides the user through a discovery process. In addition, KOSs allow the organisers to answer questions regarding the scope of a collection and what is needed to round it out.

All digital libraries use one or more KOS. Just as in a physical library, the KOS in a digital library provides an overview of the content of the collection and supports retrieval. The scheme may be a traditional KOS relevant to the scope of the material and the expected audience for the digital library (such as the Dewey Decimal System or the INSPEC Thesaurus), a commercially developed scheme such as the Yahoo or Excite categories, or a locally developed scheme for a corporate intranet.

The decision of what knowledge organisation system to use is central to the development of any digital library. The KOS must be applicable, either automatically or by human catalogers, to the resources included in the digital library. Once the material is included in the collection, the KOS must be meaningful to its users.

This section outlines the characteristics of KOSs, describes the common types, and discusses their origins and traditional uses.

Common Characteristics of Knowledge Organisation Systems

It is often said that humans are inherent organisers. From an early age, children play sorting and matching games. We cope with our ever-changing world by comparing new objects of experiences with those with which we are familiar identifying patterns and categorizing what is new into our existing frame of reference. The emphasis on developing comprehensive KOSs can be seen in the writings of our earliest philosophers, many of whom continue to influence our view of the world. For example. Aristotle's effort to categorise knowledge into groups (such as physics, politics, or psychology) is reflected in our language, our education, and our science. The original classification scheme of the Library of Congress, used between 1800 and 1814, was based on the philosophical works of Sir Francis Bacon and inherited from the English tradition. Beginning in 1814, the influence to Thomas Jefferson can be seen on the Library of Congress collection. Jefferson, who reclassified the library, reflected a more humanist philosophy (Lesk 1997).

There is not single knowledge classification scheme on which everyone agrees. Michael Lesk speculates that while a single KOS would be advantageous, it is unlikely that such a system will ever be developed. Culture may constrain the knowledge classification scheme so that what is meaningful to one culture is not necessarily meaningful to another (Lesk 1997). Therefore, we live in a world of multiple, variant ways to organise knowledge.

Despite their diversity, KOSs have the following common characteristics that are critical to their use in organising digital libraries.

- The KOS imposes a particular view of the world on a collection and the items in it.
- The same entity can be characterized in different ways, depending on the KOS that is used.
- There must be sufficient commonality between the concept expressed in a KOS and the real-world object to which that concept refers that a knowledgeable person could apply the system with reasonable reliability. Likewise, a person seeking relevant material by using a KOS must be able to connect his or her concept with its representation in the system.

Types of Knowledge Organisation Systems

A review of some typical knowledge organisation systems shows their scope and applicability to a variety of digital library settings. While there are specific definitions for many of these KOSs in the computer science and information science literature, and even in standards documents, there is debate over these definitions. Terms are often used, particularly in the popular press and in the book trade, in nonstandard ways. Reflecting the scope of this practice, a recent National Information Standards Organisation (NISO) workshop on electronic thesauri emphasised the need to improve the definitions of "terminology relating to terminology" (NISO) 1999).

The descriptions given here provide an overview of possible systems for organising digital libraries. The descriptions are based on characteristics such as structure and complexity, relationships among terms, and historical function. The list is not comprehensive, nor are the definitions of these terms contained in specific standards documents. They are grouped into three general categories: term lists, which emphasise lists of terms often with definitions: classifications and categories, which emphasize the creation of subject sets; and relationship lists, which emphasize the connections between terms and concepts.

Term Lists

Authority Files. Authority files are lists of terms that are used to control the variant names for an entity or the domain value for a particular field. Examples include names for countries, individuals, and organisations. Non-preferred terms may be linked to the preferred versions. This type of KOS generally does not include a deep organisation or complex structure. The presentation may be alphabetical or organised by a shallow classification scheme. A limited hierarchy may be applied to allow for simple navigation, particularly when the authority file is being accessed manually or is extremely large. Examples of authority files include the Library of Congress Name Authority File and the Getty Geographic Authority File.

Glossaries. A glossary is a list of terms, usually with definitions. The terms may be from a specific subject filed or from a particular work. The terms are defined within a specific environment and rarely include variant meanings. Examples include the Environmental Protection Agency (EPA) Terms of the Environment.

Dictionaries. Dictionaries are alphabetical lists of words and their definitions. Variant senses are provided where applicable. Dictionaries are more general in scope than are glossaries. They may also provide information about the origin of a word, variants (by spelling and morphology), and multiple meanings across disciplines. While a dictionary may also provide synonyms and through the definitions, related words, there is no explicit hierarchical structure or attempt to group them by concept.

Gazetteers. A gazetteer is a list of place names. Traditional gazetteers have been published as books or have appeared as indexes to atlases. Each entry may also be identified by feature type, such as river, city, or school. An example is the U.S. Code of Geographic Names. Geospatially references gazetteers provide coordinates for locating the place on the earth's surfaced. The term *gazetteer* has several other meanings, including an announcement publication such as a patent or legal gazetteer. These gazetteers are often organized using classification schemes or subject categories.

Classifications and Categories

Subject Headings. This scheme type provides a set of controlled terms to represent the subjects of items in a collection. Subject heading lists can be extensive and cover a broad range of subjects; however, the subject heading list's structure is generally very shallow, with a limited hierarchical structure. In use, subject headings tend to be coordinated, with rules for how they can be joined to provide concepts that are more specific. Examples include the Medical Subject Headings (MeSH) and the Library of Congress Subject Headings (LCSH).

Classification Schemes, Taxonomies, and Categorization Schemes. These terms are often used interchangeably. Although there may be subtle differences from example to example, these types of KOSs all provide ways to separate entities into "buckets" or broad topic levels. Some examples provide a hierarchical arrangement of numeric or alphabetic notation to represent broad topics. These types of KOSs may not follow the rules for hierarchy required in the ANSI NISO. Thesaurus Standard (Z39.19) (NISO 1998), and they lack the explicit relationships presented in a thesaurus. Examples of classification schemes include the Library of Congress Classification Schedules (an open, expandable system), the Dewey Decimal Classification (a closed system of 10 numeric sections with decimal extensions), and the Universal Decimal Classification (based on Dewey but extended to include facets, or particular aspects of a topic). Subject categories are often used to group thesaurus terms in broad topic sets that lie outside the hierarchical scheme of the thesaurus. Taxonomies are increasingly being used in object-oriented design and knowledge management systems to indicate any grouping of objects based on a particular characteristics.

Relationship Lists

Thesauri. Thesauri are based on concepts and they show relationships among terms. Relationships commonly expressed in a thesaurus include hierarchy, equivalence (synonymy), and association or relatedness. These relationships are generally represented by the notation BT (broader term), NT (narrower term), SY (synonym), and RT (associative or related term). Associative relationships may be more detailed in some schemes. For example, the Unified Medical Language System (UMLS) from the National Library of Medicine has defined more than 40 relationships, many of which are associative. Preferred terms for indexing and retrieval are identified. Entry terms (or non-preferred terms) point to the preferred terms to be used for each concept.

There are standards for the development of monolingual thesauri (NISO 1998: ISO 1986) and multilingual thesauri (ISO 1985). In these standards, the definition of a thesaurus is fairly narrow. Standard relationships are assumed, as is the identification of preferred terms and there are rules for creating relationships among terms. The definition of a thesaurus in these standards is often at variance with schemes that are traditionally called thesauri. Many thesauri do not follow all the rules of the standard but are still generally thought of as thesauri. Another type of thesaurus, such as the *Roget's Thesaurus* (with the addition of classification categories), represents only equivalence.

Many thesauri are large; they may include more than 50,000 terms. Most were developed for a specific discipline or a specific product or family of products. Examples include the Food and Agricultural Organisation's *Aquatic Sciences and Fisheries. Thesaurus* and the *National Aeronautic and Space Administration* (*NASA*) Thesaurus for aeronautics and aerospace-related topics.

Semantic Networks. With the advent of natural language processing, there have been significant developments in semantic networks. These KOSs structure concepts and terms not as hierarchies but as a network or a web. Concepts are thought of as nodes, and relationships branch out from them. The relationships generally go beyond the standard BT. NT. and RT. They may include specific whole part, cause-effect, or parent-child relationships. The most noted semantic network is Princeton University's WordNet, which is now used in a variety of search engines.

Ontologies. Ontology is the newet label to be attached to some knowledge organisation systems. The knowledge-management community is developing ontologies as specific concept models. They can represent complex relationships among objects, and include the rules and axioms missing from semantic networks. Ontologies that describe knowledge in a specific area are often connected with systems for data mining and knowledge management.

All of these examples of knowledge organisation systems, which vary in complexity, structure, and function can provide organisation and increased access to digital libraries.

The Origin and Use of Knowledge Organisation Systems

In the physical library, classification schemes such as Library of Congress (LC), Dewey Decimal System, and the Universal Decimal Classification reflect, among other things, the need to store a single item at a single location on a shelf. To provide multiple access points beyond the limits of as single physical location, subject headings are applied. Libraries use subject heading schemes such as LCSH. Sears, or other specialized schemes developed for specific content or specific collections. At the level of specific content, libraries have used authority files to control variant forms of personal, organisational, and geographic names.

However, KOSs can be found in settings other than libraries. An awareness of the KOSs available from alternative sources is valuable when considering the development of digital libraries for a specific audience.

Abstracting and Indexing Services

Abstracting and indexing (A&I) services developed as an outgrowth of traditional bibliographies and the explosion of journal literature. In the sciences, the development of A&I services was spurred by the Post-World War I concerns about inadequate access to scientific information. In the 1950s, investment in A&I services was fueled by the Cold War and Sputnik. Abstracting and indexing services in the humanities, such as the Bibliography of the History of Art or the Modern Languages Association (MLA) Bibliography, generally took a different growth path than did heir scientific and technical counterparts, but they also quickly became important resources for scholarship in the online environment. The scope of A & I services varies from broad discipline-oriented services (*e.g.*, chemistry, architecture, biology, and physics) to narrowly defined aspects of the literature (*e.g.*, peaceful uses of nuclear energy) and sub-disciplines (*e.g.*, aquatic sciences).

Special KOSs, such as thesauri and subject categories, were developed to support A&I services and their specific products and audiences. These organisations applied increasingly complex schemes to provide subject access to the literature in a variety of subjects. By the 1960s, A&I services were moving from the provision of print-only products to print and online services through large online vendors such as Dialog. Later, the products were distributed on CD-ROM and now, increasingly, on the Web. In many cases, the KOSs migrated from print to electronic media following the products they supported. While increased computing power, more sophisticated search engines, and more independent end-user searching have led to changes in some KOSs, most have retained their importance, even in the Web environment.

For many years, the KOSs related to A&I services were applied only by catalogers and indexers trained in using the KOS indexing for a particular product or products. The primary users of KOSs were librarians and other professional searchers. However, the proliferation of electronic data, the explosion of electronic publishing and increasing concerns about the difficulty of locating information have led to a renewed interest in these KOSs for use not only by professionals but also by end users.

Publishers

As publishers have migrated to electronic composition systems, they have become increasingly involved in the production of A&I products. Large journal publishers such as Academic Press and Elsevier have developed their own systems to provide bibliographic records linked to the full text of documents. As the content of online journals has grown, it has become necessary to move from systems that provide browsing by table of contents and journal issue to systems that support searching by both free text and by KOS. Electronic journals have resulted in additional KOSs, particularly classification and categorisation schemes. For example, Elsevier's Web site has a subject categorisation scheme to provide access to individual Web sites of its more than 2,000 titles.

Trade, Professional, and Governmental Organisations

A variety of authority files and classification schemes are used to support business and commerce. They range from the Standard Industrial Classification (SIC) code and the North American Industrial Classification System (NAICS), used in procurement and government statistics, to disease codes used to communicate patient illnesses and treatments among physicians, hospitals, and insurance companies. As more organisations develop Web sites, additional KOSs are being developed to support them.

Internal Projects

Organisations are among the most prolific creators and users of KOSs. Developers of corporate intranets and knowledge management systems have discovered hundreds of specific classification schemes, glossaries, categorization schemes, and other vocabularies in use within organisations. Many of these are geared toward specific tasks and are, therefore, very narrow both in subject scope and target audience. However, for these audiences, they can also be rich sources of information.

For example, the Department of Energy (DOE) Environmental Management Science Programme (EMSP) and the Office of Scientific and Technical Information are developing a digital library to support EMSP programme managers. Programme managers and researchers have developed" "needs categories" and "science categories" to organise the Environmental Science Network (ESN). The categories are used primarily to support the process of grant submission and award; however, the ESN also uses them to provide access to related material from within DOE and from other distributed databases from the EPA, the Department of Defense, and NASA. Vocabulary is currently being organised around these categories for use with a Web mining tool that will provide highly relevant Web resources for project managers in specific areas.

LINKING DIGITAL LIBRARY RESOURCES TO RELATED RESOURCES

This section emphasizes the ability of knowledge organisation systems to link digital library resources to other related resources. The basis for this linking is the identification of information within a digital resource that can be extracted and used to search and locate information within a KOS. The KOS may then be used to expand codes to more explanatory full text, to provide more descriptive records, or to link entity names to resources of physical specimens.

Expanding Codes to Full Text

Practitioners of a discipline use coding schemes to facilitate communication within that discipline. It is often helpful to connect these coding schemes to the full names for which the code stands. The examples provided here include links between databank registration codes and the biological sequence data, and between industrial codes and the full name that the code represents.

Linking Sequence Numbers to Biosequence Databanks

The lengthy biochemical and genetic sequences that molecular biologists, biotechnologists, and geneticists identify each day are kept in databanks. Several databanks have been developed, for example, to cover protein sequences, nucleotides, and cell lines. One of the largest databanks contains information on the mapping of the human genome. As molecular biologists began to discover these sequences, they reported them in scientific journals. Difficulties in composing, proofreading, and printing the text soon arose. Through an ad hoc standards process, major biomedical publishers agreed to require the inclusion of codes or databank numbers for these sequences in articles when they are published. In addition, the sequence itself must be registered in a databank before the paper can be published.

Some of the most frequently referenced databanks are listed on the Web site of the National Centre for Biotechnology Information. They include GenBank and the Research Collaboratory for Structural Bioinformatics Protein Data Bank. Each sequence number is different, but all begin with a persistent code identifying the databank.

How can the link be made between the literature and the databank?

Through a search profile, a text analysis programme, or keyword indexing, the text can be analysed and the sequence databank numbers identified. An active link can be embedded. The active link consists of a search strategy (possibly written as a CGI script) to locate that sequence number in the databank where the actual sequence is stored. When the user clicks on the active link the script is generated and launched from the user's browser. The Web-enabled database is searched, and the sequence record is returned to the user. Depending on the services provided by the databank site, the user can analyse the sequence using a number of tools provided by the databank or download the sequence for local manipulation.

This type of connection exists between the National Library of Medicine's (NLM) search service, PubMed, and GenBank at the National Centre for Biotechnology Information. If a search in PubMed yields records that have GenBank numbers, the user can automatically search and display the sequence records from GenBank.

Linking Individual Industrial codes to the Full Scheme.

In business, classification schemes serve to communicate important facts about a company or product. These codes are generally controlled by a government, professional, trade or international standards organisation. They often serve as shorthand for users interested in material in a particular area of industry or a specific business sector.

Perhaps the most familiar scheme is the SIC code, which was last updated in 1987. The SIC codes have been used by the U.S. government, economists, financial markets, regulators, and procurement offices to identify manufacturing, agriculture, and service sectors of the economy. In 1997, a new scheme was approved for use within the United States. The North American Industrial Classification System was developed with Canada and Mexico as a means of providing an agreed-upon scheme for the collection, reporting, and analysis of information about the economy by sector, bothin within and across borders. Information about NAICS is available from the Web site of the U.S. Census Bureau (see references for address).

The digital library can provide related information by using the authority files for the coding schemes as a linked authority file. If a company or economic sector mentioned in the digital library's collection can be linked to an SIC or NAICS code, the code can be searched against the official tables of definitions maintained by the U.S. Census Bureau. These files provide definitions of the codes and place each code in the classification scheme with other economic sectors.

The digital library's content can be further enhanced by making a link between the SIC and NAICS codes. If the digital library resource has the SIC code, it can be extracted and searched against the Census Bureau's *1997 NAICS and 1987 SIC Correspondence Tables*. The table returns the corresponding code from the alternate scheme.

Linking to Descriptive Records

Linking the name of an entity, such as a personal name, organisation, or location, to additional information about that entity was one of the first uses of hyperlinking. Knowledge organisation systems such as dictionaries, glossaries, and classification schemes can be used to link the entities in one resource to richer descriptions of that entity in another resource. This is particularly helpful for users who are new to a topic and in cases where the additional information can make the user's task more efficient.

The examples that follow are from three disciplines. The first example links organism names to records that not only describe the species more fully but also put it in the context of the overall classification scheme for living organisms. The second example links chemical names to descriptive records and molecular structures. In the third example, proper names are linked to the biographies for the person.

Linking Organism Names to Taxonomic Records

Genus-species names are the Latin names for organisms—*e.g.*, plants, animals, and microorganisms. Taxonomists, who study and classify living organisms, create records for each of these organisms. Generally, these records are linked relationally to the other organisms in a hierarchy. Beyond the organism name and the information that it and its placement in the hierarchy convey, taxonomic records use other elements to describe the organism. These may include distribution patterns the authority for naming and classification and the date the organism was identified. Scientists base the information on specimens that are retained because they serve as the physical evidence of the description. Natural history museums, private collections, and individual scientists number, or code, the specimens in their collections. Sometimes specimens are supported by photographs or line drawings, which may be digitized.

By using a taxonomic authority file as an intermediate authority file, one can link a text or an image file containing a name or picture of an organism to additional related information. By automatically processing the text or embedding a link from the organism name in the text or from the image to the taxonomic authority record, one can extend the knowledge conveyed by the text. The text can include the descriptive and historical information in the taxonomy record and, ultimately, link to a photograph, a drawing, or appropriate video of audio segments.

Because of the ambiguity organism names, many examples of this type are now created manually. However, depending on the extent of the files involved, the ambiguity of the Latin and common names for organisms can be overcome. An example of a taxonomic intermediate file is the Integrated Taxonomic Information System (ITIS). ITIS a partnership of U.S., Canadian, and Mexican government agencies, private organisations, and taxonomic specialists cooperating to develop an online, scientifically credible list of biological names of North American plants and animals. It is used by many U.S. government agencies for consistent naming of plants and animals for regulatory and monitoring purposes. To link textual material in a digital library to the ITIS record, the organism name can be identified manually or automatically in the text and submitted as a query to the ITIS database. When a match is found, ITIS presents the ITIS record, which provides essential information about the organism. The information includes synonymous names, including some common names, and an indication of the placement of the organism in the larger taxonomic classification scheme.

Linking Chemical Names to Molecular Structures

The unique identification for a chemical substance is not its name but its molecular structure. However, chemical names are commonly used in research documents, project plans, catalogs, and directories all of which may be resources in a digital library. There are competing systems of nomenclature (*i.e.*, that of the Chemical Abstracts Service [CAS] and of the International Union of Pure and Applied Chemistry) as well as common and commercial synonyms.

The ambiguity is resolved by providing links between the chemical names in the text and the molecular structure. This is done through a chemical registry number or code that is connected to a particular chemical name (using certain nomenclature standards) and an authority record that provides additional information about the chemical. This information includes the chemical's synonyms and some of its chemical and physical properties. Most important in today's research environment is the link from this authority file to a chemical structure file. Structure files, used with the appropriate software, graphically depict the molecular structure. This sophisticated software allows for three-dimensional visualization, rotation, and substitution of the chemical bonds.

An example of the use of the chemical registry number to link chemical names with molecular structures can be seen in the work of BIOSIS, the world's largest not-for-profit producer of biological and biomedical databases. In 1993, BIOSIS began processing it bibliographic citations (titles and keywords) to automatically identify chemical names (Hodge, Nelson, and Vleduts-Stokolov 1989). BIOSIS assigns CAS Registry Numbers (RNs) to the chemical names identified in this process. In the STN International online system, hosted in the United States by CAS, a user of BIOSIS can select one or more of the records resulting from a search and extract the RN. The extracted RN can be applied against the CAS Registry File, which contains more than 21 million substances, including organics, inorganics, biosequences, metals, and alloys. The registry file record for the chemical name, including the link to the synonyms for the chemical name and the structure file itself, can then be accessed. With special tools developed by CAS, the structure can be viewed and manipulated. It can be imported into modeling tools that allow the chemist to manipulate the structure and thereby envision new chemicals. Alternatively, the user can start with any database that contains CAS RNs and extract the resulting RNs to perform a search for complementary bibliographic records in the BIOSIS database.

Linking chemical names to structures using RNs on a large scale is neither inexpensive nor easy. There are two approaches to identifying chemical names in text. Some journal articles include the CAS RN for the major chemicals discussed. In this case, an analysis of the text for the terms "RN", "CAS RN", and variations preceding numerics can identify RNs that can be used as a link. Alternatively, a programme to identify chemical names in text, similar to that developed by BIOSIS, could be devised. Developing the identification programme, as well as searching chemical databases, is costly; however, if the digital library has license agreements for chemistry databases, this type of linkage may be possible. In addition, many organisations have small chemical files of their own that may include RNs and other information of particular relevance to the organisation's research. It may be possible to link to these local databases using methods that are more direct.

Linking Personal Names to Biographical Information

A common type of authority file is the personal name authority, which controls variants of personal names. For example, the Library of Congress Name Authority File (LCNAF) is used to control variant personal names for authors editors, artists, and others. The Union List of Artist Names (ULAN), developed by the Getty Vocabulary. Programme, is another example, Name authorities serve as tools for catalogers and indexers. They ensure that the proper form of the name, rather than an unapproved variant, is used and bring together all works by or about the person.

A name authority file can also be used to link a bibliographic record or document containing the person's name to a variety of other related materials. If the digital library's resource has a standardized form of the name, it can be identified and searched against the authority file to locate varints. The standardised and variant forms can be joined in a search against a variety of other resources that can provide related information.

For example, in the case of a digital library of images of artists' works or biographical or critical text, a name authority file such as the ULAN or the LCNAF can act as an intermediate file to provide additional information. The file, which contains integrated variant names, can be searched by the name appearing in the digital library collection. When the record is found, the information about the artist can be displayed, providing a wide range of contextual material for the use. Citations to significant biographical or critical works about the artist, some of which may also be available on the Web, may also be provided in the name authority file.

The variant names from a name authority can also be used to locate and provide automatic links from the personal name in the text to a biography, without requiring that the name be presented in the same fashion in the two resources. One such resource that could be linked to for biographical information is Gale's Biography Resource, which contains more than 1,42,000 biographies and related citations from more than 1,000 periodicals.

However, to produce this kind of link, there must be a mechanism for locating personal names in text. Several programmes can do this type of text analysis; among those that have been developed commercially are NameFinder from the Carnegie Group and the Intelligent Agent from IBM. In addition, variant names can be extracted from the name authority itself, grouped, and run as a search against the text to locate name occurrences.

Linking Entity Names to Physical Specimens

In some cases, it is possible to go another step and connect entity names in the digital library resources to physical specimens. The curation of physical specimens or artifacts is critical to the advancement of many disciplines. Exhibition catalogs describe the art objects in a particular exhibition. Museum catalogs provide inventories of the art, natural history, or cultural objects held by a particular museum. These catalogs, increasingly available as computerized databases, are knowledge organisation systems that not only provide descriptive records but also point to the location of the object in a museum, an archive, or another collection.

For example, in biology, a physical specimen is particularly important when it is the result of the discovery and description of a new organism or of the reclassification of a known organism. A type specimen is the example collected from the field by a taxonomist to serve as the prime example for the description of the organism and the validation of its taxonomic classification and naming. These specimens are held by natural history collections, and their deposit is required by the rules of various taxonomic societies.

As part of the curatorial activity, the collections assign identification codes. While the primary use of identification codes has been to organise the physical collections, numerous projects are under way in the natural history community to digitize photographs of specimens and create database records for the specimens, including their identifiers, and thereby make them more readily accessible. The degree of digitization varies from specially to specialty. For example, in botany, virtually all significant research herbaria are digitally cataloging their type collections instead of maintaining paper records. Many are also making digital photographs of the type specimens available over the Web.

The publication of identification codes in the journal literature is also changing. Historically, identification codes have been presented in the "Materials Used" sections of journal articles. The level of specificity of the identification code has varied, depending on the biological discipline. For example, botanical journals tend to list only the institution and the catalog, while vertebrate journals provide the code to the specimen level. The current trend is to require lists of specimens that are more detailed. As the lists become longer and the printing costs increase, journal publishers are beginning to request links to independent Web sites maintained by the researchers or their organisations that carry all the specimens used in the study and provide some level of identification.

If the digital library collection contains resources that include the identification comes, these codes can be extracted and matched against the Web-based catalogs or databases. This link can provide users with location and contact information to allow them to access the physical object mentioned in the digital library resource.

Curators or registrars of artistic, archaeological, and cultural history collections also assign inventory or accession numbers to items in their collections. Identification numbers may also be found in scholarly catalogues raisonnes. Links similar to those described for natural history can be made between text related to works of art and the physical work in a particular collection. An article about a work of art can be linked to additional information about the physical specimen by linking the identification number in the text with an online catalog containing the number and additional information about the work.

As museums digitize their collections to establish a presence on the Web or to reduce the handling of the physical objects. KOSs that can link the digital library resources to the physical object are being developed. If there is a museum with a collection that complements that of the digital library, it is worthwhile to discuss ways in which the digital library and digital museum collections may "co-evolve."

MAKING RESOURCES ACCESSIBLE TO OTHER COMMUNITIES

Someone recently compared the Web with a large room filled with books that were scattered all over the floor. They Web is the world's largest mass of bits and bytes. It is a meeting place that brings to gather disparate communities. The "Internet Commons," as this meeting place has been called, requires connections between and among disparate communities in order for an "economy" to develop (Weibel 1999). This economy will provide the framework within which both commercial and noncommercial transactions can occur. KOSs are one means of connecting these disparate communities. Knowledge organisation systems can be used to (1) provide alternate subject access, (2) add modes of understanding to digital library resources. (3) support multilingual access, and (4) supply terms for expansion of free-text searches in domains that are relatively unknown to the user.

Providing Alternate Subject Access

Alternate subject access refers to the provision of one or more additional subject orientations that make the resources of the digital library accessible to different audiences. This approach is particularly valuable when the digital library resources appeal to groups that do not share a common terminology. It can be a system of subject headings, a classification scheme, or any other subject-oriented system. Alternate subject access can be provided by

- indexing or classifying the resources using multiple schemes,
- retaining original schemes from organizations that contribute to the digital library, or
- mapping between the primary scheme and an alternative scheme.

Indexing the Material with Multiple Schemes

The most direct method for providing alternate subject access to a collection is by classifying or indexing the resources with multiple schemes, but it may also be the most costly. This approach requires redundant cataloging or cataloguers who are knowledgeable in both schemes. It may also require modifications to the cataloging tools and procedures. However, if the cataloging is at a high level (resources versus individual documents), or if the schemes are not difficult or detailed, it may be a reasonable approach.

Retaining Alternate Indexing from Contributors

If the digital library is being built through contributions from a variety of sources, the originating organisation may have applied an alternate scheme that could be used. For example, the NASA database on aeronautics and astronautics receives relevant bibliographic records from other U.S. agencies,- such as the Department of Defense and the Department of Energy. The controlled vocabulary terms assigned by the contributing organisation are processed through a machine-aided indexing process to create candidate indexing terms from the *NASA Thesaurus* for review by NASA's indexers. However, the final records contain both the *NASA Thesaurus* terms and the controlled vocabulary terms from the contributing organisation, with the alternate indexing terms retained in a separate data element in the bibliographic record. The terms collected from other organisations can be viewed as an alternate access point, so that at least part of the collection is accessible through another discipline's terminology.

Mapping Multiple Schemes

The third method for providing alternative subject access is the most indirect, that of mapping one or more schemes. Several examples of this approach can be found among A&I services. Both BIOSIS, the world's largest private sector A&I service in the life sciences, and the NLM apply MeSH to BIOSIS documents. The records that BIOSIS contributes to NLM's TOXLINE database are processed automatically to have appropriate MESH terms added. This is based on a mapping of the natural language terms that occur in the toxicology literature and BIOSIS' normalized natural language keyword indexing with the MeSH terminology. In the new BIOSIS relational indexing structure, BIOSIS builds and maintains authority files that connect natural language disease names to the MeSH-controlled disease terms. When the BIOSIS indexer assigns the free text keyword for the disease name, the appropriate MeSH term is also added to the record as an alternate access point (BIOSIS 1999). The assignment is based on the development over time of a mapping between the terminology used by BIOSIS and the MeSH-controlled terms.

In addition to providing alternate access points to BIOSIS products, the inclusion of the MeSH terms makes it possible to perform cross database searching on the indexing field with MEDLINE and other databases that include MeSH terms. From 1999 forward, users can search BIOSIS databases using MeSH disease terms. The disease terms can be extracted from the MeSH authority file or from a MEDLINE record and then used in a search against the BIOSIS files, or vice versa. This helps users find relevant records that are unique to either BIOSIS or MEDLINE. The inclusion of terms from an alternate KOS, such as MeSH, therefore supports the use of BIOSIS by medical librarians and practitioners who are familiar with MeSH terminology.

A more extensive example of mapping variant schemes is the metathesaurus developed by the NLM's Unified Medical Language System (UMLS). This system has linked more than 40 separate KOSs from various medical specialties. They range from MeSH to coding and classification schemes used by insurance companies and physicians to describe treatments and diseases on patient records.

The UMLS is licensed by many other organisations for inclusion in applications that can bridge various health care communities.

How can digital libraries use alternative indexing? While many digital libraries do not have the A&I resources of large database producers such as NLM and BIOSIS, the concept of applying alternate indexing can be scaled to fit. While the systems described deal with item-level bibliographic records, alternate indexing can be applied at several levels. Alternate subject access can be applied only at the resource level, for the database, electronic book, electronic journal, or image collection, so that other communities can identify resources of interest that must then by searched or browsed individually. This concept is conducive to use with portals that provide access to the same resources with different views for different audiences. Alternatively, if the digital library has bibliographic records or metadata records at a very detailed level, it may be possible to develop switching programmes that will translate concepts from the original organisation of the digital library or resource to that of the alternate scheme.

Adding New Modes of Understanding to the Digital Library

People perceive the world through many modes, including textual and graphical. Some people comprehend information more easily in one mode than another. Most people benefit from a variety of modes that reinforce one another or that can be used when appropriate to the context. Many digital library projects remain text-based; however, this text-only dimension is changing as digital libraries become oriented more to multimedia and as other modes of information presentation become viable on the Internet.

KOSs can be used to bring new dimensions to an information resource or a collection in a digital library. In the digital library environment, these dimensions can be viewed as layers that can be added on top of one or more objects. Various tools and services can be developed that are geared to a particular mode. For example, the results of a text search can be presented in graphical or visual form, based on the number of occurrences of a term or concept or on the occurrences of documents from a particular country, journal title, or author.

A more complex dimension that can be added is the geospatial dimension, which emphasises access by place. A "geolibrary" is defined as a digital library consisting of "geoinformation," or material that can be accessed by place (National Research Council 1999). This so-called georeferencing can be either direct (by a geospatial footprint, a series of latitudes and longitudes for the location) or indirect (by a textual place name). Georeferencing of textual objects is facilitated by a gazetteer, which brings together the place name and the spatial footprint for its location. Many gazetteers also include feature types for each footprint. The vocabulary used for the feature types varies among gazetteers, but may include terms such as "airport," harbor," and "railroad station."

Although many organisations, including federal and state agencies, are currently required to provide geospatial referencing as part of the National Spatial Data Infrastructure Programme, the geospatial referencing is not readily available for older works. How can the data sets of today be integrated with the textual information of yesterday? The answer is by adding geospatial referencing to the text resource. Geospatial referencing requires that the text name for a place have an associated spatial footprint. This can be achieved by using a georeferenced, digital gazetteer that provides geospatial footprints for place names.

Through this type of knowledge organisation system, place names in a library catalog or bibliographic database can have footprints assigned (Blair 1999; Tahirkheli 1999). If one or more of the library's resources have latitude or longitude coordinates in the catalog record or in the full text but no place name the coordinates can be extracted and submitted to the gazetteer service. The service will return the place name for the footprint. Alternatively, the resource may have a textual place name. This place name can be extracted and searched against the gazetteer, and the footprint can be provided to a mapping application. The latter search may result in more than one footprint, since place names may be ambiguous. Therefore, it is important that the user interface be designed to allow the user to distinguish the locations. Once the footprint has been determined, a user can access the text resource through a geographic mapping tool. Alternatively, a user of the text resource can find a set of results and have the place names displayed as footprints on a map.

In disciplines such as economy, environmental science, and even public health and epidemiology, it would be beneficial to build a digital library with access to such a digital gazetteer service. Users could then access the system through the text mode or the geographic mode, depending on their comfort level and the type of information needed. Presenting the results on a map allows users to make new associations and analyse the results more easily. Through a geospatial KOS, they can see connections between disparate data, because the data are presented in an alternate mode.

Providing Multilingual Access

A third way that KOSs can support the use of digital libraries by disparate communities is to provide multilingual access. A variety of sources, including multilingual dictionaries and multilingual thesauri, can support this type of access.

One of the most extensive multilingual thesaurus efforts is the Generalized Multilingual Environmental Thesaurus (GEMET) from the European Environment Agency (EEA), produced by Italy's research council, the Consiglio Nazionale delle Ricerche (CNR). The GEMET is available in 12 languages, and plans for a global environmental thesaurus in many more languages were recently announced. GEMET is available by agreement with the EEA.

The European Topic Centre on Catalogue of Data Sources in Germany is developing a system that will link data sources and metadata information in a virtual library. GEMET will be used to convert a search in one language into searches for the same concepts in other languages. Users will retrieve documents not only in their native language but also in other languages. This will allow data systems from throughout the EEA and beyond to be accessed as a virtual library collection with both controlled vocabulary and free-text term searching in multiple languages.

Expanding Free-Text Search Terms

Free-text searching is the main method of searching on the Web. Only a small percentage of Web resources have metadata, and an even smaller percentage have controlled vocabulary assigned. However, variations in natural language make free-text searching problematic. Even a knowledgeable user may not know all the terminology (synonyms or related terms) that can be used in the literature to express a concept. The problem is exacerbated when the user is unfamiliar with the topic or is interested in an interdisciplinary area. How can the user expand his or her search to overcome these terminology differences? One possibility is to use KOSs as aids to the selection of free-text keywords.

The Getty Vocabulary Project emphasizes support for searching as a significant application of its vocabularies. Harpring (1999) reports that the vocabularies are increasingly being used in search engines to look for different terms that refer to the same concept. The Getty vocabularies (the Art and Architecture Thesaurus, the Union List of Artists Names, and the Thesaurus of Geographic Names) are particularly rich in equivalence relationships. "When these equivalence relationships are exploited in search engines, there are typically two possible scenarios: the user may be allowed to first query the vocabulary database, locating appropriate terms and then applying those chosen terms in a query across target databases; or there may be little or no user interaction with the vocabulary, when the vocabularies are used behind the scenes [to expand the search]..." (Harpring 1999). Getty developed a prototype called *a.k.a.* to experiment with the use of equivalence terms to broaden or narrow searches across databases on the Web.

In addition to expanding routine search queries, KOSs can be used in Web mining tools. Northern Light has developed a Web mining tool that reportedly returns a high degree of relevant hits. The KOS that supports the Northern Light site was built by ingesting large existing vocabularies and thesauri, The results was then organised under an extensive classification scheme developed by Northern Light. The terms can be used to extend a user's search or to distinguish between multiple meanings of the terms supplied by the user. The results of a search are organised into "folders" based on the classification scheme. These high-level categories, represented by the folders, help distinguish multiple meanings of the same term. For example, an ambiguous word such as "pitcher" might result in two folders being presented to the user. One folder would be titled "Sports" (as in baseball pitcher), the second "Decorative Arts" (as in water pitcher). The user who chooses only the Sports folder will be presented with only those Web resources that use "pitcher" in the baseball sense. The user who selects the folder called "Decorative Arts" will be presented only with those resources that are related to water pitchers.

KOSs can be very powerful in supporting free-text searching within digital libraries and in integrating Web resources into existing digital libraries. However, these systems must be used with caution. KOSs have generally been developed for a specific discipline, task, or function, or for the indexing of a specific collection or database. Therefore, depending on the domain in which the KOS is being used and the complexity of the system, it may or may not suggest relevant free-text terms. Expanding a search with related terms, rather than pure synonyms, may return hits that are only peripherally relevant to the user.

PLANNING AND IMPLEMENTING KNOWLEDGE ORGANISATION SYSTEMS IN DIGITAL LIBRARIES

This section provides general guidelines that may be useful for an organisation that wants to use knowledge organisation systems to organise a digital library. The framework described is applicable for KOSs of any type or subject.

Planning Knowledge Organisation Systems

Analysing User Needs

Of primary importance to any digital library project is an analysis of its users' needs, in terms of content and functionality. Many volumes have already been written about needs assessment, and providing detailed guidance on this subject is beyond the scope of this paper. However, when analyzing how a KOS might be used with a particular digital library, it is essential to thoroughly understand the environment of the user. One must look not only at the needs for organising the digital library materials but also at possible links between content within and outside the digital library walls. This is particularly important for KOSs that are acting as intermediate authority files, because in such cases the links may not be readily apparent. It is important to consider other views that might be valuable for users and peripheral communities that might benefit from the digital library's content were it accessible to them through a KOS.

Locating Knowledge Organisation Systems

Once the user's needs have been analysed, it is necessary to locate KOSs to meet the need. While an alternate system can be build locally, it is preferable to find an existing KOS for several reasons. First, it is costly and time-consuming to build a KOS. Second, KOSs often benefit by saving been built over time. Many of the systems described in this report have been built over decades; some existed in paper before digitisation. The value of a KOS comes from its acceptance by the user community: sources built by noted authorities such as learned societies, trade associations. Or standards groups will be viewed as more trustworthy than those built internally. Finally, the networked environment has resulted in both an explosion of primary materials, including documents, electronic journals, and Web-based databases, and in an equivalent explosion of KOSs on the Web.

There are several ways to identify KOSs that may be of interest. Many users are already aware of KOSs on the Web within their discipline. Developers may also turn to directories, librarians in the field and reference sources, or they may perform a general search of the Internet.

Planning the Infrastructure

It is necessary to make decisions about the architecture of the KOS in the context of the digital library setting. The physical location of the KOS is important. Will the system be held externally or internally? There are pros and cons to either approach.

If the system is available on the Web, it is possible to consider linking to the KOS as an external system. This architecture requires a script or some search query to locate the resource. One must then launch a query against the resource to obtain the piece of information that will serve as the key between the two files. This key could be a universal resource locator (URL) or input to another search query. A query may be necessary if the KOS is stored in a database. The script may transfer log-on information (including user ID and password) from the digital library system to the external KOS, in order to provide access to the Web-enabled database. In the case of a more direct link, the access may be by URL.

However, the use of a URL as the link has the same problem with persistence as does direct access via a URL from a browser. The organisation may move the KOS, thereby changing the URL that is being used as the key. It is important to determine how often the URLs in the KOS change, whether there is a means of notification of these changes, and whether it is possible to consider an alternative that would be more persistent. Schemes such as the Digital Object Identifier and the Persistent URL have been devised to enable resources to be physically moved among servers without having their names changed. Another alternative is the use of other Uniform Resource Identification (URI) schemes and the Uniform Resource Name (URN), which can be sent from the newer Web browsers. The benefit of linking to a remote resource is that the resource will always be up-to-date. The maintenance of the KOS is in the hands of the owner, not the digital librarian. It may also be more apparent to users that the KOS is not owned by the digital library.

Linking to a remote KOS also have disadvantages. Persistence and unexpected changes in the organisation and content of the system may cause problems. The software or telecommunications route between the digital library server and the KOS may be unreliable. In systems requiring fast response time or large amounts of data transfer, and, therefore, high bandwidth (such as full-motion video or detailed graphics), the fact that a connection must be made between the digital library and the external KOS may make the system unacceptable to the user.

Alternatively, the KOS may be obtained from the owner and loaded locally. In many cases, this requires licensing that may not be required when the KOS is accessed remotely, because a copy of the whole resource is being provided to the digital library. Loading a KOS locally also requires that one consider issues such as maintenance, local system administration, and disk storage. If the KOS uses special software, such as a database management system, loading the KOS locally will require a copy of that software, which may require additional purchase or licensing. Other considerations are the need for firewalls and interface design. On the positive side, the KOS is under more local control. Therefore, it may be possible to improve the response time by not accessing the KOS over the Internet. If the KOS is to be used behind the scenes (that is, the system is not visible to the user), concerns of speed and integration become more important. If additional modifications (including digitization) need to be made to the KOS to integrate it with the digital library, it will also be necessary to load the KOS locally.

If the digital library intends to incorporate numerous secondary KOSs, it is important to consider the degree to which the architecture is scaleable. The National Library of Medicine's UMLS incorporates more than 40 different sources. While its main purpose has been to develop a metathesaurus for moving among these vocabularies, the management of the systems, regardless of the mapping issues, has been a major consideration. Ingest has been a major concern, with the need to develop a system that can handle a variety of input formats—from ASCII text files to highly structured database output. The architecture must also accommodate the character sets of the incoming sources. This is particularly important if a mark-up language has been used to represent special characters and diacritical marks. Systems that have been developed in Unicode, which extends ASCII to accommodate diacritical marks and non-Roman character sets, cannot be handled by systems that deal only with ASCII or extended ASCII sets.

Since many digital library systems are being built as extensions or applications of existing integrated library systems (ILS), it is important to consider who the KOSs will integrate with the library system. Unfortunately, many ILS vendors have not considered links to external files or databases in their system designs. In some cases, the vendor may require that the information be stored in the proprietary format of the ILS. The system may require that the files be on the same directory or server as the accessing ILS. The fields that can be linked to the Web or searched may be limited. Outside communications may require Z39.50 client-server connections. With relatively closed systems. ILSs may be a difficult environment in which to implement alternative and nontraditional KOSs.

Digital libraries that are interested in using KOSs should consider this integration when developing requirements for the procurement of a system to support them. Vendors should be encouraged to support relatively open architectures and to consider the extension of traditional library systems to support broader digital library functionality.

In addition to these immediate concerns, it is important to consider the in corporation of future KOSs. Initial success may spur the desire for integration of additional KOSs or enhanced functionality for the existing KOS. Success may breed additional requirements and increase the strain on hardware software, and network architectures.

Maintaining the Knowledge Organisation System

For a digital library, an outdated KOS can be more of a hindrance than a benefit. Maintenance, both of content and of the system, should be considered when planning a KOS. This is particularly important if the digital library is to be self-supporting or revenue generating.

Version control of the KOS is extremely important. Reloading a new version from the system provider is one way to accommodate changes; however, this may not be acceptable if the locally held version differs substantially from that held by the system's provider. If there has been significant transformation or processing of the original KOS, it may be difficult, or impossible, to reload the original and recreate the changes that have been made.

A transaction-based approach, whereby only changes are transferred between the KOS provider and the library, is also possible; however, this requires that the system provider have the infrastructure, both machine and human, to produce these transactions. It also requires that the changes to the original KOS be identifiable in order to create change transactions. For example, Stuart Nelson of the NLM's UMLS Project recently reported that many systems can create annual transaction records to inform the UMLS about the changes that have occurred to the original system. However, the changes are often not indicated with enough detail to support automatic change transactions in the UMLS. If a change date, for example, is recorded only at the level of the concept record, it is impossible to tell whether the term has changed (a correction of a typographic error for example) or if the relationship between this concept and another concept has changed. Since the UMLS splits the incoming terminology and its relationships into a variety of files, it is often difficult to tell how the UMLS files must be change based on the changes made during the maintenance of the original KOS (NISO 1999).

Presenting the Knowledge Organisation System to the User

In addition to deciding which KOS should be used and what functions it should serve, the digital library will need to determine how to present the KOS to its users. A KOS may be exposed to the user or made relatively transparent.

The KOS can be exposed to the user in different ways. Material can be grouped into KOS-related themes or categories on the digital library's Website. The KOS may be used at a higher level to identify specific portals for different uses or users. If the content of the digital library includes metadata records, the KOS may be displayed as index terms on the records or in its entirely as a navigation aid to searching.

In other cases, the KOS may be transparent. For example, a thesaurus can be used behind the scenes to extend the user's search to include synonyms, to connect the digital library's resources to other information and resources, or to filter or rank the information obtained.

Implementing Knowledge Organisation Systems

Acquisition and Intellectual Property Issues

It is critical to properly handle the acquisition of knowledge organisation systems. The first question is whether the KOS is under copyright. If so, the copyright holder should be contacted concerning the KOS. It is important to ensure that the apparent contact is the official one. Many references have been reprinted or put on the Web without proper acknowledgement of the real owner.

Once the contact has been made, there are several points for discussion:

- If the provider maintains the KOS, how will the digital library find out about any changes that may be made in it? Is there a notification mechanism in place? How frequently must the information be updated to be of benefit to the digital library's users? Will the maintenance be self-evident, or must the agreement include notification requirements? What will the owner do if the maintenance can no longer be performed?
- What will happen if the provide discontinues the product or sells or transfers it to someone else?
- What uses can the digital library make of the KOS under the proposed agreement? As with other licensing, it is advisable to aim for the broadest permissions and the longest term possible. At a minimum, the library should be able to renegotiate the terms of the agreement relatively easily.
- In a networked environment, it is beneficial to develop mechanisms for linking to online versions rather than to maintain a local copy of the resource. This ensures that what is presented is up-to-date, and acknowledges more clearly the ownership of the KOS. However, there are numerous factors to consider. Will the KOS be used on an intranet or behind a firewall, where access to the outside or information coming into the organisation might be prohibited? Does the KOS service use "cookies" or require knowledge of the user's Internet provider address? Does it require a user ID and password?
- If the KOS is to be accessed remotely, are there service issues? Is it likely to be accessed with bandwidth, model, and computer speeds that are adequate for outside connections of this type? Is the use of such a critical nature that unreliable service on the part of the KOS or the Internet connection will cause the digital library itself to be viewed as less useful? Does the KOS require a specialized search engine or search query formulation? Can the digital library system properly display the results, or would the results be better displayed

through the KOS system? Will the resulting information be used in its native form or must it be extracted or transformed? If the KOS is to be loaded locally, in what formats can the content be received?

- If the KOS is not available electronically, can it be digitized? Is the owner interested in a cooperative venture, and are the human and financial resources for such an effort available?

Making the Link

There are two parts to establishing the link between the digital library and the KOS. The first is locating the key anchor information in the digital library's resource. The second involves the look up against the target file. The creation of this link may be more or less automatic, depending on the particular situation. The characterization of this activity is meat to be general and to allow both "on-the fly" links and embedded links.

Regardless of what function the KOS is going to serve in the digital library, the essential information contained in the digital library resource from which the link is to be made must be identified. The mechanism for doing this depends on the type of object from which the link is being made and on the information that is expected to be identified in the digital library's resource.

The first step is to review any metadata related to the digital library resource. Do the meta data carry the term (such as SIC code, artist's name, place name, geographic coordinates) that is needed to make that link? If this information is included, the level at which the metadata are assigned should be reviewed. If the metadata indicate the subject matter of the specific resource in which the user will be interested, the metadata can be used to make the links. However, in some cases, the terms that appear in the title or description at the resource level (*e.g.*, the book) may not be indicative of the subject at the individual item level (*e.g.*, the chapter). Automatically making a link on the basis of the content description for a entire book may misrepresent the content of a chapter. Whether or not the metadata can be used will depend on the amount and type of information given in the metadata and the level at which the metadata are assigned.

If a text resource in the digital library provides no appropriate metadata, the procedure for identifying the key information may involve text analysis. A programme to perform simple string searching or a search engine that can preserve hit locations can be used if the text string has distinguishing characteristics such as a database acronym, or a specific structure, such as a latitude and longitude coordinate. If the text string has no such cues, text mining or more complex text-analysis tools may be necessary. These tools use a variety of semantic and syntactic algorithms to locate key information. There have been significant advances in commercially available text mining tools. Such as IBM's Intelligent Agent, which includes specific algorithms for identification of names of places and persons.

The second step of the linking activity to make the connection to the KOS. The methods for doing this vary, depending on whether the system is being loaded locally or is referenced remotely. If the system is loaded locally, it is possible to perform a significant amount of processing to match the two files, assuming that computer resources of this type are available to the digital library organisation. If the system is only available remotely over the Web, the interaction will require knowledge of scripting and various Web-based access techniques. Scripting should be considered in both local and remote approaches, since the more integrated the inking is with the resource, the more maintenance may be required if there are changes in either the resource or the KOS. Regardless of the approach that is taken, making the link requires an analysis of both the information in the original digital library material and the corresponding information in the KOS.

If the KOS is being used as an intermediate file to bridge between the digital library's resource and another resource, it is also important to understand thedata and the process whereby the search is performed and information returned from the target resource. If the KOS must return a value to the original digital library resource, the data and process must be evaluated in a bidirectional sense.

Choosing the linking mechanism is equally important. The link may be fixed or "on-the-fly." In the case of a fixed line, a specific URL is embedded at the link point in the digital library material. However, as stated before, problems of persistence are inherent in this approach. Alternatively, a URN can be used. The URN requires the creation of a namespace on the point of the target file, and the search is to this namespace rather than to a specific URL. Persistent locators (PURLs) and digital object identifiers (DOIs) can also solve this problem. These schemes are sufficient if the material is an HTML document.

Content in databases is more difficult to retrieve. The National Library of Medicine now supports the searching of a variety of its databases through its Internet Grateful Med (IGM) URL function. IGM users can create URLs that will actually perform searches against the databases. For example, the following script would perform a search for "pneumonia" in the HealthSTAR file: http://igm-02.nlm.nih.gov./cgi-bin/IGM_robot.pl?datafile =HealthSTAR&search =Subject=pneumonia.

Information the syntax for creating such a URL is provided on the NLM Web site. While the intent is that the search URL will be bookmarked by an individual user, the same concept can be used for creating an active link at the anchor point for the link. With additional scripting, the creation of the term *pneumonia* can be automatically replaced with an active link that picks up the term where the link has been made.

THE FUTURE OF KNOWLEDGE ORGANISATION SYSTEMS ON THE WEB

As online databases moved to the Web, they began to provide their products, including vocabulary aids, in this environment. Portable documents format (PDF) versions of printed vocabulary aids are common, since PDF can be easily produced form a Postscript file and it retains the look of the printed product. With Adobe's tools for indexing and searching the PDF file can provide some level of support for linking. Many of these aids, however, remain in the form of HTML files only—there is no database structure to easily support the linking and searching. In some cases, the full structure of the KOS is not made available on the Web; the only format for a Web-based thesaurus may be an alphabetical list of terms that does not enable the user to navigate easily the hierarchical structure. As unique ways of using these resources are developed, it is hoped that more KOS providers will be encouraged to provide their systems in formats that are conducive to such networked users.

Some of the requirements for such electronic KOSs were identified at a workshop entitled "Electronic Thesauri: Planning for a Standard" and sponsored by NISO (1999). While the focus of this meeting was digital thesauri, consideration was also given to other KOSs in digital form. The identified requirements include persistent identification at the concept level, the need for a simple protocol for the distributed querying and response from a KOS, and the development of a standard set of metadata attributes for describing a remote KOS.

To facilitate the search and display of information from a previously unknown KOS, the system must have unique and persistent identifiers for each of the concepts in the system. For example, the California Environmental Resources Evaluation System (of the California Natural Resources Agency) and the U.S. Geological Survey have developed a system for remote querying and response (CERES 1999). It requires that each concept in the thesaurus have a unique identifier. In the case of the previously described ITIS, which is accessed remotely by the CERES system, the ITIS record number is used as the identifier. Other unique identifiers could include the DOI or a classification notation that has been made unique by appending the scheme name or the URL to the notation.

The second requirement is a protocol for the distributed querying and response of KOSs. This is particularly critical for highly structured systems such as thesauri, semantic networks, and ontologies. Work has been done in this area within the Z39.50 community (Z.39.50 is the NISO standard for searching distributed bibliographic databases). A profile has been proposed by the Zthes Working Group to tailor the Z39.50 protocol to operate on thesauri that follow the Z39.19 standard.

A similar effort is under way at the CERES Project. Instead of a Z39.50 based protocol, CERES has developed a structure that is based on the Resource Description Framework (RDF) and the HTTP protocol of standard browsers. The RDF's concept of containers is a natural for managing the hierarchical structure of complex systems, such as thesauri. The structure proposed by CERES is likely to be encoded using XML, a mark-up format that tends itself to structured information. This protocol for linking distributed vocabularies will support both searching and cataloging. The user will be presented with remote vocabularies that can be displayed and navigated by a local client.

The third major finding from the NISO workshop was the need for a metadata content standard for the description of KOSs. Such a standard is key to provision of knowledge organisation services over the Internet. The metadata identify the Web resource as a KOS and provide important information to allow an application to use it remotely without prior knowledge of its content or structure.

A draft set of attributes for description KOSs available in a networked environment has been developed by a task group of the Network Knowledge Organisation Systems (NKOS) Working Group, an ad hoc group of terminology experts from organisations that are interested in issues related to the use and interoperability of KOSs over the Internet. The draft attributes are based on work originally done by Linda Hill (Alexandria Digital Library at the University of California at Santa Barbara) and Michael Raugh (Interconnect Technologies).

The attributes describe the KOS so that content from the system can be transferred over the Internet and handled by a remote browser or client application. The attributes include the depth of hierarchy, the types of relationships included, the subject (described by free text or by a declared classification scheme). Storage format, copyright and rights management, and contact information. To facilitate the transfer of information, the attribute set also includes information on character set and file size. To facilitate the acquisition and licensing of the KOSs, the draft content description includes point of contact information.

During discussions about the metadata content standard, workshop attendees identified three methods for storing the metadata for a KOS. First, the metadata could be stored with the KOS as metadata elements for that resource. Second, the metadata could be stored in a physically separate knowledge organisation registry. The third possibility is a hybrid approach, where a minimal set of metadata elements is contained in a central registry (i.e., sufficient information to identify the resource, where it is located and how more information can be obtained). The more detailed information would be stored with the KOS itself.

There is significant interest in the use of KOSs to organise and search material on the Internet. It is hoped that this interest will result in knowledge organisation services that will make these sources more readily accessible to a variety of software applications and to a variety of users. As services and enabled software proliferate, it will be easier to integrate these KOSs into digital libraries.

CONCLUSION: ENHANCING DIGITAL LIBRARIES WITH KNOWLEDGE ORGANISATION SYSTEMS

Given that the digital library field is still quite new, it seems strange to be talking already about enhancing digital libraries. However, in this fast-moving environment, the initial digital libraries resulting from digitisation projects, or even virtual collections, are being enhanced as user expectations and technology capabilities allow. In the midst of this furious activity, it is valuable to analyse users' needs and interests and then to identify KOSs that can be used to enhance the digital library.

Knowledge organisation systems refer to a range of traditional and nontraditional systems for the organisation of knowledge. The systems have been developed in numerous environments outside the traditional library environment, including those of A&I services, publishers and professional organisations, and corporations. Examples exist in many disciplines and for many target audiences.

Knowledge organisation systems can enhance the digital library in a number of ways. They can be used to connect a digital library resource to a related resource. The related information may reside within the KOS itself or the KOS may be used as an intermediary file to retrieve the key needed to access it in another resource. A KOS can make digital library materials accessible to disparate communities. This may be done by providing alternate subject access, by adding access by different modes, by providing multilingual access, and by using the KOS to support free text searching.

A well-planned infrastructure of KOSs is required. This includes the resources, processes, and policies for analyzing user needs; locating KOSs to answer these needs; and acquiring, implementing and maintaining the KOS.

Traditional and nontraditional KOSs provide an opportunity to extend the boundaries of the digital library. By going beyond the initial organisation of the digital library digital librarians can use the network environment to provide additional value to its users.

NOTES AND REFERENCES

1. The term knowledge organisation systems as used in this report was coined by the Networked Knowledge Organisation Systems Working Group at its initial meeting at the ACM Digital Libraries '98 Conference in Pittsburgh, Pennsylvania.

2. A recent National Science Foundation -sponsored workshop, "Digital Gazetteer Information Exchange," addressed the issues of digital gazetteers. One of the critical issues is that there is not standard for the interchange of information, either to provide gazetteer information physically to another gazetteer or to interoperate with one or more distributed gazetteers through the Internet. The workshop participants distributed gazetteers through the Internet. The workshop participants emphasised the need for such protocols and for enhancements to current gazetteers. (Many gazetteers do not include coordinates or are incomplete in this regard.) The goal is to develop a digital gazetteer service that can be accessed by any application.

   Such a service is central to the vision of a geolibrary. A report on distributed geolibraries from the National Research Council (1999) envisions the geolibrary as a physical globe. One would walk into such a geolibrary and be confronted not by a card catalogue or an OPAC terminal but by a large physical globe. The user would indicate his or her area of interest by pointing to a place on the globe. The librarian would use the geospatial location information to retrieve and present materials related to that place. By comparing feature types, the user could ask for other place names and locations that were similar to the original.

Significant work into digital gazetteer services and geospatial libraries has been conducted by the Alexandria Digital Library (ADL) Project at the University of California at Santa Barbara, with support from the National Science Foundation's Digital Library Initiative-1 (Hill and Zheng 1999). An ADL Gazetteer was created by merging place name authority files from the National Image Mapping Agency and the U.S. Board on Geographic Names of the U.S. Geological Survey. The project also added controlled feature types to the gazetteer. With the aid of a visualisation tool, the information can be provided on a map and accessed using other geogrpahic visualisation tools.

BIBLIOGRAPHY

Aaronson, A. And Carroll, J.M. 1987, Intelligent Help in a One-Shot Dialog: A Protocol Study. Proceedings of ACM Human Factors in Computing Systems and Graphics Interface (CHI + GI) '87, 163-168.

Ackerman, M.S. and Malone, T.W. 1990. Answer Garden: A Tool for Growing Organisational Memory. *Proceedings of ACM Conference on Office Information Systems*, 31-39.

Allen, T. 1977. *Managing the Flow of Technology*. MIT Press, Cambridge, MA.

Arms, W.Y., D. Hillmann, C. Lagoze, D. Krafft, R. Marisn, J. Saylor, C. Terrizzi, and H. Van de Sompel. A spectrum of Interoperability: The Site for Science prototype of the NSDL. *D-Lib Magazine*, 8(1), January 2002.

Arms, W. *Digital Libraries.* MIT Press, Cambridge, MA, 2000.

Borgman, C. From Gutenberg to the Global Information Infrastructure: *Access to Information in the Networked World.* MIT Press, Cambridge, MA, 2000.

Committee on Intellectual Property Rights and the Emerging Information Infrastructure. *The Digital Dilemma: Intellectual Property in the Information Age.* National Academy Press. Washington, DC, 2000.

Crane, G., D.A. Smith, and C.E. Wulfman. Building a hypertextual digital library in the humanities: A case study on London. In *Proceedings of the First ACM+IEEE Joint Conference on Digital Librarie*, pages 426-434, Roanoke, VA, 24-28 June 2001.

Curtis, P. and Nichols, D.A. 1993. MUDs Grow Up: Social Virtual Reality in the Real World. Xerox PARC. Manuscript.

El-Beltagy, S.R., W. Hall, D.D. Roure, and L. Carr. Linking in context. In *Proceedings of the 12th ACM Conference on Hypertext and Hypermedia*, pages, 151-160, Arhus, Denmark, August 2001.

Endig, M. M. Hoding, G. Saake, K. Sattler, and E. Schallehn. Federation Services for Heterogeneous Digital Libraries Accessing Cooperative and Non-cooperative Sources. In *Proceedings of Kyoto International Conference on Digital Libraries: Research and Practice*. IEEE Computer Society Press, 2000.

European Workgroup on SGML. *MAJOUR Header Manual*, 1.0 edition, 1991.

Faensen, D., L. Faulstich, H. Schweppe, A. Hinze, and A. Steidinger, Hermes – a notification service for digital libraries. In *ACM/IEEE Joint Conference on Digital Libraries*, Roanoke, Virginia, USA, June 24-28 2001.

Faulstich , Lukas C. and Myra Spiliopoulou. Building HyperView wrappers for publisher web-sites. *International Journal on Digital Libraries*, 3(1):3-18, 2000.

Fischer, C.S. 1982. *To dwell among friends: personal networks in town and city.* University of Chicago Press, Chicago.

Fox, E.A. 1993, Source Book on Digital Libraries. Virginia Tech, Department of Computer Science, TR 93-35.

Fox, E.A. and Lunin, L.F. 1993. Introduction and Overview. *Journal of the American Society for Information Science*, 44 (8), 441-446.

Gaizauskas, G., P. Herring, H Oakes, M. Beaulieu, P. Willett, H. Fowkes, and A. Jonsson. Intelligent access to text: Integrating information extraction technology into text browsers. In *Proceedings of HLT*, San Diego, CA, 2001.

Giles, C.L., K. Bollacker, and S. Lawrence. CiteSeer: An automatic citation indexing system, In *Proceedings of the 3rd ACM Conference on Digital Libraries*, pages 89—98, Pittsburgh, PA, 1998.

Griffel, F., C. Zirpins, and S. Muller-Wilken. Generative softwarekonstruktion auf basis typisierter komponenten. In U. Killat and W. Lamersdorf, editors, *Proceedings 12, GI-Fachknonferenz Kommunikation in Verteilten System* (KiVS), Informatik aktuell, pages 325-338, Berlin Heidelberg New York, Feb 2001. Springer-Verlag.

Hutchins, E. 1990. The Technology of Team Navigation. In J. Galegher and R. Kraut ed. *Intellectual Teamwork: Social and Technological Foundations of Cooperative Work.* Lawrence Erlbaum, Hillsdale, NJ.

Kahle. B. Preserving the Internet, *Sci. Am.* (Mar. 1997); see www.sciam.com/0397issue/0397 kahle.html.

Kenney, A. and Rieger, O. Moving Theory into Practice: Digital Imaging for Librarian and Archives. Research Libraries Group, Mountain View, CA, 2000.

Lagoze, C. and H.V. de Sompel. The Open Archives Initiative: Building a low barrier interoperability framework. In *Proceedings of the First ACM+IEEE Joint Conference on Digital Libraries*, pages 54-62, 2001.

Lesk, M. *Practional Digital Libraries: Books, Bytes, and Bucks* Morgan Kaufman Publishers, San Francisco, 1997.

McCray, A., Gallagher, M., and Flannick, M. Extending the role of metadata in a digital library system. In *Proceedings of the IEEE Forum on Research and Technology Advances in Digital Libraries* (Baltimore, May 19-21). IEEE Computer Society, Los Alamitos. CA, 1999, 190-199.

Michael Ley. DBLP – Digital Bibliography & Library Project, 2001.

National Information Standards Organisation. *The Dublin Core Metadata Element Set: Draft Standard Z39:85.*

Ousterhout, J.K. 1993. Tcl and the Tk Tookit. Book manuscript.

Pollack, M.E. 1985. Information Sought and Information Provided: An Empirical Study of User/Expert Dialogues. *Proceedings of Human Factors in Computing Systems* (ACM CHI'85), 155-159.

Rothenberg. J. Avoiding Technological Quicks and: Finding a Viable Technical Foundation for Digital Preservation. Rep. to Council on Library and Information Resources, Jan. 1999.

Schallehn, E., M. Endig, and K. Sattler. Citation Linking in Federated Digital Libraries. In M. Rantree, W. Hasselbring, and S. Contrad, editors, *Proc. 3rd Int. Workshop on Engineering Federated Information System, EFIS'00* Dublin, Ireland, June, pages 53-60, Berlin, 2000, Akadem. Verlagsgesellschaft.

Smith, D.A., A. Mahoney, and J.A. Rydberg-Cox Management of XML documents in an integrated digital library. *Markby Languages: Theory and Practice* 2(3): 205-214, 2000.

Sproull, L. and Kiesler, S. 1991. *Connections: New Ways of Working in the Networked Organisation.* MIT Press, Cambridge, MA.

St. Pierre, M. and LaPlant, Jr., W. *Issues in Crosswalking: Content Metadata Standards.* National Information Standards Organisation, 1998.

Strand, E., Mehta, R., and Jairam, R. Applications thrive on open systems standards. *Standardview 2,3* (Sept. 1994), 148-154.

Suchman, L.A. 1987. *Plans and Situated Actions: The Problem of Human-Computer Communication.* Cambridge University Press, New York.

Swick, R.R. and Ackerman, M.S. 1988. The X Toolkit: More Bricks for Building User-Interfaces. *Proceedings of Winter 1988 Usenix,* 5-17.

Waters, D. *The Digital Library Federation: Programme Agenda.* A Programme of the Council on Library and Information Resources, June 1998.

Zirpins, C., H. Weinreich, A. Bartelt, and W. Lamersdorf, Advanced, concepts for next generation portals. In *Proc. First International Workshop on Web Based Collaboration WBC'01.* IEEE, 2001.

Index